SOCIO-ECONOMIC STATUS OF WIDOWS

SOCIO-ECONOMIC STATUS OF WIDOWS

DR. K. PADMANABHAN
Reader and Head (Retd)
Department of Economics

SERIALS PUBLICATIONS
NEW DELHI

First Published - 2006

ISBN: 81-86771-98-0

Published by

SERIALS PUBLICATIONS
4830/24, Prahlad Street, Ansari Road
Darya Ganj, New Delhi-110002 (India)
Phone : 23245225
Fax : 91-11-23272135
E-mail: serials@satyam.net.in

"When women whom we call abala become sabala, all those who are helpless will become powerful"

– Gandhiji

DEDICATED TO :

All those widows, who undergo the pains patiently, and holding high the light of chastity, protected and preserved by the culture and tradition of this age old nation.

CONTENTS

ACKNOWLEDGEMENT

The project on, Socio-Economic Status of Widows (Mudaliar Community) of Tamil Nadu–A Three Generation Study, is conceived, planned, formulated and implemented with a view to find solution to a number of problems faced by the specific caste widows in Tamil Nadu. On the basis of household or group approach, a strategy to solve the social problems, a study on the widows declared by the Government as socially and economically advanced, has been specifically taken as a subject for analysis.

The revelations made by the study are quite appealing. It shows the holocaust and sacrifice endured by widows for a long time. Illiteracy, unemployment, moneyless, loneliness, assetless etc., have added to the degradation of widows status and enhance their dependence. Age, old customs and conventions have inflicted certain indelible mark of attitudes in them, which remains unchanged. They simply accept the social norms attributed to them. during the era of human rights. It is become necessary to empower the widows by changing their mindset vis-à-vis the mind-set of the society who meted out inhuman treatment to them Economic empowerment, will lead to social empowerment. both of them depend on the development of literacy, education, and skills.

Various efforts like legislations, welfare measures, social activism have had little impact on the society's attitude towards widows, particularly, belonging to the Hindu upper castes. The present study, an eye-opener to the cruel society, that meted out inhuman treatment to women, who lost their husbands. A society should be rich not only in wealth but also it should show compassion and consideration to unfortunate sisters, who are made to oscillate between fate and bitter society. The suggestions made in the study and the action plan, if adopted, would lead to the acceptance of widows as human beings and relieve them from the pains of widowhood.

The study would be incomplete, if it does not draw inspiration and encouragement from various quarters, whose unstited cooperation should be acknowledged. The Indian Council of Social Science Research , New Delhi, and its expert committee deserve my gratitude and thanks for approving the project and for sanctioning the fund for carrying out the project.

I feel greatly indebeted to the Members, Advisory Board for their valuable suggestions and scholarly advice.

The management, particularly, the Rector, Rev Dr. Arokiam Kanaga SDB M.A., Ph.D., the Principal, Rev.Dr. C.M. Varghese SDB M.Sc., Ph.D., the administrator, Rev. Fr. Siluvai Muthu SDB M.Phil., the Vice-Principal Rev. Dr. C. Antony Raj and all the college council members for providing all the facilities in the college to carry on the research project, to whom I owe my deep debt of gratitude and thanks.

My Special thanks are due to Rev. Dr. A.T. Thomas S.D.B. M.A., M.Phil, Director, the Librarian and the assistante of the Sacred Heard College Library for providing all possible help for the project.

The staff and students of the Department of Economics deserve my thanks for their critical comments on the project.

Mr. G. Jothi Nehru M.A., M.Phil., and Ms. S. Sumathi M.A., are the two pillars of the project, with out whose support and hard work, the project would not have been completed in time. I take this opportunity to thank them profusely and wish them a glorious career in their life.

I thank the Social Work Department, particularly, Dr. Christopher M.A., Ph.D., and Dr. S. Sagayadoss M.A., M.Phil., Ph.D., and their assistante for undertaking the statistical analysis of the collected data.

My thanks are due to the Mudaliar Associations in Tamil Nadu as well as at Vellore for extending full support to the project.

I also thank all the respondent widows, who came forward voluntarily to open out their heart to the investigator in spite of the reservations and reticence.

Finally, I thank the Bright Computers for their neat typing and the VP for the elegant binding works.

I thank the Almighty for giving me enough strength to undertake this project even after my retirement and complete it within the stipulated time.

Dr. K. Padmanabhan

1
INTRODUCTION

GENERAL VIEW OF WOMEN

The concept of women has been best described in an ancient Sanskrit saying.."Yatra Nary Pujante." Women have been given the ascription of mother goddess and is considered the source of SHAKTI. A women mirrors the wealth and prosperity of the society to which she belongs. Her role has been duly recognised by the civilised societies and developed economies. The level of development of a country can be best judged by the status it attributes to women. A country progresses with women or regresses with her.

India is the second largest country in the world in terms of female population, which constitutes about half of the population. A women is not only a daughter, wife or mother, but, she is also a social being. A mother's role is more important as she has to mould the children into a dutiful member of the society. Modern women are highly endowed with intelligence, foresight, dignity and thoughtfulness to face difficult situations in their homes .

Women is an endless source of power. She is a formidable force that can change the complexion of growth, rejuvenate the human resource, absorbs the strains of modernisation and fight the forces of destruction [2].

Concept of Widow

Mukesh Ahuja defines a widow as "one who has no issue and who has been widowed one or two years of her marriage or she may be one who becomes a widow after a period of five to ten years and has one or two small children to support or she may be one who is above 50 years of age[3].

WIDOWHOOD

Widowhood is a crisis in a women's life, involving new social adjustment for the family as well as for herself. The life of the women whose husband dies while she is alive has been institutionally made miserable by the norms of patriarchy. She faces emotional trauma, familial exploitation and social stigma. She has to adjust with in-laws, find some job for supporting her young children, adjust with sons and daughters-in-law, and has to face the male gaze seductive overtones and even molestation attempts[4].

PROBLEMS OF WIDOWS

Widows came to be regarded as inauspicious and had to suffer great disabilities. Many widows committed 'Sati' voluntarily to avoid inhuman sufferings at the hands of their relations including sons. They did not receive any sympathy from society. The greatest danger that can overtake a women is widowhood, says Ramayana. Within twelve days of widowhood, the sindoor and bindi in her forhead are smudged, her bangles, nose-ring, the coloured sari and mangalesutra removed. Her long black stress are cropped short. Among the orthodox Brahmin widows, in the south, they must shave their heads. A white sari will replace her coloured one. A widow is ill-omen. She is not allowed to attend marriages in some villages in the south. A prostitute is given a higher status in our society than a widow[5].

The problem of widows with examples of three cases: One is the case of a girl who becomes a widow within one or two years of marriage and has no children. Next is the case of a women who becomes widowed after a marital span of 5 to 10 years and has one or two small kids for support. And, last is the case of a women who is a widow and is of 50 years of age or even above. Similarities in the three cases are that: (a) all possess the status of a widow, (b) all have to face problems of adjustment in terms of expected roles they have to perform and (c) the possibility that like the third type, the second and even the first type of widows will spend the rest of their life in widowhood. But what is important is the difference in the three roles.

The first widow has no obligations as such but she is faced with the problem of economic, emotional and sexual adjustment.

The second widow has social obligation of bringing up children and performing even the role of a father for them. Of course, she has also to face the problem of social, psychological and biological adjustment too.

The third widow has no obligation of supporting the young children. Neverthless, she is confronted with some problems. Further the first and second type of widows are not as welcome in their husband's family as the third type.

Widowhood is both a crisis, and a problem. When it occurs, its suddenness and intensity make it a crisis and as the individual finds ways of coping it becomes a problem.

Economic Deprivation

One of the most immediate problems following widowhood is economic deprivation. The widows face deprivation due to the economic disadvantages rather than widowhood itself. Almost all widows face two big problems, both closely related (i) Money (ii) Finding jobs, because of their inexperience in dealing with financial matters, and their lack of occupational skills. This makes their economic condition worse.

Emotional Deprivation

The widow becomes physically weak and mentally distressed. Sometimes, a widow becomes so highly disturbed that she even doubts her husbands death. Emotional reactions may include anger, guilt, depression, anxiety or adjustment due to individual hindrances like nervousness, moods of depression and morbidity, tendency to worry and general emotional instability.

The widows face physio - psycho problems and she loses interest in her daily life and neglects her health. Along with these, lack of social contacts, sense of insecurity, isolation and other factors affect her health adversely. She becomes restless, irritated and frustrated due to her distress of mind pathetic and over-whelmed with the sense of emptiness of life. Widows, particularly young, show withdrawal from friends and relatives and suffer from personal loneliness in life. Loneliness may reflect social isolation, psychological isolation, or a combination of both.

Cultural Deprivation

In general, a Hindu widow is deprived of wearing the tali, flowers, glass-bangless, nose-ring and applying kumkum. A widow can not wear the above insignia of sawbhaghya under any circumstances. However, the life of an orthodox Brahmin widow had to face, much against her will, the horrible and inhuman rite of tonsure. Even today, widows are discouraged from taking part in any auspicious ceremonies and ritually sacred activities[6].

OBJECTIVES

Overall Objectives

To analyse the socio-economic status of Mudaliar Community widows in three generations and to find out the change in their status and to suggest measures for their improvement.

Specific Objectives

1. To find out the social status of widows in the Mudliar Community. The social status relates to the nature of households, singles, nuclear or joint families, pattern of living in terms of dresses, food, entertainment, performing rituals, attending marriage, visiting relatives and friends, going to theatres and parks, role in the family - bread winner, cooking, childcare, washing and cleaning.
2. To study the economic conditions of widows in the Mudaliar community. The economic status will be analysed in terms of family income, expenditure on food, non-food items like rent, cloths, education, entertainment,

travel, saving and investment, debt incurred, sources of borrowing etc.

3. To ascertain the role of widows in the decision making in the family. The decision making relates to buying and selling of daily requirements, purchase and sale of movable and immovable items including land, building, marriage of daughters, sons and other relatives, celebration of festivals, ceremonies, investments, from whom to borrow, where to save, whom to approach for health assistance etc.
4. To examine the impact of women welfare programmes on the status of widows belonging to the Hindu Mudaliar community in Tamil Nadu.
5. To find out the problems faced by Mudaliar community widows in Tamil Nadu. The problems relate to economic, emotional, physical, mental and cultural etc.
6. To suggest measures to empower widows socially and economically.

HYPOTHESIS

From the above objectives the following hypothesis are prescribed for testing.

1. The widows in the Mudaliar Community continue to face deprivation, exclusion and social stigma in spite of the social movements and social legislations protecting their rights.
2. The widows continue to depend on the earnings of the members of her family or in-laws.
3. The decisions making of widows is related to their income.
4. The attitude of others towards widows depends on their income.

SCOPE OF THE STUDY

The problem of widowhood has elicited considerable interest in the minds of researchers in recent times. The widowhood is a combination of the problems of the women and the widow. Hence, in order to understand the complex phenomenon of widowhood, a systematic study of various problems faced by widows, the causes, the consequences and the effects on the personality of widows, the difficulties in adapting to widowhood and how they manage to overcome the problems become essential.

The study will be useful to the policy makers, sociologists, women's organisations, administrators, academicians and social scientists. It will help them to frame a proper perspective planning for the empowerment of widows. This study will awaken the conscience of the orthodox and blind community and it will persuade them to accept the widows as a person and recognise her faculties and utilise her energy for development and acknowledge her as a partner in all the ventures which will be planned for the 21st century.

LIMITATIONS

1. The problems, the widows face, the treatment they receive from the family and the society and such other issues vary from religion to religion, and with in castes in a region. Therefore, it has been decided to focus attention on widows from a single religion and also from a single caste viz, the Hindu Mudaliar community.
2. The information furnished by the respondents were not from written records but from their memory. The recall bias is unavoidable in this study. But this defect is minimised by the investigator's frequent visit to the villages and development of rapport with the widow's family.
3. Since the present study is location specific, the findings of the study is applicable only to similar problems elsewhere.
4. In the original proposal, the whole of Tamil Nadu was treated as a unit of study. But later it was found that the Mudaliar community is scattered all over Tamil Nadu and they are called by different names in different district. Therefore, it was decided to select a representative district which has largest number of Mudaliar population. As such, vellore district emerged as a representative district with largest number of Mudaliar population. Different sub-castes of Mudaliar community like Agamudiar,

Chenkunther and Thulu Vellalas are in existence in this district. All the sub-caste of Mudaliar community is included in this study.

The fund allotted for this project is far from adequate in view of the escalation in wages and salaries paid to the project staff as well as steep rise in the transport cost which prompted this researcher to restrict the sample to 500 as against the sample size proposed in the proposal. It is a deviation from the original proposal. It may be ratified.

PLAN OF THE REPORT

1. The first chapter, introduction, covers a general view of women as widows, statement of the problem, objectives, hypothesis, scope and limitations.
2. The second chapter, review of literature, deals with important concepts used in the study and a brief review of the past studies.
3. The third chapter, description of the study area, gives a brief account of the Vellore District.
4. The origin and spread of the Mudaliar community is espoused in the fourth chapter.
5. The fifth chapter, research methodology, represents the methods used in this study.
6. The sixth chapter deals with the social status of the Mudaliar widows in Vellore.
7. The seventh chapter presents a spectrum of economic status of the Mudaliar widows.
8. The eighth chapter pertains to the role of the Mudaliar widows in decision making.
9. Ninth chapter relates to the impact of the welfare programmes on the status of the Mudaliar widows.
10. The tenth chapter deals with the problems faced by the widows of Mudaliar community in the study area and the suggestions for their improvement.
11. The final chapter presents the important findings, conclusions and policy implications.

NOTES

1. Maya Majumdar (2001), "Protecting Our Women", Vol.III., Domiant Publishers andDistributers, New Delhi, pp. 361 -368.
2. Tusharkant Mishra (1988), "Make Women Equal Partners in Development", Yojana, Vol.32., May, p. 18.
3. Mukesh Ahuja (1996), "Widows - Role Adjustment and Violence", Wishwa Prakashan Publishers, New Delhi, p. 11.
4. M.A. Fritz (1979), "A Study of Widowhood in Sociology and Social Research", Yojana, Vol.XIV, No.1., January, p. 53.
5. M. Rajkumar (2000),"Encyclopedia of Women and Development", Vol.16., Anmol Publications, New Delhi, pp.1-10.
6. D. Godavari (2000), "A Study on Deprivation of Hindu Widows", Gyan Publishing House, New Delhi, pp. 27-29.

2
REVIEW OF LITERATURE

A review of concepts and previous studies is useful to define precisely the concepts used in the present study, to place the problem in proper perspective and to decide the frame work for analysis. Precise definition of the concepts would enable both the collection of relevant data, and meaningful interpretation of the results of analysis.

CONCEPTS

The following concepts and terms, used in the present study, are given below:

Widow

The English word widow is related to a Latin root meaning to place apart; widows are often treated as distinct from married women.

The Oxford English Dictionary defines, 'widow as a women whose husband is dead and who has not married again and a wife bereaved of her husband'[2].

N. Dutt (1968) defines, 'widow as a women whose husband is dead and who has not married again'[3].

Mukesh Ahuja (1996) defines, a widow as 'one who has no issue and who has been widowed one or two years of her marriage or she may be one who becomes a widow after a period of five to ten years and has one or two small children to support or she may be one who is above 50 years of age[4].

Agarwal (2000) describes, widows, who in the learned tongue are called 'vidhava', a word akin to the latin 'vidua' are given less respect than a 'sumangali' and when they happen to have no children, they are generally looked upon with the utmost scorn. The very fact of meeting a widow is considered to bring ill luck[5].

Widow in the present study, is defined as a women belonging to Mudaliar community, whose husband is dead and has not married again.

Widowhood

The term, 'widowhood', is used, in this work, to refer to female widowhood specifically.

Leslie (1979) remarks that widowhood is a long term proposition. Widowhood and the accompanying deep sense of loss and frustration come to an end with remarriage or with death[6].

Widowhood is a crisis in a women's life, involving new social adjustment for the family as well as for herself[7].

Widowhood is almost always accompanied by deep sense of shock, due to the sudden and unexpected death of the husband. The death of a husband entirely changes the social identity of a women[8].

Morgan (1981) viewed widowhood as a complex transition with multiple possible consequences[9].

Widowhood is a life event that removes not only persons, closest support persons but also reduces the size of informal support network at the same time[10].

According to Greg, widowhood is an event that brings about the greatest change in the status of a women, for, it is often accompanied by deleterious consequences[11]. In India, widowhood represents the last and lowest stage in life for the Hindu women.

Widowhood implies a shift in position from that of a wife with economic, social and emotional security to an economically dependent and socially and psychologically insecure women (with few exceptions)[12].

Widowhood can be viewed as a social category consisting of individuals whose life partner is dead[13].

Hyman (1983) observes that widowhood is one of the sad facts of existence. Millions of women experience this misfortune and generally bear its burden for many years[14].

Rosow says that widowhood hits women, particularly, harder than men. A widower, being economically independent, does not feel the stigma, and the loss of the spouse, as much as a women. Widowhood is primarily, a female phenomenon[15].

Brubaker opines that widowhood is a family event and the loss reverberates throughout the later family network. The spouse has lost a mate; children a parent, siblings a brother or sisters. Further, he points out that widowhood represents cut-off of former roles and relationships and commencing of a new set of relationships and expectations[16].

Radhadevi observes that widowhood brings about both subjective and objective consequences. Where as, subjective consequences can be almost the same for widows and widowers. The objective consequences differ due to the distinctively different roles between men and women. The social consequences brought about by widowhood have a damaging effect on the self-concept of a widow[17].

In the present study widowhood indicates the status of a widow belonging to the Hindu Mudaliar Community, who is subjected to deprivation and is dependent, socially and economically.

Household

A household is defined as a group of persons who usually stay together and take food from a common kitchen. These persons participate in the socio-economic and cultural activities and share the responsibility of the household they have been included[18].

Nuclear Household

Widows living with their unmarried sons.

Filial Household

It may be defined as household consisting of a widow, atleast one of her married sons and possibly other persons.

Filial Stem Household

A widow lives with only one married son.

Filial Joint Household

A widow lives with several married sons[19].

Oxford Dictionary (1997), defines household as a group of people living together in shared accommodation and with common domestic expense. A household usually, but not always, contains people who are related or cohabiting. Whereas the individual is the recipient of incomes, the household is the unit through which a lot of consumption expenditure is decided[20].

Dictionary of Economics (1999) defines 'household' as an economic unit consisting of a single person living alone, a married couple or a complete family, each unit with a source of income and responsibility for its disposal[2].

A.M. Shah (1973) meant a 'household' as a residential unit composed of one or more persons living under the same roof and eating food cooked in a single kitchen[22].

A 'household' is defined as a group of persons who commonly live together and take their food in a common mess unless the exigencies of work prevent any of them from doing so[23].

Encyclopaedia of women (1998), found that women's and men's role in society is inseparable from their roles in the household and family. Changes in size and structure of household and families therefore have important implications for social and economic policies[24].

A widow's household in the present study is taken as with whom the widow chooses to live, for example, with the in-laws, parents, sons or filial etc.

Dependency

Dependency refers to a relationship between a person and another person, symbol, substance or material object characterized by physiological or psychological withdrawal pains contingent upon its unavailability and the absence of subjectively perceived alternatives[25].

G.S. Bidarkoppa (1971), has pointed out that in India, even today, a women is dependent on her husband for support, decision and protection. She has no independent identity, whether she works in the house or in the farm or in a factory, because here the man is the head of the family, owner of property and he is in charge of the family exchequer. Under such circumstances, when a husband dies, the wife, who is unprepared for such a situation, faces several problems connected with finance, property and other matters. She has to depend upon herself except for the help received from parents, kinsmen, and others which may not be either adequate or a constant source to depend upon. Her plight is heightened when she is uneducated, poor and ignorant[26].

Economic dependency is only one of the two variables which have important independent effects upon the decisions to leave an abusive relationship. The relation in unemployed cohabiting male economically dependent upon employed female may actually increase the likelihood of the female partners being abused in the first place. Widows can not have a separate establishment for they are not trained to lead an independent life. If a widow is young or middle-aged with minor children, she has to live with her near relatives. She often needs help to manage the property of the husband but frequently there every relatives may plot against her and exploit her helpless situation. If the widow is aged, she has to live with her sons, over whom she has no authority. The widow's life in their family and with close relations becomes miserable, if they do not have any property. Often due to conflicts between mother-in-law and daughter-in-law, they are made to cook separately.

After the death of the husband their lives become economically disorganised and they become dependent upon traditional support networks like joint family, or some specially created societal resources like widow homes, etc[27].

In the present study, Mudaliar Community widows is deemed to depend upon her children–son/daughter or parents/parents-in-law for her social and economic support.

Decision Making

According to Joshi (1973), in the joint family, decision making is centred in the hands of the eldest male person. But in the nuclear family, decision making is dispersed and women are also supposed to take part in it. In the extended family system, women tend to participate more in the family decision making[28].

Ranjana Kumari (1981), identified decision making in terms of who among the family members takes day to day as well as social decisions[29].

Decision making is the oft-repeated instrument applied in studies on marital power. Expenditure on food, clothing, entertainment, going to movies, visiting friends, children's education, and giving presents to friends are taken by the head of the family[30].

To Michael Mann (1983), decision making is a process whereby decisions are arrived at over questions of general in an organisation or over the practical implementation of an established policy. For sociologists the main focus of interest is the degree to which different groups with an interest in the outcome of the decision are able to participate in and influence the process. Decision making has long been used, especially in the pluralist tradition, as a measure of where power lies[31].

Women are an important segment of the family's economy, because of their active participation in home and farm activities. They play a vital role in decision making regarding household resources, which are specifically used by them. Their influence and decision making in household affairs is affected due to certain factors like the degree of economic independence, socio-cultural pressures, demographic factors and physical settings etc[32].

Dubes (1955), observed that in an ideal home, the final say in all matters connected with the family is always with the husband[33].

A widow has to take number of decisions after the death of her husband. Those decisions may relate to personal affairs, family, finance, wealth and employment. Those decisions may affect the individual and the family as a whole.

Attitude

According to Davis (1964), "an attitude is an inferred factor with in the individual, which involves a tendency to perceive and react"[34].

Thodarson and Thodarson (1969), found that "an attitude is an orientation towards certain objects (including persons other than oneself) or situation"[35].

According to Krech and Crutchfield (1948), "an attitude can be defined as an enduring organisation of motivational, emotional, perceptual and cognitive processes with respect to some aspects of the individual worlds"[36].

Thurston (1946), defined attitude as the degree of positive or negative effects associated with some psychological objects[37]. Edward (1957) found that for a quick, convenient and reliable quantitative measurement of attitude of large groups, an attitude scale would yield fruitful results. An attitude scale therefore serves as means of assessing the degree of positive or negative disposition of an individual towards a psychological object. The behaviour of in-laws or of sons, relatives, employers, etc., to the widow depends not only upon the widow's contribution to their need gratification but also their general attitude towards widowhood. The widow's own reaction to the behaviour of others to her also depends upon her attitude towards widowhood[37].

To Kluck Hohn Clyde (1951), attitudes are more individualistic. Attitude are related to value[38].

Rokeach (1979), argued that an attitude represents several beliefs focused on specific object or situation. The significance of attitude and value lies in the fact that temperamental and dynamic qualities are integrated into patterns of perceiving and acting. In a broader sense, an individual's entire personality structure and his behaviour may be thought of as organised around a central value system that comprises many related attitudes. Values and attitudes are inter-related and complementary to each other. He says that attitude is an organisation of several beliefs[39].

Krishna Kumar (1987) referred attitude to the respondent's degree of favourableness or unfavourableness towards the psychological object. Hence, it is operationally defined as the mental disposition of the respondent to respond favourably or unfavourably towards widow's remarriage, employment after widowhood, participation in social activities etc[40].

In the present study, attitude is taken to refer to the widow's thinking or feeling about herself or towards her in-laws or other members of the family, vice-versa, social activities about re-marriage and employment.

Social Stigma

Social stigma and financial crisis combine to make loneliness the hallmark of widowhood. Their changed and reduced social status as widows, makes establishing new relationship difficult. The stigma of widowhood becomes aggravated when she deviates from the traditional attitude of a widow. The deviation gets socially transferred from generation to generation as they get fixed with the generalised familial status. Such families become part of 'avoidance' for matrimonial purposes and also international arena[41].

Goffman (1963), refers social stigma to a relationship of devaluation in which one individual is disqualified from social acceptance' stigma can be physical, documentary, contextual, ascribed, or achieved. In some instances the stigmatised person has relatively little control over the character or display of his/her disfigurement: In other words, the appearance may be so organised that revelation is suppressed or ambiguous in its impact. Its sociological significance resides in its importance for the analysis of information, management, ascribed deviance and conventional character of social control.

Widows in all communities, suffer from limited freedom to participate in religious and auspicious social functions. They carry the stigma of inauspiciousness and hence have to keep away from functions. They are not allowed to touch those objects used during marriage or religious ceremonies. A widow can not cook rice fed to a prospective bride or bridegroom, nor can she attend or even witness a marriage ceremony. In fact, a widow is not even entitled to perform the ritual to welcome her own daughter-in-law[42].

Ranjan Kumari (1981), found that a widow is held personally responsible for the death of her husband and is treated as the personification of the inauspicious and the profane. Her presence at any kind of social function and festival ranging from marriage and child birth, to sowing of crops is considered to be very inauspicious. Loss of the property and under utilisation of the resource base are two of the most frequent consequences of the discrimination practiced against them[43].

In the present study, the Hindu Mudaliar widows are restricted from wearing 'Tali', flowers, bangles, bindi, eating good food, wearing colourful dress, sowbakya tilak, etc. These are taken as social stigma.

Social Exclusion

Widows are not to laugh or even talk loudly and not to speak with outsiders. They are impressed upon to visit the temple in the evening and eat the prasad of parched rice and dhal. If possible, they do some religious work for their spiritual welfare. Therefore, they may devote free time to bajans, visiting temples and places of pilgrimages. After the death of the husband, they are not to think of other men. They should never re-marry[44].

Social restrictions on the life-style of women tend to become more rigid as one moves up in the caste hierarchy. For instance there is more exclusion of females among upper castes than among lower castes. With in the upper - caste communities in north India, women are strictly secluded and denied access to gainful employment outside their homes. Low caste women have greater freedom to take up gainful employment[45].

Martha Alter Chen (1998), said that the well-being of widows is not just a question of economic security, but also one of dignity, self respect and participation in society. Many widows in his sample suffered from different forms of social isolation, psychological abuse or emotional distress. He found that the social marginalisation of widows frequently took one or more of the following forms.

1. Rumours and accusation: Widows are often accused of being responsible for the death of their husband, regarded as sexually threatening, and generally considered as inauspicious.
2. Enforced dress and behaviour codes: Many widows are under strong pressure to observe restrictive codes of dress, appearance and behaviour. Some of the traditional restrictions have become quite rare, even among the upper castes, but other remain widespread.
3. Social ostracism: A widow is often excluded from the religious and social life of the community due to her perceived inauspiciousness.
4. Physical violence: Violence against widows primarily takes the form of sexual harassment or property-related violence[46].

In the present study, a widow is forced to face social exclusion when she is restricted from participating in employment outside the home, access to education, training, credit or technology.

Social Status

Social status refers to the position of an individual in family and in society. This is determined by social factors like education and caste and economic factors like employment, income and consumption.

According to Lakshmi Menon (1969), the social status of women in any community is largely dependent on the culture and tradition of the community. That a women's primary responsibility is to her family has wide social acceptance all over the world[47].

Social status is the position occupied by a person, family, or kinship group in a social system relative to others. This determines rights, duties and other behaviours, including the nature and extend of the relationships with persons of other status.

Social status has a hierarchical distribution in which a few persons occupy the highest positions. The simplest theoretical model of the social system would be a distribution in which position was determined competitively by the possession of abilities relative to the demand for abilities in the society. The institution of private property, inheritance, differential taxation and social services will modify the form of distribution of status.

Social status is determined by education, income, possession and the social valuation of occupation and of other activities in society[48].

Social status is the position of an individual within social relationships. Social status can be both, high or low. There is an order of social status in society. In the past, Brahmins enjoyed greater respect and were considered superior to other castes.

The social status of an individual is that particular position in relation with other individuals, by virtue of which he is the recipient of respect and prestige, and wields influence and which can be recognised by symbols of prestige accruing to him and his actions.

The social status of an elderly person is determined by several factors such as physical health, marital status, level of education, position in society, economic status etc. The widow experiences not only traumatic sorrowful pain but most of them live a miserable and in human social existence. For subjective experience of grief and sorrow is both inwardly felt physic state due to material-physical de-linking of closest relationship and socially induced subjectivity of a permanent social status, where in, she is redefined a widow as distinct from married[49].

The social status of women in society is measured in terms of the level of education, health as well as the role played by them in the family, community and in society[50].

The social status of the Hindu Mudaliar Community widows, in the present study, is taken to mean the customary rituals like attending marriages, religious functions, visiting friends and relative's house, writing letters to friends and relatives and watching TV and radio in group in the houses.

Economic Status

Paul Chowdhry (1992), pointed out the income / employment of an individual determines his / her economic status[51].

Joachim (1989), related economic status to the nature of occupation done by the Christians of scheduled caste origin, total income, assets possessed by them and their level of indebtedness i.e. assessing whether they are below poverty status or above it[52].

Padmavathi (1992), refers the term 'economic status' to the income available per head for the household of an individual and the expenses incurred per month per head on food. This term also refers to the level of saving and borrowing by the individual[53].

In the present study, the economic status of the Mudaliar Community widows is meant to include ownership of property, employment, income, expenditure and borrowings.

Generation

A generation is normally taken to mean thirty years[54]. In the present study, the respondent widows are classified as 'young' below 40 years, 'middle-aged' between 41 to 60 years of age and 'old' above 60 years of age.

Investment

Taruna Sareen (2001), defines investment as "an addition to the stock of capital goods in the public or private sector over a given time period[55].

Abba.P. Lerner (1985), defines "investment as the spending on additions on our real capital. Buying goods that are not currently consumed[56].

Raymond Bye (1985), defines, "from the point of view of the society, it is the process of producing wealth that will yield income in the future[57].

In the present study, the investment is taken to refer to the widows investment's towards land, building, plant and machinery, lives stocks and share capital.

Saving

J.M. Keynes defines, "savings as the excess of income over expenditure on consumption"[58]. He also explained "savings as the sum of differences between the money income of individuals and their money expenditure on current consumption"[59].

In the present study, saving is taken to refer to the monthly and yearly saving habit of the Hindu Mudaliar community widows in various sources like banks, post offices, financial institutions etc.

Remarriage

Oxford English Dictionary (1978), defines, "re-marriage" as a second or subsequent marriage"[60].

Oxford English Dictionary (1980), defines, "re-marriage" as to enter again into matrimony"[61].

Caste

Caste is derived from the Portugese casta,.meaning race, lineage or pure stock, which is in turn derived from the Latin castus, meaning clean, pure or pious.

It is coined to refer to the traditional Hindu-based system of social organisation in and around India. This originated in the 2nd or 1st millennium B.C and was largely in place about 500 AD. It includes endogamous marriage, strict rules regarding social and personal contacts, occupational homogenity, and structured economic and ritual practices within each caste.[62]

In the present study, Mudaliar together with its sub-caste are taken into analysis.

Generation

In any society an aggregation of persons who are of more or less the same age is termed as a generation. This concept, like that of social class, allows the analysis of the influences at work on those occupying a similar social position, in this case of age.

The concept may be used narrowly in relation to those born at different times of the same parents within a family unit, or broadly in relation to those born within a period, usually about thirty years, within one society. Each generation, by the virture of the different collection of experiences it has undergone, will perceive historical events from a different perspective. Difference between generations form one source of social change and for this reason theorists or reformers, interested in change, give great importance to the young generation[63].

The respondent widows, in the present study, are divided into three age groups–below 40 years, 41 to 60 years and 60 years and above–are treated as three generation for the purpose of analysis.

REVIEW OF PAST STUDIES

Age at Widowhood

Sandhiya had made a study on widows in Ambala division, Haryana during the year 1994. There were 324 widows in her sample frame which comprised of 124 rural, 100 urban, and 100 industrial. Descriptive percentage method was used to analyse the data.

The study reports that the age of widowhood below the age of 20 were more (16 Percent) in the rural areas. The widowhood, that befell on women between the age of 21 and 40 years, was almost equal in rural, urban and industrial sample. The widowhood after 40 years was observable more in industrial and urban subjects[64].

N.S. Krishna kumari had made a study of status of single women in India-Spinsters (working and non-working), widows (working and non-working) and divorced (working and non-working). The study was conducted in Bangalore city in the year 1987. 300 widows were interviewed. Structured questionnaire was used to collect the data. Simple percentage method was used to draw inferences.

She found that early marriage was a common feature among all the respondents. Unlike non-working widows, who had enjoyed, long years of married life, working widows had a short period of married life and they were widowed at a very young age. The non-working respondent had lost their husbands at a much older age than working widows[65].

In her study on the 'Hindu Widows' (a study of deprivation) in Dharwad District (Karnataka State), Godavari D. Patil has analysed their social, economic, cultural and psychological deprivation. The primary data was collected from 300 sample widows (150 rural and 150 urban) using the interview method, chi-square test, 'T' test and simple descriptive percentages were used to analyse the data.

He found in his study that the mean age at widowhood of rural widows was 38.11 years and of urban widows was 41.50 years. The mean duration of widowhood life for rural widows was higher (14.20 years) than that of the urban widows (12.65 years)[66].

T.N. Kitchulu had made a study of the socio-economic conditions of widows in the union territory of Delhi. The study was conducted in Delhi from both urban and rural areas. 500 widows were selected from all the major religious communities. The widows selected were below 45 years. The data was collected with the help of interview schedule. Simple descriptive percentage method was used for the analysis of data.

The above study established a direct correlation between the age of marriage and the age of widowhood. The wide age difference between the husband and wife was found to be the reason for the high incidence of widowhood[67].

B. Hanumandha Rayappa and K.S. Umarani had conducted a study on the 'incidence of widowhood in Karnataka' with the following objectives. (i) The present trends and differentials in the incidence of widowhood from 1921 onwards. (ii) the causes and consequences of widowhood. Trends were mostly obtained from census data and the differentials were taken from survey data. The study included 182 sample widows drawn at random from Lingayats, Vokkaligas, Brahmins, Schedule tribes, Schedule casts, Kurumba, Kujan, and other casts and other religions. They estimated that the mean age at widowhood for those got widowhood by the age of 45, ranged from 30 years in the decade 1901-1911 to 35 years for the decade 1961-1971[68].

In his study on Widows–Role Adjustment and Violence, Mukesh Ahuja had analysed the widowhood - social position in family and society. The study was made in Jaipur city, Rajasthan. The number of widows interviewed for this study were 190. Interview Schedule was used for collecting data from the respondents. The study was focused on Hindu widows. Coefficient tests and chi-square tests were used for the analysis of data. He found that the mean age of becoming widow was 33.2 years in Jaipur city in comparison to the average age of 36.2 years of widowhood at the national level. The mean period of living the life of widowhood was 15.9 years at the time of interview[69].

K. Malathi (2001), had conducted a study on Socio-Economic Status of Hindu Naidu widows in Walajapet Taluk, Vellore District, Tamil Nadu-A Three Generation Study. There were 340 widows in her sample frame which comprised of 100 young, 114 middle and 126 old generation widows. Descriptive percentage and other statistical methods were used to analyse the data.

The study reports that the mean period of widowhood of the respondents of young widows was 13.5 years, middle-aged widows was 14.7 years and the old generation was 10.7 years. She also found that the old generation widows had a long married life and hence had a shorter duration of widowhood. Conversely, the young and middle-aged widows have a short span of married life, hence they have a longer period of widowhood[70].

Nature of Household

Jeuti Barooach had made a study on Single Women in Assamese Hindu Society covering the area of Guwahati comprising of working widows, divorces and un-married women. 110 single women (40 widows, 30 divorces and 40 un-married) were covered in this study. Structured questionnaire was used for collecting data from the respondents. The descriptive percentage method was used for the analysis.

The study reported that 28.2 percent of widows belonged to denuded nuclear families. 21.8 percent of them were belonged to joint families and 8.2 percent belonged to extended families[71].

Martha Alter Chen and Jean Dreze had made a study on widowhood and their well-being in north India. The study was conducted in Palanpur, Uttar Pradesh during the year 1992. The number of widows interviewed was 262. Percentage method was used for analysis of data. According to the study, the proportion of widows who lived in households headed by themselves or by one or their sons was over 80 percent. The vast majority of the households were of three types: nuclear households (widows living with their unmarried children), filial households (defined as household consisting of a widow, atleast one of her married sons and possibly other persons), and very few widows lived with their in-laws, daughters, parents, brothers etc.[72].

H.V. Nagesh and A.P. Katti had made a study on the Socio-Economic Status of Widows in Hubli city and 8 villages from Dharwad Taluk. 167 widows (50 from urban and 117 from rural areas) were covered in this study. Structured questionnaire was used for collecting data from the respondents. The descriptive percentage method was used for analysis. The study reported that about 30 percent of the rural and 10 percent of the urban widows were living with their parents[73].

In her study on the Socio-Economic Status of Hindu Naidu widows in Walajapet Taluk, Vellore District, Tamil Nadu- A Three Generation Study, K. Malathi has analysed social, economic, decision making and attitude of the widows of three generations.

The study reported that 22 percent of young respondents were living with their parents, 16 percent were living with their in-laws, 29 percent were living with their children and 33 percent were living independently. Among the middle-aged group 8.77 percent were living with parents, 12.53 percent were living with in-laws, 40.35 percent were living with children and remaining 40.35 percent were living independently. In case of old generation widows, 48.81 percent were living with their children. 51.59 percent were living independently. The study also reported that the old generation widows did not prefer to live either with parents or in-laws but they preferred to live with their children, who were married and had children[74].

Dependency

Mukesh Ahuja in his study (1996), found that out of 190 respondents, 48.4 percent were depending on children, 28.4 percent were depending on in-laws and children, 11.4 percent were on in-laws, 6.8 percent living alone, 3.7 percent on parents and 1.6 percent on brothers[75].

In her study Godavari D. Patil (2000), found that 8 percent of the urban sample widows were dependent due to inability to earn against 32.67 percent of the rural respondents[76].

In her study, K. Malathi (2001), found that in the young generation, 21 percent of the widows depended on parents compared to the 14 percent who depended on in-laws and 10 percent who depended on sons/daughters. Among the old generation widows, 54.76 percent of the respondents were dependent only on sons/daughters. It is because these respondents who have already reached old age, preferred to live with sons/daughters[77].

Social Stigma and Social Exclusion

Godavari D. Patil, in her study, had analysed the social stigma and the social exclusion of the widows. She found that after widowhood 61 percent of the urban and 76 percent of the rural respondents were wearing simple cloths. Change in the food habit was noticed after widowhood among 66 percent of the urban respondents and 78 percent of the rural respondents.

The sowbhagya tilak like 'Kumkum' 'Mangalsutra' and 'flowers' were not worn by a majority of widows. Most of the widows did not attend marriage ceremonies both in rural and urban areas[78].

The study, made by Martha Alter Chen and Jean Dreze (1992), reported that widows had very little freedom to return to their parental home. They were expected to remain in their husbands village. It was also pointed out that widows faced severe employment restrictions due to gender divisions of labour[79].

In the study made by Krishna Kumari (1987) working widows preferred to attend religious functions rather than social functions because of ill-treatment and lack of respect in the latter. Among the non-working widows many of them did not like to attend both religious as well as social functions[80].

T.N. Kitchulu noticed in his study (1982) that after widowhood there were drastic changes in the life style of women. About 62 percent of the widows had undergone change in dress and they were not allowed to use Kumkum or Sindhur and 28 percent of the widows had to change to simple diet after widowhood[81].

H.V. Nagesh and A.P. Katti, in their study (1997), observed that the participation of women in religious activities had decreased after widowhood in rural areas from 97 percent to 43 percent and in urban areas from 64 percent to 58 percent[82].

K. Malathi (2001) in her study, observed that the younger generation widows preferred to wear cos1tly dress-sari with blouse–compared to middle-aged and old generation widows, who preferred to wear ordinary and simple dress–white sari with blouse. About 75 percent of young respondents were preferred rich type of dress than middle (64 percent) and old generation widows (16 percent). She also found that the young respondents enjoyed more freedom in the choice of dress compared to the other two generations of widows. She also reported that the young respondents preferred rich and special food. The middle-aged and old generation respondents preferred simple ordinary food which was customary for a widow to eat. In her study she also reported that 46 percent of young respondents were used cosmetics and 54 percent were refused to use it. In the same way 88 percent of the young generation widows were used jewels as against 75.44 percent of middle-aged generation and 5.56 percent of old generation. Going to theatres for entertainment was preferred by 75 percent of the young respondents, 64.04 percent of the middle-aged respondents and 7.94 percent of the old respondents[83].

Decision Making

Godavari D. Patil (2000) had analysed the decisions taken by the widows in urban and rural areas. She found that about 3.6 percent of the urban and 54 percent of the rural respondents consulted their relatives. About 12.87 percent of the urban and 4.67 percent of the rural respondents consulted their adult children[84].

Mukesh Ahuja (1996) reported that 44.4 percent of the respondents were never consulted by their sons, daughters, in-laws on important issues or even in giving gifts to others or selling and buying things[85].

Krishna Kumari, (1987) pointed out that the majority of non-working widows felt handicapped while taking decisions regarding the education and the marriage of their children. 26 percent of the respondents reported that they missed the friendship, emotional warmth and moral support provided by their husbands at the time of distress[86].

K. Malathi, found that less than half of the respondents, (young 41 percent, middle-aged 44.74 percent and old 41.27 percent) alone could take independent decisions. The rest of the respondents had to depend on others to take decisions[87].

Economic Status

T.N. Kitchulu, reported that about 78.48 percent of the widows started working after widowhood due to economic necessity. Among rural widows 33 percent faced the problem of getting jobs in comparison with 14.29 percent of urban widows. Almost all widows had faced two big problems viz., (i) Money and (ii) Finding a job because of the inexperience in dealing with financial matters and due to lack of occupational skills[88].

On the other hand, N.S. Krishnakumari, reported that a majority of 56 percent of the respondents belonging to the working category had joined the work force after the death of their husbands and therefore they were solely dependent on their own income for their livelihood and for the maintenance of their families unlike non-working widows whose major sources of husband's pension and a combination of these two[89].

Godavari D. Patil pointed out that both urban and rural widows, irrespective of their castes, had started working after widowhood due to sheer economic necessity. It was found that a little over half of them (25.67 percent) started working. It is also significant to note that a greater number of urban widows (16 percent) as compared to the rural widows (12 percent) started working after becoming widows. In both urban and rural areas, a majority of widows (46.67 percent) are helped by their parents / brothers in getting employment, and about 40.74 percent of the urban widows, as against 66.67 percent of their rural counterparts faced problems in getting jobs due to lack of proper education. It is also interesting to note that among working widows a significant majority of those based in rural areas (87.33 percent) are not satisfied with their present employment[90].

The study made by H.V. Nagesh and A.P. Katti, (1987) reported that the average size of household among total respondents was 3.3 at the time of the study. In the rural area, it was 4.6 and in the urban area 3.7 on an average. 1.4 (urban) and 1.1 (rural) members in the households were working. This might have naturally caused economic hardship to the households of the widows.

The average annual individual income was Rs. 649 at the time of widowhood and it went up to Rs. 877 at the time of studying in rural area and in urban area it went up to Rs. 1041 from Rs. 506. It indicated that the respondents were not economically active, generally when their husbands were living, but they have been forced to take some job after they lost their husbands. Some of the respondents, who were not working when their husbands were alive, were forced to work after the death of their working parents. The proportion increased to 14.5 percent from 1.2 percent in rural areas. In urban areas the proportion of respondents being economically active increased in each category of workers.

About 68 percent of the rural and 94 percent of the urban respondents had developed a sense of insecurity after they lost their husbands. It appears that widows feel insecure mostly because (i) rural widows suffered the loss of income due to the demise of the bread winner and (ii) urban respondents suffered from the absence of anyone who can give shelter and support during widowhood[91].

The study made by K. Malathi, (2001) reported that 40 to 45 percent of the respondents were belonging to the lowest monthly income bracket of Rs. 100 to 200. The non-earners range between 36 to 45 percent. Similar to individual income, 26 to 36 percent of the respondents family income per month ranges between Rs. 1000 to 2000. Those who belonged to the family income bracket of Rs. 2001 to 3000 ranges between 12 to 24 percent. Those whose monthly family income falls in the income bracket of Rs. 3001 to 4000 ranges between 2 to 11 percent. The non-earners had no source of income. She also reported that the family annual expenditure on food for 44 to 47 percent of the respondents varies from Rs. 501 to 1000, 30 to 39 percent of the respondents had spent Rs. 1001 to 2000 per month on food and 3 to 7 percent of the respondents had spent between Rs. 2001 to 3000 per month. While 63 to 73 percent of the respondents had spent between Rs. 200 to 400 on cloths per year. The remaining respondents had spent between Rs. 400 to 600 annually on cloths. 25 to 30 percent of the respondents had not incurred any expenditure on education. Those respondents who had to repay debts were 17 respondents from young, 24 respondents from middle-aged and 22 respondents from old generation. The debt varies from a minimum of Rs. 3000 to a maximum of Rs. 5000. Some of the debts were incurred by their deceased husbands. The respondents had borrowed for meeting the medical, education and marriage expenses of their children[92].

Social Status

H.V. Nagesh and A.P. Katti (1987), in their study, reported that the average size of household among total respondents was 3.3 at the time of study. In the rural areas, it was 4.6 and in the urban areas it was 3.7. About 79 percent of the rural respondents and 58 percent of the urban respondents were illiterate. 4 percent of the rural and 1 percent of the urban respondents had studied between seventh standard and

Matriculation. Educational attainment of the urban respondents was slightly better than that of rural respondents, in the rural areas respondents had, on an average of 2.5 children at the time of widowhood and 2.5 children in urban areas.

Most of the respondents had to face many problems like food, shelter, clothing, education and marriage of their children, loss of status etc. Only 10 percent of the rural and 2 percent of the urban respondents reported that they did not face any serious problems. About 78 percent of the rural and 72 percent of the urban respondents had received some help from certain sources mainly relatives and friends[93].

T. Rajaretnam and E. Gandhi had made a study on Socio-Economic and Demographic Aspects of Widowhood in Athoor and Batlagundu Blocks in Tamil Nadu. The number of samples covered by the study was 1027 widows in Athoor Block and 977 in Batlagundu Block. Interview Schedule was used for the collection of data. The collected data was analysed by using simple descriptive percentages. It was found that eiderly widows aged 50 and above were mostly illiterate[94].

The study made by Krishna Kumari (1987), reported that 79 percent of the working widows held a very low status in society in their caste or community. Only 14 percent opined that they were accorded equal treatment with other married women. 5 percent reported sympathetic treatment from their caste people, 2 percent were unable to decide the status ascribed to them.

A vast majority of non-working widows (87 percent) claim that they have a low status in their caste and community. 11 percent of non-working widows reported an equal status with other married women, the remaining 2 percent of the respondents received sympathetic treatment from their caste[95].

T.N. Kitchulu, in his study, 'Widows in India', reported that a majority of Hindus considered performing all the customary ceremonies on a widow essential as these were prescribed by the social customs (breaking of bangles, removal of married signs, serving food to Brahmins etc.)[96].

The study made by K. Malathi (2001), reported that there was not much change in the practice of girls being given in marriage took in all the three generations of the community in the study area. As the respondents grow older they prefer independent living. In the pattern of living wide variation could be noticed among the respondents between generations. 10 to 20 percent were living in huts, 40 percent were living in thatched houses, 30 to 40 percent were living in tiled houses and rest were living in terraced houses. Regarding dressing pattern, food habit, use of cosmetics, use of jewels and entertainment the young respondents had high preference as against the middle-aged and old generation widows. In doing customary things like performing rituals, attending marriages, writing letters to friends and relatives, visiting friends and relatives and visiting temples the younger generation respondents had greater preference than the middle and old generation respondents. The respondents role in the family reveals that more than 50 percent of them were sole earners, 34 to 43 percent were doing self cooking, 48 to 65 percent of them were engaged in child care, 26 to 41 percent of them would make purchases. Washing and cleaning was done by 33 to 47 percent of the respondents[97].

Re-marriage of the Widows

Godavari D. Patil (2000) reported that 80 percent of widows favoured widow re-marriage and 39.32 percent stated one year as the ideal gap between widowhood and re-marriage. 39.08 percent of the respondents hold the opinion that young widows should re-marry and 81.67 percent of them accept re-married widows. 46.34 percent of the respondents have opined that it would be difficult for a married women to adjust to a second marriage. The widow's disapproval of re-marriage clearly pointed out that religious and social sanction for re-marriage were lacking[98].

H.V. Nagesh and A.P. Katti (1988) reported that 47 percent of rural and 64 percent of urban respondents would approve of re-marriage of other widows. The re-marriage of 43 percent of the rural widows was not approved by elders from husband's side and 72 percent of rural widows said that elders from father's side did not approve of re-marriage. In urban areas 16 percent approved re-marriage from husband's relatives and 24 percent of urban widows reported that relatives of father approved re-marriage. 58 percent of the urban respondents felt that children will be neglected and they will not tolerate re-marriage. A few were afraid of society, custom and other things[99].

Krishna Kumari, in her study (1987), reported that 32 percent of non-working widows and 18 percent of working widows have positive attitude not only if the widow is young and children but also in other instances. Instances of widow re-marriage in the family were unknown in the majority of both the working and non-working widows families.

It is noted that a higher proportion of non-working widows advocate re-marriage than those who would actually consider it for themselves, if an occasion arose. The consistency in attitude and action seems to be more among working widows than among non-working widows. This may be due to their being practical in view of a society which does not advocate re-marriage. Only 3 to 6 percent cases (Bangalore) are willing to re-marry[100].

In her study "Socio-Economic Psychiatric Study of Widows" in two districts of Ambala division, Sandhiya (1994), reported that only a very few cases encouraged re-marriage. They advocated re-marriage of young widows with out issue[101].

CONCLUSION

The review of the above studies reveal that the present study, on the Socio-Economic Status of Hindu Mudaliar Community Widows–A Three Generation Study, is different from them both in content and dimensions. The present study is confined to a community which has been declared 'forward' both socially and economically. The study relates to three generation of widows–young, middle-aged, and old. It is possible to identify the changes that have occurred on the socio-economic status of the Hindu Mudaliar community widows over a period of time. The methods adopted for the present study is presented in the fifth chapter.

NOTES

1. Serinity Young (1998), Encyclopedia of Women and World Religion, Vol. II, Macmillian Reference USA, New York, p. 1029.
2. K. Malathi (2001), An Published Ph.D Thesis; Socio-Economic Status of Hindu Widows in Walajapet Taluk - A Three Generation Study, University of Madras, Chennai, p. 44.
3. N. Dutt (1968), Origin and Growth of Caste in India, Vol.I, Firma Publications, Calcutta, p. 247.
4. Mukesh Ahuja (1996), Widows: Role Adjustment and Violence, Wishva Prakasham Publishing House, New Delhi, p.36.
5. G.R. Lesile (1979), The Family in Social Context, Oxford University Press, New York, p. 614.
6. M.A. Fritz (1929), A Study of Widows in Sociology and Social Research, Vol. XIV, No.1, p. 553.
7. B.M.M. Aradhya (1987), What is Means to be a Widow, Social Welfare, Vol. XXXIV, No.9, p. 3.
8. L.A. Morgan (1981), Economic Changes at Midlife Widowhood–A Longitudinal Analysis, Journal of Marriage and the Family, Vol. 43, No. 4, p. 899.
9. K. Malathi (2001), Op.cit, p. 46.
10. Ibid, p. 46.
11. Mukesh Ahuja (1996), Op.cit, p. 21.
12. B.M.M. Aradhya (1987), Op.cit, p. 3.
13. H.H. Hyman (1983), Of Time of Widowhood, Duke Press Policy Studies, Durham, p. 3.
14. K. Malathi (2001), Op.cit, p. 48.
15. Monica Das Gupta et.al (1995), Women's Health in India, Oxford University Press, Mumbay, pp. 267-268.
16. Godvari.D. Patil (2000), A Study in Deprivation – Hindu Widows, Gyan Publishing House, New Delhi, pp. 27 - 29.
17. Idid, pp. 28,29.
18. Ibid, p. 29.
19. Raj Kumar (2000), Encyclopedia of Women and Development, Vol.16, Anmol Publications, New Delhi, p. 7.
20. Ibid, p. 7.
21. K. Malathi (2001), Op.cit, p. 48.

22. M.C. Median (1999), Dictionary of Economics, Himalaya Publishing House, Mumbai, p. 132.
23. K. Malathi (2001), Op.cit, p. 49.
24. Ibid, p. 49.
25. Ibid, p. 50.
26. Mukesh Ahuja (1996), Op.cit, pp. 59-64.
27. Lalitha Srinath (2000), An Indian Book Review, Vol.3, No.4, Sage Publications, New Delhi, p. 27.
28. Ranjana Kumari (1981), Widow Headed Households on Rural India, Radiant Publishers, New Delhi, p.40.
29. D. Baskara Rao (1998), International Encyclopaedia of Women, Vol. I, Discovery Publishing House, New Delhi, p. 6.
30. M. Indra Devi (1987), Women, Education and Employment Family Living, Gian Publishing House, New Delhi, pp. 130-132.
31. K. Malathi (2001), Op.cit, p. 55.
32. Idid, p.55.
33. Mukesh Ahuja (1996), Op.cit, p. 51.
34. K. Malathi (2001), Op.cit, p. 56.
35. M. Rokeach (1979), Understanding Human Values-Individual and Societal, The Free Press, New York, p. 2.
36. K. Malathi (2001), Op.cit, p. 57.
37. Mukesh Ahuja (1996), Op.cit, p. 43.
38. K. Malathi (2001), Op.cit, p. 58.
39. Ranjana Kumari (1981), Op.cit, p. 60.
40. Monica Das Gupta et.al (1995), Op.cit, pp. 279,280.
41. Ram Singh (1994), Decision-Making in Home and Farm Related Activities, Kurukshetra, Vol. XLII, No.10, p. 37.
42. M. Indra Devi (1987), Op.cit, pp. 130-132.
43. K. Malathi (2001), Op.cit, pp. 61,62.
44. Ibid, p. 62.
45. Ibid, pp. 63,64.
46. Mukesh Ahuja (1996), Op.cit, p. 22.
47. K. Malathi (2001), Op.cit, p. 65.
48. Ibid, p. 65.
49. Ibid, P.66.

50. Ibid, p. 41.
51. Ibid, pp. 66,67.
52. Taruna Sareen (2001), Encyclopaedic Dictionary of Economics, Vol.2, Sarup and Sons, New Delhi, p. 378.
53. Ibid, p. 378.
54. Ghodake (1985), Encyclopaedic Dictionary of Economics, Vol.3, Mittal Publications, New Delhi, pp. 640-641.
55. Ibid, p. 640.
56. Ibid, p. 641.
57. Ghodake (1985), Op.cit, p. 944.
58. Ibid, p. 944.
59. Ibid, p. 944.
60. The Oxford English Dictionary (1978), Vol.VIII, POY-RY, Oxford, London Glasgow, p. 325.
61. Ibid, p. 325.
62. MacMillan Student Encyclopedia of Sociology (1983) edited by Micheal Mann, p. 33.
63. Ibid, p. 145.
64. Sandhiya (1994), Widowhood: A Socic - Psychiattic Study, Mohit Publications, New Delhi, pp. 82- 98.
65. N.S. Krishna Kumari (1987), Status of Single Women in India, Uppal Publishing House, New Delhi, p. 85.
66. K. Malathi (2001), An Published Ph.D Thesis; Socio-Economic Status of Hindu Widows in Walajapet Taluk - A Three Generation Study, University of Madras, Chennai, p. 67.
67. Ibid, pp. 67,68.
68. Ibid, pp. 70,71.
69. Mukesh Ahuja (1996), Widows: Role Adjustment and Violence, Wishva Prakasham Publishing House, New Delhi, p.35.
70. K. Malathi (2001), Op.cit, pp.71 to 73.
71. Ibid, p. 70.
72. Ibid, pp. 69,70.
73. Mukesh Ahuja (1996), Op.cit, p. 59.
74. K. Malathi (2001), Op.cit, p. 71.
75. Ibid, pp. 72-75.

76. N.S. Krishna Kumari (1987), Op.cit, p. 90.
77. Ibid, p. 92.
78. Ibid, pp. 94,95.
79. K. Malathi (2001), Op.cit, p. 72.
80. Ibid, p. 73.
81. Mukesh Ahuja (1996), Op.cit, p. 63.
82. Ibid, p. 67.
83. K. Malathi (2001), Op.cit, pp. 73,74.
84. N.S. Krishna Kumari (1987), Op.cit, p. 82.
85. Ibid, p. 89.
86. Ibid, p. 95.
87. Ibid, p. 75.
88. K. Malathi (2001), Op.cit, p.73, 74, 75, 76.
89. Ibid, pp. 75, 76.
90. Ibid, pp.77, 78.
91. Ibid, p. 80.
92. Idid, p. 77.
93. N.S. Krishna Kumari (1987), Op.cit, p. 85.
94. Ibid, pp. 87, 88.
95. Ibid, p. 95.
96. Ibid, pp. 86, 87.
97. K. Malathi (2001), Op.cit, p. 79.
98. Ibid, p. 80.
99. Ibid, pp. 80, 81.
100. N.S. Krishna Kumari (1987), Op.cit, p. 98.
101. Sandhiya (1994), Op.cit, p. 261.

3
PROFILE OF THE STUDY AREA (VELLORE DISTRICT)

The Socio-Economic factors such as population, literacy, nature of population, religion, crop pattern, rainfall, soil and irrigation, land utilisation, industrial development and welfare schemes form the infrastructure of the area of the study. Therefore, a brief description of the study area including the above factors, presented here, would provide the backdrop for the analysis of the problem.

BRIEF HISTORY OF THE VELLORE DISTRICT

Vellore District was also known as "Thondalmandalam region" in early south Indian history. The pages of South Indian History replete with incidences that the region has witnessed many thrilling fights for supremacy between the local chieftains and rulers on the one hand and the French and English invaders on the other. Places of historical importance in this district like Arcot, Vellore and Wallajah etc., have seen several small and big battles. The great Philosopher and former President of India, Dr.Sarvapalli Radhakrishnan, Sir. C.P. Ramaswamy Iyer, a well known administrator Dr.A.Lakshmanaswamy Mudaliar, Vice-Chancellor of the University of Madras for a record period of 27 years in India, Dr. RamasamiMudaliar, great trade unionist, were also sons of this district. The Vellore district is benefitted under various plan schemes introduced by the Tamil Nadu Government.

From the earlist times for which evidence is available, the Vellore District formed part of the Pallava Kingdom during the second half of the ninth century A.D. Kanchipuram in Chengalpattu MGR District was then the capital of Pallavas. In the succeeding periods, the district came under the rulers of Cholas, the Rashtrakutas, the Thanjavur ruler Raja Raja and the Hindu ruler of Vijayanagar. The district then fell under the rule of the Mohamedan Nawabs of the Carnatic, whose head quarters was Arcot. The British had introduced many Socio-Economic changes here in the 19th century. The Vellore jail has become famous inview of its importance in the history of the freedom struggle and also due to internment of many great leaders in the jail. The district has been making great strides in all spheres since then. The world famous CMC Hospital located at Vellore is known for its specialised medical services. The main aim of Dr. Ida Scudder, the founder of this institution, was to serve the poor. Many leading private industries, manufacturing particularly leather products, are located around Vaniyambadi and Ambur in Vellore district.

LOCATION AND AREA OF THE VELLORE DISTRICT

Vellore District lies between 12°15′ of the Northern Latitude and 78°20′ and 79°50′ of the Eastern Longitude. On the East, it is bounded by Kancheepuram district, on the south by Tiruvannamalai district, on the west by Dharmapuri district and on the North by Chittoor district of Andhra Pradesh. Map, showing the location of vellore district, is enclosed. The total area of the vellore district is 6,077 Sq.Km. It contains 4.67 Percent of the state's area. Vellore District is the fifth largest districts of Tamil Nadu. It's Headquarter is at Vellore, which is an important educational center in the state, and the economy of the district is essentially agrarian in character.

PHYSICAL FEATURES OF THE VELLORE DISTRICT

Topography

The area covered under forest in the Vellore District is about 1.98 Sq.Km. The district has well-marked natural divisions in Tirupattur taluk, the Jawadu Hills contains Sandal Wood. It gives good revenue to the government. The broken masses of the Jawadu Hills stretching about 40 Kms North-South and 24 Kms East-West, forms part of the Western Ghats. The Jawadu Hills is about 2,500 feet high above Mean Sea Level (MSL). The Yelagiri Hills lies in the central part of the Tirupattur Taluk. The general elevation of the Yelagiri Hills is about 1048.5 feet above Mean Sea Level (MSL). The district is covered mostly by rocky hills. The spherical rock masses of these hills throw off rain water without retaining them, thus, helping to generate a number of tanks. There are large number of hills scattered around the district.

Soils

In general, the soils in the vellore distric can be classified into two main groups, black and red. But a more useful classification would be as loamy, sandy, clay groups. The clay variety is found to exist in limited area in the neighbourhood of the lakes. Important soil typs, found in the district, are red ferugenous loamy and sandy loamy. Black soil is generally limited to the Palar, Ponnaiyar river basins. Most of the best land in the district has loamy soil. The red soils are best suited for dry crops but the availability of irrigation facilities have enabled the ryots to raise paddy, sugarcane, flower plants and other crops.

Climate

The district has generally experienced tropical climate. The period from April to June is generally hot. A uniform climatic condition prevails through out the district. Generally November to February would be fairly cool months. The taluks lying in the eastern region with little or no forest or mountains; experience a comparatively more equal climate than the remaining areas. The taluks falling in this group are: Arakkonam and parts of Walajapet. The Arcot, Vellore, Walajapet and Gudiyattam taluks, which are surrounded by hills and mountains, are exposed to different climate and slightly cold during the winter season. In Tirupattur and Vaniyambadi taluks, climate is rather slightly cold during winter, but moderate during other seasons. The average minimum and maximum temperature in the district is between 16° celsius and 38° celsius respectively.

Rainfall

Another important parameter, which contribute to the growth of the economy, is rainfall. As it is in the case of Tamil Nadu, rain fall in vellore district is scanty. The normal average rain fall in vellore district during 2003 was 1012.4 mm as against the state normal average rainfall of 925.2 mm. The seasonal fluctuation in rain fall is also common in vellore district, this may be seen in table 3.1 below.

Table - 3.1
Monthly and Seasonal Rainfall in Vellore District (1997-1998)

(mm)

Seasons	*Months*	*Normal*	*Actual*	*Percentage*
South-West Monsoon	June to September	432.1	454.3	48.73
North-East Monsoon	October to December	365.9	434.7	46.63
Winter Period	January to February	23.4	0.3	0.03
Hot Weather Period	March to May	105.3	42.8	4.59
Total		926.7	932.1	100

Source: Tamil Nadu Economic Appraisal, 1997-98, P.S-19.

The annual as well as month wise distribution of rainfall has not been uniform during the years 1995 to 2000. Wide deviation from the normal rainfall could be noticed in these years. While the actual rainfall during the years 1995, 1996, 1998 was higher, it was much lower than the normal year during the year 1997, 1999 and 2000.

Rivers

The Palar river is the most important river of the region which takes its origin near Nàndidurga in Karnataka state. It enters North Western corner of the Tirupattur taluk. The Ponnaiyar river, Koddas and Kaundanya rivers are the tributaries of Palar river.

Table – 3.2
Month wise Distribution of Rain fall in Vellore District between 1995 and 2000.

Months	*Normal*	*1995*	*1996*	*1997*	*1998*	*1999*	*2000*
January	30.9	28.05	–	–	–	8.9	–
February	8.9	4.05	–	–	–	1.1	47.9
March	11.5	11.82	1.60	–	–	–	–
April	24.3	0.45	53.60	14.00	18.50	20.5	24.4
May	70.8	250.15	9.60	52.50	20.80	53.9	51.8
June	58.1	93.52	144.90	130.50	23.20	56.8	60.5
July	87.6	131.20	34.20	56.20	104.80	30.8	70.3
August	132.9	270.90	156.60	103.40	181.30	85.5	130.7
September	160.5	111.10	161.10	102.90	211.30	73.9	219.7
October	166.2	99.60	150.90	117.60	159.00	142.3	210.7
November	158.4	36.80	131.40	183.50	212.30	105.2	68.0
December	61.0	13.80	277.60	84.40	100.20	56.9	60.0
Total	971.1	1051.44	1121.50	934.90	1031.40	635.8	964.0

Source: Vellore District Official Records.

Forest

The forest area in vellore district is estimated to be 1924.61 Sq.km during 1997-98. Out of this, 1713.78 Sq.km is reserved forests, 49.61 Sq.km is reserved lands and 161.22 Sq.km is estimated as unclassified forests.

Flora and Fauna

The ordinary trees found in the district are tamarind trees, teak wood, some sandalwood, ven-teak, casurina, bamboo etc. As regards fauna, the western region, and in particular the mountainous tracts possess some wild animals. Bison is seen in small numbers on the Javadi ranges, and tiger is seen occasionally. Leopards are found all through the rocky hills, black bears, hyenas, sambar, spotted deer, jungle sheep, barking deer, antelope, varieties of snakes including the king cobras are spread over different regions of the district.

Elephants were previously seen and captured near Chengam forests. Monkeys exist in several places in the district. The skeleton of gigantic elephant caught in the Chengam forest region is kept in the national museum at Chennai. The common birds of South Indian species are seen in the district. The peafowls and jungle fowls exist in the forests of the district.

Revenue Administration

The Revenue Administration of the district is divided into four divisions, Viz., Revenue Divisions, Revenue Taluks, Revenue Firkas and Revenue Villages. There are three Revenue divisions, namely Ranipet, Vellore and Tirupattur. Eight Revenue Taluks namely, Arcot, Walajapet, Arakonam, Vellore, Gudiyattam, Tirupattur, Vaniyambadi and Katpadi. Fifty two Revenue Firkas and eight hundred fourty three revenue villages are part of the revenue administrative divisions of the vellore district. The administrative divisions of the vellore district is kept below.

Local Administration

The local administration of the district is classifiedd into municipalities, town panchayats, panchayat unions and village panchayats. At present there are nine municipalities, 27 town panchayats, 20 panchayat unions and 753 village panchayats in the system of local governance of the vellore district. Apart from the local bodies, there are 12 Legislative and three Parlimentary constituencies in the district.

SOCIO-ECONOMIC INDICATORS

Human Wealth

The size and quality of population is a major factor which determines regional variation in development. The census of 2001 for vellore district is compared with other districts in Tamil Nadu with special reference to size of population, composition, density, rural urban popolation and literacy etc.

According to 2001 census, the population in vellore district is enumerated as 34,82,970 comprised of 17,43,871 males and 17,39,099 females. In size of population, vellore district ranks 3rd among 29 districts of Tamil Nadu. It accounts for 5.60 Percent of the total state population. The decadal growth of population is estimated as 15.09 Percent in vellore district between 1991-2001. The decadal growth rate is just above the state average decadal growth rate of 11.19 Percent. The fluctuation in decadal growth of population in vellore district, may be seen in table 3.3.

Table – 3.3
Decadal Growth of Population in Vellore District During 1901-2001

S. No.	*Year*	*Decadal Variation in Percentage*
1.	1901-11	9.30
2.	1911-21	2.88
3.	1921-31	12.89
4.	1931-41	17.23
5.	1941-51	16.40
6.	1951-61	8.44
7.	1961-71	22.74
8.	1971-81	17.79
9.	1981-91	15.14
10.	1991-01	15.09

Source: Census of India 2001 – Tamil Nadu Series, Paper 1 of 2001, P.20.

Rural Population

The Percentage of rural population to the total population in vellore district is calculated as 62.15 Percent in 2001. Vellore district is one of those districts whose rural population is higher than the state average rural population of 56.14 Percent. In rural population vellore district ranks 16th among 29 districts of Tamil Nadu.

Urban Population

With regard to urban population, vellore district is behind many other districts of Tamil Nadu. The percentage of urban population to the total population in Vellore district is calculated as 37.85 percent in 2001. Vellore district is one of those districts whose urban population is below the state average of 43.86 Percent. In urban population, Vellore district ranks 15th among 29 districts of Tamil Nadu. One of the reasons for low ratio of urban population in Vellore district is due to its slow growth of urban agglomeration.

Sex Ratio

The sex ratio in Vellore district has been higher than the state sex ratio both in 1991 and 2001 census. In 1991 census, the sex ratio for Vellore district has been estimated as 978 females for every 1000 males as against the state average of 974 females for every 1000 males. In 2001 census the sex ratio of the district is 997 females for every 1000 males as against the state average of 986 females for every 1000 males.

Density

The density of population in Vellore district is estimated as 573 persons per Sq.km. as against the state average density of 478 persons per Sq.km. in 2001 census. In density of population, Vellore district ranks 9th among 29 districts of Tamil Nadu. The high density may be attributed to higher rate of growth of population in Vellore district.

Literacy

The literacy of persons in Vellore district has increased from 60.87 percent in 1991 to 73.07 percent in 2001. The literacy of men has increased from 72.94 percent in 1991 to 82.67 percent in 2001. The female literacy rate has also increased from 48.58 percent in 1991 to 63.53 percent in 2001. The litercay rate in Vellore district (73.07 Percent) is lower than the state average literacy rate (73.47 Percent). In addition to this, the illiteracy of the district is also reduced from 39.13 percent in 1991 to 26.93 percent in 2001. The illiteracy of men has reduced from 27.06 percent in 1991 to 17.33 percent in 2001. The female illiteracy has also rapidly reduced from 51.42 percent in 1991 to 36.47 percent in 2001. The literacy is an important indicator of development. Various new educational programmes have been adopted recently, such as, functional literacy programme, adult literacy programme, distance education and open university system. These may bring about the desired change in the literacy rate in Vellore district. The introduction of nutritious noon meal seheme is another notable programme which serves not only to improve the nutritional standard of children but also provides education to all children, by minimising potential dropouts.

Occupational Pattern

The overall engagement of the people in the district in different sectors, of the economy, namely agriculture, industry and service sectors is brought out in the occupational pattern. Agricultural labourers form 27.48 percent, cultivators form 17.64 percent followed by household industries of 11.33 percent. The employment of human labour in the district is mostly contributed by agricultural labourers and other workers. It accounts for 88.47 percent of the total employment, this may be seen in table-3.4.

Table – 3.4
Occupational Pattern in Vellore District (2001)

S.No.	*Occupational Pattern*	*No. of Workers*	*Percentage*
1.	Cultivators	2,51,688	17.64
2.	Agricultural Labourers	3,92,206	27.48
3.	Household Industries	1,61,704	11.33
4.	Other Works	6,21,405	43.55
	Total	14,27,003	100

Source: Census of India 2001–Tamil Nadu Series, Paper-208, 2001, P.151.

Language

The people in the vellore district could speak languages like Tamil, Telugu, Marathi, Kannada and Urdu. Tamil is the local language spoken by majority of the people.

Land Use-Pattern

Since majority of the people in vellore district are agriculturists, the land use pattern elucidates the land-man relationship. The table-3.5 provides the land use pattern in vellore district during 1997-98. Out of the total geographical area of 14,74,746 hectares, only 22,00,56 hectares were sown which formed only 14.92 percent of the total area. The area sown in vellore district is much lower than the area sown in the state. The area under forest cover is far below the minimum requirements of ecological standards. The area under forest comes to 10.93 percent of the total area. The barren and uncultivable land comes to 1.76 percent of the total area and 5.60 percent of the land is utilised for non-agricultural purpose. Current fallow land forms 2.50 percent while 0.46 percent of the land is declared as cultivable waste. The land put to other uses like pastures, grazing land and miscellaneous tree crops comes to less than 1 percent of the total area.

The land use pattern shows that there is lot of scope for increasing the area sown provided irrigation facility is created in vellore district. That will pave the way for generating more employment and income.

Table–3.5
Land Use Pattern in Vellore District During 1997-98.

S. No.	*Items*	*Area in Hectares*	*Percentage*
1.	Geographical area	592018	40.14
2.	Forest area	161229	10.93
3.	Barren uncultivable land	26054	1.76
4.	Land put to non- agricultural uses	82681	5.60
5.	Cultivable waste	6825	0.46
6.	Permanent pastures and other grazing lands	3833	0.25
7.	Land under misce.tree crops and groves not included in net area sown	1830	0.12
8.	Current fallows	36976	2.50
9.	Other fallow lands	52534	3.56
10.	Net area sown	220056	14.92
11.	Area sown more than one	35327	2.39
12.	Gross croped area	255383	17.31
	Total	14,74,746	100

Source: Tamil Nadu Economic Appraisal 1997-1998, P. S.21.

Irrigation

Sparse rainfall in an area calls for more attention to irrigation. Much importance has been given to irrigation in Tamil Nadu state since 1950-51. Various measures and schemes like major irrigation, minor irrigation, well irrigation, lift irrigation, sprinkler irrigation etc. have been launched. But there is wide variation in the utilisation of irrigation potential in the state. The net area sown and irrigated in vellore district is estimated to be 54.13 percent in 1997-98; this is higher than the state average of 52.77 percent. It is interesting to note that vellore district with 1,17,769 wells is in the top of the list of all the districts using wells for irrigation.

The net area irrigated by wells in the district is 91,973 hectares. The main reason for such incongruity, largest number of wells and lower area irrigated, may be due to the small size of holdings and the wells remain dry for a long period. Each well irrigates below its capacity. Hence ther is ample scope for extending the area irrigated under each well in vellore district in the future. Apart from well irrigation, tanks also play an important role in the irrigation of the district. There are 1355 tanks located in vellore district for various irrigation purposes.

Table –3.6
Cropping Pattern in Vellore District

S. No.	*Crops*	*Area in (ha)*	*Production in Tons*
I.	Food Crops		
1.	Paddy	52,332	2,35,562
2.	Millets	37,184	52,253
3.	Pulses	37,242	23,906
4.	Cotton	4,962	1,754
5.	Sugarcane	27,249	2,45,241
6.	Oil seeds	59,592	1,01,575
	Grand Total	2,18,561 (100 %)	6,60,291

Source: Dept of Agriculture, Vellore.

Cropping Pattern

Crop pattern in a place is determined by the agro-climatic conditions of the area. It would also determine the profitability of the crop and employment pattern of agricultural labourers. The cropping pattern, as shown below, gives the crops grown in the farm at a particular point of time. The area and production of crops during the year 2000-2001 is furnished in table-3.6 below.

The area under food crops command 58 percent of the total cropped area compared to 42 percent of the non-food crops. The important food crops grown in the district are paddy, millets and pulses. Cotton, sugarcane and oil seeds are the important non-food crops grown by the farmers in vellore district. The production of various crops in the district indicates that paddy tops among other food crops. Among the non-food crops, sugarcane stands first followed by oil seeds.

Livestock Population

The livestock census of vellore district gives a wide sepectrum of animals grown by the farmers (see table-3.7). There were 5,02,514 cattles, 1,14,802 buffaloes, 3,06,818 sheeps, 2,03,270 goats, 16,923 pigs, 94,285 dogs and 2,665 other animals in the vellore district. The livestock population will provide employment and income to the farmer.

Table – 3.7
Livestock Population in Vellore District During 1997-1998

S.No	*Items*	*Number*
1.	Cattle	5,02,514
2.	Buffaloes	1,14,802
3.	Sheep	3,06,818
4.	Goats	2,03,270
5.	Pigs	16,923
6.	Dogs	94,285
7.	Others	2,665
	Total	12,41,277

Source: Tamil Nadu Economic Appraisal 1997-1998, P. S. 45.

Milk Production

The district has a large number of livestock population, hence, the milk production is also very large in the district. During the year 1997-1998, the district has produced 225.4 tonnes of milk. It accounts for 5.56 percent of the state average milk production. The milk production of the vellore district during 1995-98 are presented in table-3.8.

Table-3.8
Milk Production in the Vellore District

(in 000' tonnes)

S. No	Year	Milk Production of the State	Milk Production of the District
1.	1995-96	3790.5	190.9
2.	1996-97	3976.5	210.4
3.	1997-98	4061.1	225.4

Source: Tamil Nadu An Economic Appraisal 1997-98, P. S-47.

The milk production of the vellore district is gradually increasing from 5.03 percent in 1995-96 to 5.29 percent in 1996-97 and 5.55 percent in 1997-98.

Egg Production

During the year 1997-98, the district has produced 358.5 lakh eggs. The egg production of the district is lower than the state average egg production of 32134.3 lakh eggs. The district accounts for 1.19 percent of the state average egg production.

Employment

The employment in public and private sector is furnished in the table-3.9 below.

Table – 3.9
Public Sector and Private Sector Employment in Vellore District

Sector / Year	1993-94	1994-95	1995-96	1996-97	1997-98
Public Sector	118176	119267	125204	130085	124793
	(74.57)	(72.88)	(72.08)	(71.08)	(70.56)
Private Sector	40303	44376	48487	52933	52080
	(25.43)	(27.12)	(27.92)	(28.92)	(29.44)
Total	158479	163643	173619	183018	176873
	(100)	(100)	(100)	(100)	(100)

Source: Director of Employment and Training, Chennai.

The public sector employs more labourers compared to the private sector. But due to the change in government policy, the importance of public sector has gone down. As a result, the employment in the public sectior is declining. But the activities of private sector generates more employment.

Female Participation

Female participation in economic activity is considered as sine-quo-non for development. The low female participation is considered as a sign of under development in the third world countries of today. The distribution of female workers among various activities shows that 16.07 percent are cultivators, 42.54 percent are agricultural labourers, 17.34 percent are engaged in housing, industry and manufacturing activities, and other 24.05 percent belonged to other works in vellore district during the year 2001.

Industry

The position of vellore district with regard to industrial development is analysed in relation to large and small scale units.

Large Scale Industry

There were 954 large scale factories in vellore district as on 1995-96, with a fixed capital of Rs. 69,552 lakhs and Rs. 54,171 lakhs worth of net value added. The total number of workers working in these factories is 51,354. The employment of fixed capital in vellore district forms only 2.28 percent of the state total fixed capital. The total value of inputs by the large scale industry in the districts is 2,81,943 lakhs and the value of total output is 3,43,843 lakhs. The industrial activities concentrated by the large scale industries in vellore district are as follows.

1. Fertilizer Production
2. Chemicals
3. Textile Products
4. Sugar / Jaggery Manufacturing
5. Asbestos Manufacturing
6. Explosive Manufacturing
7. Finished leather and leather Products

8. Footwear for export
9. Manufacture of food products
10. Synthetic fibers
11. Food Processing and Cement Production.

Small Scale Industry

Theré are 14,927 registered SSI units in vellore district as on 1998. The vellore district forms 5.05 percent of the total state registered units. The classification of registered SSI units in vellore district is furnished in table-3.10.

Table – 3.10
Classification of Registered SSI Units in Vellore Dustrict (1998)

S. No	*Code No*	*Small Scale Units*	*N. o. U in 1997*	*N. o. U in1998*
1.	20-21	Food products	1711	1831
2.	22	Beverages, Tobacco and Tobacco Products	149	151
3.	23	Cotton Textiles	333	367
4.	24	Woolsilk and Synthetic Fibre Textiles	122	124
5.	25	Jute, Hamp amd Mesta Products	7	7
6.	26	Hosiery and Readymade Garments	2598	3168
7.	27	Wood and Wooden Products	498	525
8.	28	Paper and Paper Products	519	546
9.	29	Leather and Leather Products	1021	1103
10	30	Rubber and Plastic Products	344	353
11.	31	Chemicals and Chemical Products	1110	1123
12.	32	Non-Metalic Mineral Products	344	362
13.	33	Basic Metals and Alloy Industries	229	233
14.	34	Metal Products and Papers	1013	1029
15.	35	Machinery and Parts	967	1013
16.	36	Electrical Machinery and Apparatus	956	968
17.	37	Transport Equipment and Parts	506	507
18.	38	Other Manufacturing Industries	1216	1517
		Total	13643	14927

Source: Tamil Nadu An Economic Appraisal 1997-98, P. S-19.

Khadi and Village Industries

The Khadi and Village Industries Board plays a very important role in promoting industrial development in vellore district. The khadi and village industries units are presented in the table 3.11 below.

Table – 3.11
Khadi and Village Industries Units in Vellore District

S. No.	*Category*	*Number of Units*
1.	Khadi Units	25
2.	Village Industries	10
3.	Co-operative Societies	12
4.	Village Spinning Units	15
	Total	62

Source: Tamil Nadu An Economic Appraisal 1997-98, P. S-19.

Leather Industry

Leather industry plays a very vital role in vellore district. It provides employment opportunities to the people, and revenue for the development of the district. There were 1103 leather units producing leather and leather products in vellore district as on 1998.

SOCIAL INFRASTRUCTURE

Education

Educational scenario of the vellore district brings out the Educational institutions at various levels. It may be seen in table - 3.12

There were 134 high schools, 88 higher secondary schools, 60 aided schools in vellore district. Apart from schools, there were 12 colleges, three self-financing colleges and five government and management enginering colleges in vellore district. There is one University and one Deemed University, which also comes under the educational system of the district. Regarding the technical education, there is one government polytechnic and six Government aided polytechnic located in the district.

Table – 3.12
Educational Institutions in Vellore District During 2001

S. No.	*Educational Institutions*	*No. of Institutions*
1.	Govt High Schools	127
2.	Municipal High Schools	4
3.	Adidravada High School	3
4.	Govt Higher Secondary Schools	79
5.	Municipal Higher Secondary Schools	3
6.	Adidravada Higher Secondary Schools	6
7.	Aided Schools	60
8.	Colleges	12
9.	Self-financing Colleges	3
10.	Govt and Management Enginering Colleges	5
11.	University	1
12.	Deemed University	1
13.	Govt Polytechnic	1
14.	Govt aided Polytechnic	1
15.	Private Polytechnic	5

Source: Tamil Nadu An Economic Appraisal 1997-98, P. S. 29.

Health

Hospitals like educational institutions are service organisations. Efficient and successful management of these institutions are essential for the creation of a healthy society. There are 13 Government hospitals in vellore district with 1637 beds and 179 doctors. The population per bed accounted for 2128 and the population per doctor accounted for 19,458 during the year 2001-2002, there were 64 primary health centres functioning allover the district. Besides government hospitals, there are private hospitals mostly located in urban centres. The Christian Medical College and hospital located at vellore, is a multi-specialty hospital which meets the health care needs of the people not only in India but also in Asia.

Drinking Water

The main sources of drinking water for the people of vellore district are wells and tanks. These are the drinking water sources of the district during the year 2001.

ECONOMIC INFRASTRUCTURE

Roads

Roads connect all the villages in the district. The details of road length in kilometers during 2000-2001 are given below.

Table – 3.13
Length of Roads in Vellore District

S.No.	*Details*	*Length in Km*
1.	Mud Road	33.14
2.	Metal Road	171.19
3.	Tar Road	2571.45
4.	Cement Concrete Road	99.60
5.	Corporation and Municipal Roads	452.22
6.	Panchayat Union and Panchayat Roads	3176.32
7.	Town Panchayat and Township Roads	421.58
8.	Village Roads	131.25
9.	State Highways	531.00
10.	National Highways	191.00
	Total	7778.75

Source: District Statistical Office, Vellore.

Railways

In vellore district of Tamil Nadu, the railway lines run all through from north to south and from west to east. The railway route between Chennai and Jolarpet is a busyone, and also an important one, from the point of view of the economy, as well as connectivity with the rest of the nation.

Though Jolarpet is a small town, it gains importance because of its railway junction. All the trains that ply to North India, West India, North East India and South India pass through Jolarpet. From Jolarpet one can reach any part of India by train. Besides passenger trains, a number of cargo trains too pass through Jolarpet. At this junction, goods wagon destined to different parts of India, are seperated and are linked with other goods trains. This facility of separating the wagons is a unique one and is not available at other junctions.

Other important junctions in the district are Katpadi and Arakkonam. At Katpadi, trains leaving for Andhrapradesh are diverted and at Arakkonam, trains, destined for west India like Bombay, pass through.

The district of vellore has to its credit of 197 Km of broad gauge line and 56 Km of meter gauge line. The main train routes leading to Kerala and Bangalore are electrified. This has made the people of vellore district move faster and quicker. Double electric lines covering the entire length of vellore district is an added advantage for the speedy movement of men and materials in the district. The railway lines and roads is kept below.

Motor Vehicles

The motor vehicles on road, classified as commercial and non-commercial vehicles, are presented in table 3.14 below. There were 14,262 commercial vehicles as against 1,19,175 non-commercial vehicles on road in vellore district by the end of march 2001. The details are presented in table-3.14.

Table – 3.14
Registered Motor Vehicles in Vellore District
(As on 31st March 2001)

S.No.	*Items (Commercial)*	*Numbers*
1.	Stage carriers : Public	914
	Private	400
2.	Mini Bus	2
3.	Auto Rickshaw	3216
4.	Motor Cab: State	236
	All-India	107
5.	Maxi Cab: State	436
	All-India	11
6.	Ordinary Taxi	76
7.	Omni Buses: State	6
	All-India	5
8.	Private service vehicle	120
9.	Light commercial vehicle	289
10.	Lorry: State Permit	5423
	National Permit	1635

S.No.	Items (Commercial)	Numbers
11.	School Buses	31
12.	Ambulance	39
13.	Fire Fighter	20
14.	Arti culated vehicle: State	121
	National	26
15.	Tractor and Trailor	1149
*	Sub - Total	14,262
S.No	*Items (Non-Commercial)*	*Numbers*
16.	Motor Cycle	26,218
17.	Scooter	14,054
18.	Mopeds	65,306
19.	Tricycle	96
20.	Motor Car	9711
21.	Jeep	1097
22.	Station Wagon	5
23.	Tractor	2454
24.	Three Wheeller	48
25.	Four Wheeller	90
26.	Road Rollers	11
27.	Others	85
**	Sub - Total	1,19,175
	Grand Total * + **	1,33,437

Source: Commissioner of Transport, Chennai.

Communication

There were 938 post offices and 24,428 Telephonees are the important communication network of the district as on 1997-98, apart from that, there were large number of Internet centres, Telegraph offices, Letter boxes, Public call offices and Telephone exchanges located in each and every part of the district.

INDUSTRIAL INFRASTRUCTURE

Electricity and Power

The Mettur Hydro–Electric Power and the Madras Thermal Power Stations meet the energy needs of vellore district. The distribution of power is made through the electricity system of Chengalpattu, Vellore and Thiruvanamali towns. There is a very good network of power transmission lines in the district. As on 2000-01, all the census towns, villages, hamlets and Adi-Dravidar colonies of the district were given power connection. Barring very few places, which are either interior or inaccessible areas, where there is little or no demand for power, the district enjoys power connection in all areas.

The details of consumption of electricity in vellore district during 2000-01 in each category are presented in table–3.15 below.

Table – 3.15

Category Wise Power Consumption in Vellore District

S. No.	*Category*	*In MillionUnits*	*Percentage*
1.	Domestic	4472	15.48
2.	Commercial	2676	9.27
3.	Public Lighting	400	1.39
4.	Industrial	12482	43.22
5.	Agricultural	7680	26.60
6.	Miscellaneous	1166	4.04
	Total	28,876	100.0

Source: District Statistical Office, Vellore.

It can be seen from the above table that consumption of power is the highest in respect of industries in vellore district and agriculture with 26.6 percent is the next important category, and the lowest in respect of public lighting with 1.39 percent during the year 2000-2001.

Trade and Commerce

Vellore district is an important commercial center. The movement of the mercandise is carried through road transport by lorries and carts drawn by bullocks. The mercantile consignments include all items from iron and steel and sundry shopping goods. Most of the commodities that move out of the district are general goods, grains, sugar, jaggery, fertilizers and chemicals.

The commercial banks, co-operative banks and Private money lenders provide finance for the trade. The outlets for consumer-goods consist of co-operative consumer stores.

Banking (Financial Institutions)

The district is served by 199 commercial bank branches, besides branches of the District Central Co-operative Bank, Urban Co-operative Banks and Tamil Nadu Industrial Investment Corporation.

The Vellore Central Co-operative Bank is the most important financial agency extending credit facilities to the agriculturists through its 343 Primary Co-operative Societies. In many cases, short term loans are converted into medium and long term loans for various reasons including drought, to help the farmers to repay the loans with least inconvenience.

Urban Co-operative Banks of the district are under the control of Joint Registrar of Co-operative Societies, Vellore. It has 13 branches in taluk head quarters and extends jewel loan facilities to the agriculturists

The vellore district branch of the Tamil Nadu State Co-operative Land Development Bank meets the long-term credit requiremernts of the agriculturists through 17 Primary Land Development Banks in the district. The over due position in these banks is very high. The poor recovery hampered the operations of these institutions to a very large extent. However, due to revised regulation of advances, the bank is able to meet not only the term-loan requirements of agriculturists but also the allied activities of the small and marginal farmers in large number.

Regional Distribution of Commercial Banks

The regional distribution of commercial banks is furnished in table 3.16 below

In vellore district the regional distribution of commercial banks shows that they are in favour of rural areas. Thanks to the nationalisation of banks.

Table – 3.16
Regional Distribution of Commercial Banks in Vellore District

S.No.	Type	Distribution of Commercial Banks (As on March 2001)				
		No. of Banks	Rural	Semi Urban	Urban	Total
1.	State Bank Associates	4	20	12	6	38
2.	Public Sector Banks	14	68	42	7	127
3.	Private Sector Banks	11	15	8	11	34
	Total	29	103	62	34	199

Source: District Statistical Office, Vellore.

Distribution of Bank wise Consumption of Loan

There is a great demand for consumption loan in vellore district. It is mainly for the purchase of durable products and to meet the expenditure in connection with ceremonies. The table–3.17 below gives the bank wise distribution of consumption loans in vellore district during the year 2001-2002.

Table – 3.17
Bank wise Distribution of Consumption Loans During 2001-2002

S.No.	Name of the Bank	Consumption Loans (Amount Rs. in 000's)			
		A/C	Unit	Amount in Rs.	Percentage
1.	Canara Bank	2	2	350	2.06
2.	Dhanalakshmi Bank	4	4	4	0.02
3.	Indian Overseas Bank	23	23	360	2.13
4.	Indian Bank	34	34	130	0.76
5.	State Bank of India	320	320	3020	17.76
6.	VCC Bank	1	1	300	1.76
7.	Urban Co-operative Bank	4980	4980	12836	75.51
	Total	5364	5364	17000	100

Source: Indian Bank–District Credit Plan, 2001-2002.

Out of the total loan of Rs. 1,70,00,000 the Urban Co-opeative Banks have sanctioned 75.51 percent of the consumption loans as against 17.76 percent by the State Bank of India. It reveals that most of the people living in urban areas are the borrowers of consumption loans mainly for the purchase of home durable products.

Small Savings in Vellore District

The small savings is an important component of development. The small savings drives have been undertaken every year. The net amount collected from such drives is furnished below.

Table – 3.18
Small Saving Collection (Net) in Vellore District From 1992-1998

S. No.	*Year*	*Saving Collections (Rs in Crores)*
1.	1992-93	15.27
2.	1993-94	22.15
3.	1994-95	27.48
4.	1995-96	18.29
5.	1996-97	14.65
6.	1997-98	19.89

Source: Director of Small Savings, Chennai-6.

The small saving collection in vellore district has not been steady between 1992-93 and 1997-98. Though the collection has increased from Rs. 15.27 crores in 1992-93 to Rs. 27.48 crores in 1994-95, it declined to Rs. 18.29 crores in 1995-96 and it further declined to Rs. 14.65 crores in the year 1996-97. but it picked up during the year 1997-98.

ADMINISTRATIVE SERVICE

The administrative service of the vellore district is divided into police stations and courts. There are 56 police stations with 2134 police personnel who form the protective strength of the district as on 1997-98. Apart from that, there are municipal courts at the taluk level and the district court is located in vellore.

STANDARD OF LIVING OF THE PEOPLE

The standard of living of the people could be judged by the items of food they consume. The average telephone connections in vellore was recorded as 5.05 percent of the population, telephone users accounted for 56/1000, televisions

583/1000, computers 7/1000 and internet users 4/1000. Though 50 percent of the population views television, in the consumption of other items of information technology, the district remains at a very low level, but there is a sign of improvement in their consumption.

PLACES OF WORSHIP

Lord Jalagendeswar Temple (Vellore), Lord Rathinageri Murugan Temple (Rathinagri), Lord Narasiman Temple (Sholingar), Lord Vallimalai Murugan Temple (Vallimalai), Magadeva Malai Temple and Lord Anjaneya Temple are the important places of worship in the district.

FESTIVALS

There are number of festivals celeberated by the people in vellore district. Some of the important festivals are Vellore Chitrapournami festival, Pushpa Pallaku festival, Gudiyattam Gangiyamman festival and May-Jun Kodaivizha festival in Yelagiri Hills.

IMPORTANT TOURIST PLACES IN VELLORE DISTRICT

Vellore

The fort at vellore is one of the great attractions in the district. It's said to have been built by Chinna Boomi Nayaka, a subordinate under Sadasivaraya of the Vijayanagar kingdom in mid 16th century A.D. The fort was the bone of contention for many powers. The fort contains both secular and religious structures including Tippu Mahal, Begum Mahal, Kandi Mahal, Jalakanteswara Temple, A Mosque and a Church. Museums are also recently established in this fort by the Archealogical Survey of India (ASI) and State Department.

Vellore has the renowned Christian Medical College and Hospital where patients from all corners get advance medical treatment.

Vallimalai

Vallimalai has been one of the important Jain centres during the early medieval period. The hilly area with fountains must have been very much favoured by the Jain monks. One of the natural caverns with jaina thirthankaras image at the top of the hill was later converted into a shirne dedicated to Lord Subramanya. It is an important place as it is said to have witnessed the marriage of Lord Subramanya and Goddess Valli.

Arcot

Arcot was the head quarters of Nawab of Carnatic, who ruled this region in 18th century A.D. The fort enclosing the Arcot town was on the bank of river Palar. It was built by Daud-Khan, Nawab of Arcot. The fort was a huge one and had a circumference of 8 Kms. The invasion of TipuSultan of Mysore resulted in the complete destruction of the fort. A part of the ramport is remaining. Besides a fort around the town, the Nawab had also built mosques.

Rathanagiri

13 Km from Vellore, Ratnagiri is famous for the Murugan Temple situated on a small hillock. It is said that the temple was built in the 14th century A.D. but renovations were made recently.

Tirupattur

It is famous for the Christukula Ashram, the earlist among the Christian Ashrams. It was founded by Dr.S. Jesudason and Dr. Ernest Forest Paton in August, 1922. To identify with indigenous south indian architectural patterns the church has been built in an oriental style. In its quiet and prayerful surroundings it attracts devotees from all over the district.

Yelagiri Hill

Yelagiri Hill is one of the hill stations of Tamil Nadu. Yelagiri Hill can be reached by a winding ghat road, that has 14 hairpin bends. Places of tourist interest include Punguanoor Lake which is an artificial lake made in an area of 56.706 square metres. Other attractions are the childrens park, Velavan Temple, a Herbal farm and a Telescope house. There are avenues for organising adventure tourism activities like Trekking, Mountaineering, Rock Climbing and Hanggliding in the hills and the slopes.

Jalagamparai Water Falls

'Attaru' river passes through the Yelagiri Hills from a height of 30 meters at Jadaiyanur on the other side of the hills. Adjacent to the Jalagambarai falls, there is a Murugan Temple located within a building constructed in the shape of a lingam.

Kavalur

The biggest Solar Observatory is Vainupappu situated in Kavalur, 25 Km from Yelagiri Hills. It could also be accessed from Vaniyambadi (30 Kms). Prior permission is required to visit the observatory. All are welcome on Saturdays from 4.pm to 6 pm without seeking prior permission. A large variety of deer roam around the observatory.

Amirthi Forest

24 Km south of vellore is the panoramic Amirthi forests, rich in its variety of flora and fauna. Half of this jungle is cleared to serve as a tourist spot while the other half is developed as a wild life sanctuary. A trek for a Km leads one to a full view of seasonal water falls.

Javadu Hills

Jamanamaruthur in Javadu Hills is famous for its sandalwood and fruit bearing trees. It is at an altitude of 300 to 1000 metres. The Beemanmadavu water falls in the thick reserve forest, 2 Km from here is worth a hard-trek. A night's stay here is a new experience due to the solitude of the hills.

Palamathi Hills

Palamathi, about 14 Km from Vellore and is famous for its Murugan Temple recently built on the hill about 1800 feet above the sea. A travel through the enchanting eight hair pin bends at palamathi hills is an unforgettable experience.

WIDOWS WELFARE SCHEMES IN VELLORE DISTRICT

The Widows Welfare Schemes in Vellore District is presented in the Chart below.

Widows Welfare Schemes in Vellore District

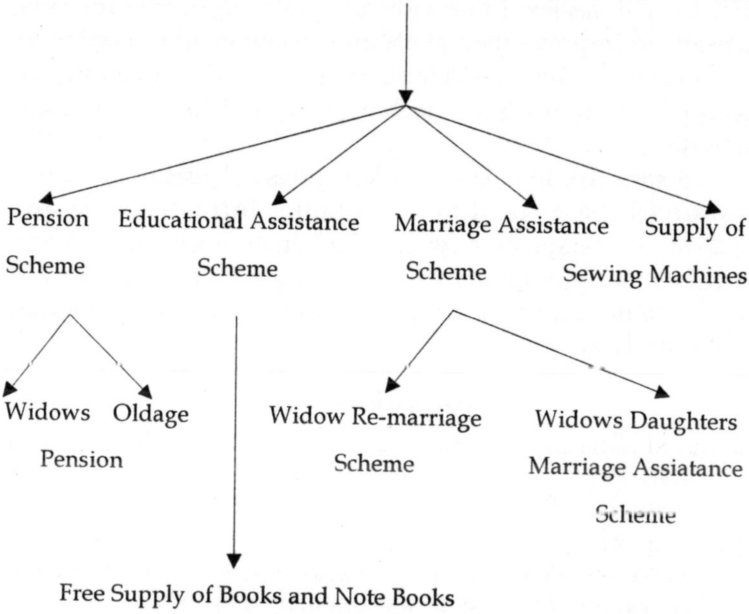

Specific Schemes to Assist Women and Widows

The following schemes are specifie schemes to assist women and widows in vellore district.

1. Moovalur Ramamirtham Marriage Scheme.
2. EVR Maniammai Widows Daughters Marriage Scheme.
3. Tamil Nadu Government Female Children Protection Scheme.
4. Anjugam Intercaste Marriage Scheme.
5. Annai Teresa Destitute Daughters Marriage Scheme.
6. Dharmambal Marriage Scheme (Widow Re-marriage).

DEVELOPMENT PROGRAMMES

Various development programmes like Integrated Rural Development Programme (IRDP), Training of Rural Youth for Self-Employment Programme and National Rural Employment Programme (NREP), were introduced in vellore district with a view to provide adequate support to the rural artisans to improve their skills and to create additional work opportunities. The District Industries Centre (DIC) Vellore, has been providing necessary technical support to develop these activities.

To sum up, the size, location, physical features, human resources, basic facilities available, infrastructure and institutions established, welfare schemes implemented and development programmes adopted in the Vellore district will provide a backdrop for the analysis of the problem of widows in the study area.

REFERENCES

Census of India 2001 - Tamil Nadu, (2001), Provisional Population Totals, Paper - 2 of 2001, Rural Urban Distribution, Series - 34, Controller of Publications, Civil Lines, New Delhi, pp. 151-161.

Census of India 2001 - Tamil Nadu, (2001), Distribution of Workers and Non-workers, Paper - 3 of 2001, Series - 34, Controller of Publications, Civil Lines, New Delhi, pp. 154-157.

Tamil Nadu - An Economic Appraisal 1997-98, Dept of Evaluation and Applied Research, Govt of Tamil Nadu, Chennai, pp. S–19 -157.

P.A. Thomas and K.Padmanabhan, (1991), District Planning, Northern Book Centre, New Delhi, pp. 18 -72.

Manorama Year Book - 2003, (2003), Tamil Nadu Series, Malayala Manorama Press, Kottayam, p. 177.

4
MUDALIAR COMMUNITY— ORIGIN AND SPREAD

INTRODUCTION

In order to understand the status of widows belonging to the Hindu Mudaliar community, a study on the origin and spread of the Hindu Mudaliar community is a pre-requisite. As such, the present chapter is devoted to the study of the Hindu Mudaliar community in Tamil Nadu particularly in Vellore district.

Two recent studies on castes in India have been made by Thurston . C and Singh K.S. Those studies are referred here to find out the origin and spread of Mudaliar Community in Tamil Nadu.

The Mudaliar is a sub-caste of Vellala Community, who lived in the districts of Madras, Chengleput, North Arcot and some parts of South Arcot. According to a version, the name Mudaliar is derived from the terms mudal meaning 'first' and ar meaning 'plough', thus representing the first ploughmen or agriculturists. Another version says that they derived the name from the word 'mudal' meaning 'wealthy', as they were wealthy people.

They speak Tamil and use Tamil script. There were both vegetarian and non-vegetarian among them.

Marrying mother's brother's daughter, father's sister's daughters are allowed. A sacred pendant (Thali), Vermilion (Kumkumam), bindi and toe-rings (Metti) symbolise married women. The Shaivite among them, who form the majority, wear 'thiruneeru thali' (a gold pendant hung down from the thali inscribed with three horizontal lines signifying sacred ashes), while the Vaishnavite inscribe namam (emblem of the Vaishnavite faith) on the gold pendant.

The practice of giving dowry in cash and kind is in vogue. Divorce is allowed for both men and women, remarriage is still considered to be a privilege of men. Property was divided equally among the sons and the eldest son acted as the head of the family.

Tonsure (Mudi Eduthal) and ear-boring (Kadhu Kuthu) ceremonies for both male and female children,. Puberty ceremony (Mangal Neeratu Sadangu) for girls on attaining menarche, seemendam for a pregnant women and naming ceremony (Peyarsootu Vizha) are significant occasions for Mudaliars.

They observe Brahminical customs while performing a marriage ceremony. They cremate the dead. Death pollution is observed for sixteen days, which is terminated with the performing of 'kariyam'.

Traditionally, the Mudaliars are agriculturists but now most of them have taken up various white-collared jobs. A good number of them are rich contractors, industrialists, academicians, lawyers and politicians. The Mudaliars mainly worship deities such as Murugar or Subramanyar, Perumal and Karumariamman and celebrate festivals such as Pongal, Diwali, Adi Keerthigai and Sivaratri. Brahmins are invited to preside over all their ceremonies. Being a community, mainly settled in urban centres, they have inter married with other communities also. They fully avail all the modern amenities extended by the Government in their localities.

MUTHALI

It's supposed by Mr. Nelson that this tribe has sprung from the Vellalas of Madura, especially as the customs of the two tribes are very similar. The Muthalis are described as a "small but highly responsible and influential agricultural caste. They are strict followers of the shiva faith; and appear to have come into the country in very recent times". The word Muthali means 'Leading or Principal man'[1].

MUDALIAR

They are one of the subgroups of the larger Vellalar community, the agriculturists and landlords of Tamil Nadu. Among the Mudaliar, four different subgroups, viz., Tondaimandala Melanadu Mudali, Tondaimandala Kilnadu Mudali, Ponneri Mudali and Pundamalli Mudali have been recorded. They use Mudaliar and Pillai as their surnames.

In Maharashtra, the Mudalairs are also known as Pillai. They are migrants from northern districts of Tamil nadu and they are concentrated in the Mullund and Vikroli areas of Mumbai. They use Mudaliar as their surname. Besides Tamil which is their mother tongue, they also speak Marathi and Hindi and use both the Tamil and the Devanagari scripts. There are both vegetarian and non-vegetarian sections among them and consume rice and wheat as their staple cereals. A Thali is the marriage symbol for woman. The practice of dowry and kanyadan exist in the community. Divorce and widow remarriage are prohibited, while widower remarriage and sororate are allowed. Only sons inherit parental property. The tonsure ceremony is performed by most of them. Puberty ceremony for girls is generally not observed but the maternal uncle gives a sari to the girl. A Brahman officiates at the marriage rituals. The important ceremony associated with marriage is the tying of the marriage pendent (thali) around the bride's neck. The dead are either buried or cremated. In case of cremation, the mortal remains are immersed in the sea. The eldest son performs the death rites for the mother and the youngest son for the father.

Traditionally, the Mudaliars are agriculturists. There are also traders, contractors and government servants among them. The Mudaliar Sangham works for the upliftment of the community by providing scholarships and pension for widows, arranging marriages, etc. As Hindus, they worship Venkateshwara, Murugan and Balram. Sacred specialists from the Brahman community perform their life-cycle rituals. They exchanged cooked food and water with communities of equal social status such as the Vokkaliga, Devanga and Ganiga. Sidha food is exchanged with all. They share water sources and crematoria, visit shrines and participate in village festivals with others. There are a good number of businessmen, white-collar personnel, professionals, defence employees and local-level political leaders among them[2].

VELLALA AGAMUDIYAR

A community of Tamil Nadu, the Agamudiyars are a group of vellala Mudaliar. They prefer to call themselves Mudaliar or Naicker. The name is derived from the words, 'aham' meaning 'pride' and 'vadaiyar' meaning possessor. Thruston (1909) describes the Agamuduyar as a cultivating caste found in all districts of Tamil Nadu who closely follow the vellalas in their manners and customs. He also mentions fourteen subgroups, namely Aivali Nattan, Kottaipattu, Malainadu, Nattumangalam, Rajaboja, Rajakulam, Rajavasal, Kallan Maravan, Tuluvan, Servaikkaran, Ganam, Manusha, Deva and Rakshasa among them. They speak Tamil and use the same script.

Language

They are also conversant with the Telugu language. The AIBAS data reveals that the average household size of the Agamudiyar of Tamil Nadu is six. The percentage of males (54 percent) is more than that of the females (46 percent). But married females (33 percent) are less than married males (38 percent). They are, on an average, of medium height and show comparatively higher proportion of broad-headed individuals with broader or flat type of noses. They are occasional non-vegetarian for whom beef and pork are strictly prohibited. Their staple diet is rice and ragi. There are two sects of vaishnavas and shaivas among the Agamudiyar.

Gotras

These two sects have their own gotras, such as Vishnugotra and Shiva Gotra. The religious sects are not a bar in matrimonial matters. The Agamudiyar prefer marriage with one's maternal uncle's daughter, paternal aunt's daughters or sister's daughter. Endogamy is practised at the community level. Symbols of marriage are a thali, toe- ring and bindi. The system of bride-price, known as Parayapanam, is still in practice. Property is equally inherited by the sons only, and the eldest son succeeds to the authority. Their women have a role in social functions and religious spheres. Birth entails pollution for sixteen days, which is terminated with the performing of the Punyavachanam ceremony. They observe tonsure and ear-boring ceremonies as birth rituals. The important marriage and nuptial ceremonies are performed at the bride's residence. The dead are buried and pollution terminates on the sixteenth day with the performing of the ritual 'karyam'.

Occupation

Agriculture is the traditional occupation and even now the majority of them are agriculturists. A few of them are daily-wage labourers, and some are engaged bidi-rolling. A traditional caste Panchayat (gramakattalai) is operational, and perudandakaran is the head of the village. They follow Hinduism and have two sects, vaishnava and shaiva. They visit the common Hindu religious shrines along with others. They do not share burial grounds. Their attitude towards family planning is favourable. Couples prefer two or three children. Dug-wells and hand pumps are the drinking-water sources. They avail the benefits of IRDP (Integrated Rural Development Programme), self-employment and other development programmes.

The Agamudiyar of Pondicherry call themselves Agamudiyan and Mudaliar. Here they are also called udayar and pillaimar. Their traditional occupation is agriculture. At present, some of them are engaged in trade and service in various private agencies. The level of education is encouraging among them. They are utilising the benefits of all developmental programmes.

Mudaliars in Andhra Pradesh

The Agamudiar, a community from Tamil Nadu, are concentrated in the bordering taluks of Chittor and Nellore districts of Andhrapradesh. The community has several synonyms like Tuluva Vellala, Arcot Vellala, Arcot Mudali, Aghamudian, Aghamudi, Agamudi Reddy and Aghamudi Mudaliar. They speak Tamil among themselves and with their kin groups and Telugu with others. Some of them are conversant with the Kannada and Urdu languages also. They are non-vegetarian who take chicken, fish, sheep and goat. Rice and ragi are their staple cereals. The Agamudiars are divided into shiva and Vishnu Gotrams. They prefix surnames along with their father's name to their personal names. The surnames and gotras regulate their marital alliances. They claim equal status with the Kapu Reddy, in the local social hierarchy and claim to be Sudra in the Varna order. They follow community endogamy. They marry their father's sister's daughter, mother's brother's daughter or sister's daughter. Adult marriage is the practice. Monogamy is the prevalent form of marriage. Dowry in cash and kind is prevalent. Divorce is permissible on the grounds of maladjustment, cruelty and adultery. Remarriage is allowed for the widower and male divorce. Junior sororate is allowed in the community. Ancestral property is divided equally among the male children. The women participate in economic activities such as daily-wage and agricultural labourers, vegetable vendors, construction workers, etc. Some of them are employed in government and private establishments.

Ceremonies and Rituals

The Agamudliar in Andhra Pradesh observe post-delivery pollution, naming and tonsure ceremonies, and puberty rites for girls. Traditionally the marriage rituals are performed at the brides residence according to the puranic rites officiated at by a Brahman priest. In the event of death, the eldest of the family is cremated while the others are buried in lying position. Death pollution is observed. The final rites are performed on the sixteenth day. The majority of them are small and marginal farmers.

The landless Agamudiar work as daily-wage labourers, construction workers, vegetable vendors, masons, commission agents, mechanics, etc. A few of them are government servants, teachers, lecturers, bank employees, etc. They are Hindu and belong to either the shiva or vaishnava sect. They have clan deities like Perumal, Puliar, Subramanya, Murugan, Ayanar and Pidari, Boyakonda Gangamma, Mariamma, Anklayamma, Sattayamma and Yellama who are the village deities. Sri Venkateswara, Murugan, Subramanaya swamy, Kamakshiamma, are the regional deities. They observe all local Hindu festivals, like Sankranthi, Pongal, Shivaratri, Ugadi, Dussehra, Ayudhapuja and Diwali. Folk songs are sung by women on ceremonial and festive occasions. Traditionally they accept water and food from the equal-ranking communities. They exchange food with the Kapu, Kamma, Balija and Yadava communities.

Attitude Towards Development

The Agamudiar receive the services of the Chakali, Mangali, Viswakarma, Satani, Jamagama and Brahman communities and pay them either in cash or kind. They have a favourable attitude towards the development programmes. Some of them have studied up to postgraduate level. They avail themselves of health, medicare and family welfare schemes. The IRDP, and schemes pertaining to agricultural and crop loans are availed by these people.

Agamudiyar Christians

The Agamudiyar Christian of Tamil Nadu believes that they migrated to the present habitat from central Tamil Nadu during the Muslim invasions and were converted to Christianity by the portuguse missionaries. They are also known as Tuzhuva Vellala, Arcot Vellala or Kodikara Vellala. They are distributed in the Coimbatore, Periyar and Salem districts. Tamil is spoken and the Tamil script is used. They have four subgroups, namely Pollukkaran, Katupanni, Attangathan and Vandikkaran. Cross-cousin marriages and sororate are permissible. A marriage pendant and toe-rings are the symbols of marriage for women. Divorce is permissible in case of maladjustment. Male equigeniture is the norm but females are given a share on demand. Succession right goes to the eldest son. The marriage rituals are performed at the bride's residence. The tying of thali and registration are important rituals associated with marriage. On death, the body is given a ritual bath before it is buried. On the thirtieth day a special mass is arranged.

Agriculture is the mainstay of the Agamudiar Christian. Weaving and betal-growing have been adopted by many; a few of them are engaged in service. Mukkandar and Koilmaniagarar are the headman and temple managers of the community respectively, who with the help of other functionaries settle disputes and adjudicate cases, etc. the Indian Christian Mukkalathor Association is the modern caste association trying to unite the Christian Agamudiyar, Kallar and Maravar communities for their advancement. Inter community marriages take place with their counter parts and other Mukkalathor communities. They share wells and water sources with other communities. Attitude towards family planning programmes is positive and generally women get sterlized.

The Agamudiyar Christian of Pondicherry prefers to adopt the title Mudaliar or Naicker. They speak Tamil and use the same script. They are non-vegetarian who do not eat beef and pork. Their staple food is rice, ragi and they use all kinds of pulses. Though they are a section of converts from Mudaliar they adhere to endogamous marriage. They practice exogamy at the surname level. Consanguineous marriages are preferred and preference is given to mother's brother's daughter or father's sister's daughter. Patrilocal is the type of residence followed. Divorce is permissible for both males and females. Widow, widower, and male and females divorce remarriage is permitted. All sons share property equally. Succession is by the eldest son. The marriage ceremony is performed at a church. The important marriage rituals include betrothal in a church, exchange of garlands, signing in register and marriage is solemnized according to the Christian custom officiated at by a father. The dead are buried. They remove the thali from the deceared person's wife on the same day to identify her widowhood. Death pollution is observed for eleven day's. Their traditional occupation is agriculture. Their attitude towards education is favourable. They use both modern and indigenous medicare systems. Their attitude towards family welfare programme is favourable. Development and self-employment programmes are utilised by them.

VELLALA, ARCOT VELLALA

A community of Tamil Nadu, they are also known as Thuluva Vellala. Pillai, Odaiyar, Mudaliar are their surnames. The agriculturists (Vellala) of the Arcot are called Arcot Vellala. They are mainly concentrated in the districts of Vellore. Tamil is their mother tongue. They are non-vegetarian. Their staple cereals are rice and ragi. Social divisions exist at the lineage level, which regulate marriage alliances and indicate descent. Consanguineous marriages with one's father's sister's daughter, mother's brother's daughter or sister's daughter are permissible. Toe-rings and a thali are the symbols of marriage. Divorce is permissible. Remarriage for widows and male divorcees is permissible. They observe Valaikappu in the seventh or ninth month of pregnancy. They observe birth pollution for ten days. They observe naming ceremony, ear boring, first feeding of cereals (Annaprashan) and tonsure. Puberty rites (Manjal Neerattu Vizha) are also observed. They observe the marriage rituals either at the bride's residence or at a Kalyanamandapam. Dead are either cremated or buried. They observe death pollution for sixteen days and final rites on the sixteenth day.

The traditional occupation of the Arcot Vellala is settled cultivation. Nowadays they are engaged in trade, business and government and private service. They have community association to work for their welfare. They are Hindus. They traditionally accept and exchange water and food with the other Vellalas and Mudaliars. Formal education is favoured for either sex. Their attitude to indigenous traditional and modern medicare as well as family planning is favourable [3].

TULUVA VELLALAS

They are also known as Saiva Vellala, Nainar, Pillaimar, Vellala or Saiva Vellalar. The titles used are Pillaimar, Nainar, Mudaliar and Udayar. They speak Tamil and are distributed in all the districts of Tamil Nadu. They are pure vegetarian. The staple cereals used are rice and ragi. Thurston (1909) has reported that Tondamandalams are the dwellers of the pallava country, i.e. the present Chingleput and Vellore districts. He has further written that the 'Tondamandalams are sub-divided into the Tuluvas, who are supposed to have come from the Tulu country; the Poonamalle (or Pundamalli Vellalas, so called from the town of that name near Madras); and the Kondaikattis (Those who tie their hair in a knot without shaving it)'. They are divided into clans (gotras) like 'Iyeayer' or 'Iyyanar', Vishnu and Siva. Besides gotras they have several surnames (Veetuperu) that govern marital alliances. Endogamy is practised at the community level. They prefer cross-cousin marriages. A marriage pendant (Thali) and toe-rings (Meetei) are the marriage symbol for women.

They observe pre-delivery rituals, such as Valaikappu and Seemantham. A birth entails pollution for eleven days. Naming ceremony, earboring (Kadiniviya) and tonsure (Thalaineekaradu) ceremonies are performed on the fifteenth day to terminate pollution. The dead are either buried or cremated. Death entails pollution for eleven days.

Agriculture is their traditional occupation. The majority of the Tondamandalam Saiva Vellala has agriculture as their main occupation. The subsidiary occupation is dairy, government service, business, daily wage labourers, etc. Traditional caste Panchayat system exists. They follow Hinduism. The sacred specialists are from the Brahman community. The community has businessmen, teachers, administrators, engineers, doctors and a few white-collar workers to promote modern intercommunity linkages. Political leadership has emerged up to regional level. Their attitude towards formal education, modern and traditional indigenous medicare and family welfare programme is favourable[4].

SALIENT FEATURES OF THE MUDALIAR COMMUNITY

The origin and spread of the Mudaliar community brings out its distinctive characteristics. Though its origin is not known, Mudaliar community is a sub-caste of Vellala community. The customs, conventions, ceremonies and habits of the Mudaliars are closely resembles the Vellalas. But the Mudaliars are rich and are concentrated in urban centres. There are lot of industrial entrepreneurs, administrators, academicians and professionals in this community. But those who live in the villages are agriculturists and they are undertaking various farming activities.

The main sub-caste of the Mudaliar community are: Vellala Agamudaiar, Arcot Vellala, and Tulu Vellala. Though they belonged to the same clan, their difference is in their faith and symbols. The shivaites and vaishnavaites have separate symbols or 'namams' and they follow different gotras. There appears no difference in the marriages and conducting ceremonies. Brahmins are the purohits who conduct ceremonies in all the sub-castes. But all of them are against widow remarriage and they are common in their hard and cruel sanctions to widows. As a result, the rich community made their women and widows dependents for ever.

NOTES

1. M.A. Sherring (1975), 'The Tribes and Castes of the Madras Presidency", Cosmo Publications, New Delhi, p. 112.
2. K.S. Singh (1998), "Indias Communities", Anthropological Survey of India, Oxford University Press, Vol.V, New Delhi, pp. 2368-2369.
3. E.Thurston (1975), Castes and Tribes of Southern India, Vol.VIII, Cosmo Publications, New Delhi, pp. 3634 - 3638.
4. E.Thurston (1975), Castes and Tribes of Southern India, Vol.VIII, Cosmo Publications, New Delhi, p. 3648.

5
RESEARCH METHODOLOGY

Having analysed the problem of widows and the objectives and the hypothesis of the study in the first chapter, the present chapter is devoted to the research design adopted for the study.

UNIVERSE OF THE STUDY

The present study relates to the problems of the widows of the Mudaliar Community and their sub-sects living in Tamil Nadu state which forms the universe of the study.

SOURCES OF DATA

Both primary and secondary data were used for the analysis of the problems faced by widows. The main sources of secondary data were published materials, particularly CSO reports, NSS reports, Government of India Statistics on widows, State Government published materials, Government of Tamil Nadu Archives, District Gazeteers, District Statistics, Social Welfare Department Statistics etc. The primary data was collected from a cross section of widows households by means of sampling method.

SAMPLING PROCEDURE

Choice of District

Tamil Nadu has got at present 29 districts. The Mudaliar Community population is scattered all over the state. The Mudaliar Community is called by different names in different places. In Vellore District, they are known as Chenkunther

Mudali, Agamudiar etc. A district with highest number of Mudaliar population was chosen purposely for the present study. The decennial census is not taken on the basis of caste, thus it is very difficult to enumerate the people included in the Mudaliar Community. But each caste maintains records of population belonging to it's caste. The Mudaliar population could be calculated from the records kept by the Mudaliar Community organisation. Vellore district emerged as a district with highest population of mudaliar community. Therefore, Vellore district is chosen on the second stage.

Choice of Blocks and Municipal Towns

In order to choose the blocks and municipal towns, all the blocks and municipal towns are listed in descending order according to their Mudaliar population. From the list, eight blocks and eight Municipal towns were chosen.

The following are the Blocks and Municipal towns chosen for the present study.

S. No	*Name of the Block*	*No.of Samples*	*Name of the Municipal Town*	*No.of Samples*
1.	Tirupattur	50	Tirupattur	50
2.	Vaniyambadi	25	Vaniyambadi	25
3.	Madanur (Ambur)	25	Ambur	25
4.	Gudiyattam	25	Gudiyattam	25
5.	Vellore	50	Vellore	50
6.	Arcot	25	Arcot	25
7.	Ranipet	25	Ranipet	25
8.	Wallajapet	25	Wallajapet	25
	Total	250	Total	250

Choice of Villages and Wards

From the selected blocks all the villages were listed in descending order with highest number of Mudaliar population. From the list, one village with highest number of Mudaliar population from each block was chosen. There were eight villages in the sample. Similarly, all the wards from the selected Municipal town are listed in decending order with highest number of Mudaliar population. From the list, one ward with the highest Mudaliar population from each Municipal town was chosen. There are eight wards in the sample.

Selection of Sample Mudaliar Widows Households

From the selected villages/wards, all the Hindu Mudaliar widows were identified and from among them, 25 widows households were chosen by means of simple random method. The ultimate sample size consists of 500 Hindu Mudaliar widows households, divided into villages (rural)-250 (10 x 25) and municipal town (urban)-250 (10 x 25). The selected Mudaliar widows were post-stratified into young (below 40 years), middle aged (41 to 60 years) and old (above 60 years of age).

Thus, the procedure adopted for the selection of the Hindu Mudaliar sample widows could be termed as multi - stage random sampling method.

The Chart below depicts the choice of the Hindu Mudaliar widows.

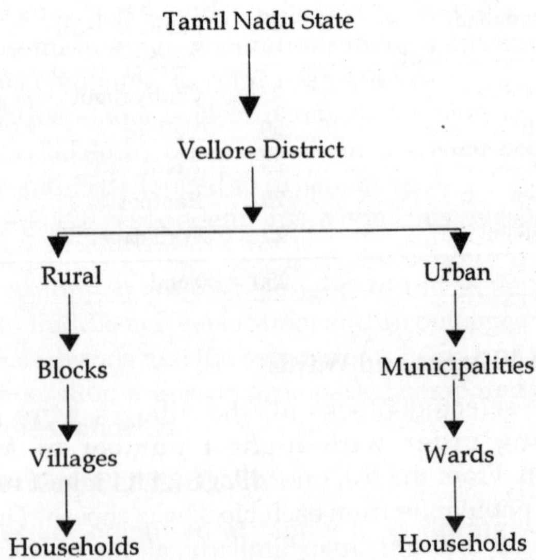

COLLECTION OF DATA

Data Requirement

On the basis of the problem, objectives and hypothesis of the study the following data were required to be collected from the respondents. They are: Personal identification, age – present age, at the time of marriage, family details, parental family, in-laws family, details about husband, social status, role in the family, help received, economic status, attitude of widows, attitude of others towards widows, problems faced by the widows, awareness of the Govt. schemes and widow's expectations.

Tools of Analysis

The collected data were analysed and interpreted with the help of statistical tools like Percentages, Averages, Standard deviation, Chi-square test and Correlation Analysis, Correlation Matrix, Regression Analysis, Deprivation Analysis etc.

Percentages

Ratio is often expressed as percentage. One figure is taken as base and is represented by 100 in calculation of percentage; and the other figure is expressed as a ratio of this base.

Average (Arithmetic Mean)

Average is an attempt to find one single figure to describe the whole of figures.

$$\overline{X} = A + \left[\frac{\Sigma fd}{N}\right] \times i$$

Where,

X = Average (Arithmetic Mean)
A = Assumed Average
Σ fd = Sum Value of f × d
f = Total Frequency
d = M – A / N (M- Mid point of Various Classes, A- AssumedAverage, N- Number of Respondents).
N = Number of Respondents
i = Step deviation

Correlation Analysis

Correlation was done to describe the relationship between the respondents age at the time of marriage and their husbands age at the time of marriage, respondents education and their husbands education. The following formula describes the correlation analysis.

The Forumla:

$$\Gamma = \frac{\left[\frac{\Sigma\, dxdy -}{n}\right] \Sigma dx \,.\, \Sigma dy}{\sqrt{\Sigma dx^2 - \frac{(\Sigma dx)^2}{n} \times \Sigma dy^2 - \frac{(\Sigma dy)^2}{n}}}$$

Where,

Γ = Correlation Coefficient

Σdx and Σdy = Sums of the deviations of x and y series respectively from their assumed means.

Σdx^2 and Σdy^2 = Sums of the squares of deviations of x and y series, respectively from their assumed means.

$\Sigma dxdy$ = Sum of the product of corresponding deviations of x and y series from their assumed means.

n= Total Number of Respondents.

Correlation Matrix of Socio-Economic Variables

A correlation matrix was done to describe the relationship among the variables education, income, occupation, attitude of widows and attitude of others towards widows.

The Equation

Correlation coefficients are calculated between variables X_1 and X_2, $X_1$and X_3, X_1 and X_4, X_1 and X_5. Also between X_2 and X_3, X_2 and X_4, X_2 and X_5 and so on.

Where:

X = Education

X_2 = Income
X_3 = Occupation
X_4 = Attitude of Widows
X_5 = Attitude of Others

The tabular arrangements of all the correlation coefficients that are calculated from all the possible pairings of the five variables X_1, X_2, X_3, X_4, X_5 are given in the correlation matrix.

REGRESSION ANALYSIS

Multiple Regression Analysis on Attitude of Widows

Multiple Regression analysis was done to predict the attitude of widows. Those variables, which had correlation with the attitude of widows were chosen and introduced in the model. The stepwise method in multiple regression was used in the analysis to arrive at the regression equation.

The Equation:

$$Y = B_o + B_1X_1 + B_2X_2 + B_3X_3 + B_4X_4 + \Sigma$$

Where,

X_1 = Present age
X_2 = Education
X_3 = Income
X_4 = Occupation
B = Beta Value
Σ = Random Error

Regression Analysis on Attitude of others

Regression Analysis was done to study the attitude of others (Parents, Brothers, Sisters, In-laws, Sons, Daughters, Co-worker, Shop keepers, Men and Women in general) towards widows. Those variables, which had correlation with the attitude of others viz., Income, Occupation and Age were chosen and introduced in the model. The step wise method in regression was used in the analysis to arrive at the regression equation.

The Equation

$$Y = B_o + B_1X_1 + B_2X_2 + B_3X_3 + B_4X_4 + \Sigma$$

Where,

Y = Decision making (Attitude of Others)
X = Present age
X_2 = Education
X_3 = Income
X_4 = Occupation
B = Beta Value
Σ = Random Error.

Regression Analysis on Decision Making

Regression analysis was done to predit the variable, which influence the decision making capacity of widows. Those variables which had correlation with the decision-making were chosen and used in the model. The step wise model in the regression was used in the analysis to arrive at the regression equation.

The Equation:

$$Y = B_o + B_1X_1 + B_2X_2 + B_3X_3 + B_4X_4 + \Sigma$$

Where,

Y = Decision making (Attitude of Others)
X = Present age
X_2 = Education
X_3 = Income
X_4 = Occupation
B = Beta Value
Σ = Random Error.

Levels of Deprivation

An attempt was made to estimate the level of deprivation based on possessions at the household level of some basic social and physical amenities of life using the data collected. Six necessities are found to determine the levels of deprivation. They determine the levels of deprivation. They are,

1. Level of Education (Illiterate / Literate)
2. Type of house (Kuccha / Pucca)
3. Nature of house (Rent / Own)
4. Availability of Land
5. Availability of TV / Radio / Bicycle (any one)
6. Availability of electricity in the house

The measurement of deprivation was done on the basis of following variables. AD, MD, JAD, and WAD.
Where:

AD = Abject Deprivation (household does not have any necessities)

MD= Moderate Deprivation (those which have one or two necessities)

JAD = Just Above Deprivation (those which have four necessities)

WAD = Well Above Deprivation (those which have 5 or 6 items)

Chi-Square Test

The Chi-Square Test was done to test the hypothesis. The following formula helps in obtaining the value of Chi-Square.

The Formula:

$$\chi^2 = \frac{\Sigma (O - E)^2}{E}$$

Where:

χ^2 = Chi-square Value
Σ = Sum of Frequencies
Σ = Observed Frequency
E = Expected Frequency

6
VARIEGATED SOCIAL STATUS OF MUDALIAR WIDOWS

INTRODUCTION

A study on the problems faced by the Mudaliar Widows in Tamil Nadu are presented in the first chapter together with the objectives, hypothesis, scope and limitations. The concept and review of past studies on the topic are presented in the second chapter. The third chapter describes the study area, Vellore district. The origin and spread of the Mudaliar community is espoused in the fourth chapter. The methods applied in the study are given in the fifth chapter. The present chapter provides the variegated social status of Mudaliar Widows. This chapter is divided into two sub sections, first section espoused the general information about the sample widows and their deceased husbands. The second section furnishes the social status of the sample widows.

GENERAL INFORMATION OF SAMPLE WIDOWS AND THEIR HUSBANDS

Classification of Sample Widows

Three types of classifications were made. All the sample widows were belonged to the Hindu Mudaliar Community. They are further divided into three sub-castes viz: Chenkunther Mudaliar, Agamudaiar Mudaliar and Vellala Mudaliar including the Tulu Vellalas small in number. Table–6.1 presents the Classification of sample widows according to their sub-castes.

Table - 6.1
Classification of Sample Widows according to their Sub-Castes

S. No.	Sub-castes	Area		
		Rural (Percentage)	Urban (Percentage)	Total (Percentage)
1.	Chenkunther	46 (18.4)	85 (34.0)	131 (26.2)
2.	Agamudiyar	133 (53.2)	147 (58.8)	280 (56.0)
3.	Tuluva Vellala	71 (28.4)	18 (7.2)	89 (17.8)
	Total	250 (100)	250 (100)	500 (100)

Source: Primary Data.

There were 131 widows belonged to Chenkunther sub-castes, 280 widows belonged to Agamudiyar sub-castes and 89 widows belonged to Tuluva Vellala sub-castes. As there was not much difference between sub-castes, this classification was not considered for further analysis.

Spatial Classification of Sample Widows

The sample widows were, classified as rural and urban, presented in table 6.2 and 6.3. All the 500 sample widows were divided equally between rural–250 and urban – 250. Table 6.2 presents the distribution of sample widows among eight rural blocks.

Table – 6.2
Distribution of Sample Mudaliar Widows in Rural Blocks of Vellore District

S. No.	Rural Blocks	Sample Mudaliar Widows	Percentage
1.	Tirupattur Block	50	20.0
2.	Vaniyambadi Block	25	10.0
3.	Ambur Block	25	10.0
4.	Gudiyattam Block	25	10.0
5.	Vellore Block	50	20.0
6.	Walajapet Block	25	10.0
7.	Ranipet Block	25	10.0
8.	Arcot Block	25	10.0
	Total	250	100.0

Source: Primary Data.

As shown in table 6.2, 250 sample Mudaliar Widows were distributed among eight blocks like Tirupattur, Vaniyambadi, Ambur, Gudiyattam, Vellore, Walajapet, Ranipet and Arcot. Similarly, the distribution of 250 sample Mudaliar widows households in various urban towns in Vellore district is presented in table 6.3.

Table–6.3
Distribution of Sample Mudaliar Widows Households in Urban Towns in Vellore District.

S. No.	*Urban Towns*	*Sample Mudaliar Widows*	*Percentage*
1.	Tirupattur	50	20
2.	Vaniyambadi	25	10
3.	Ambur	25	10
4.	Gudiyattam	25	10
5.	Vellore	50	20
6.	Walajapet	25	10
7.	Ranipet	25	10
8.	Arcot	25	10
	Total	250	100.0

Source: Primary Data.

As shown in the table 6.3 above, the sample Mudaliar Widows households were drawn from all the Municipal towns of the Vellore district viz: Tirupattur, Vaniyambadi, Ambur, Gudiyattam, Vellore, Walajapet, Ranipet and Arcot. The process of Urbanisation* of Vellore district, has influenced the socio-economic status of the Mudaliar widows, hence, the spatial classification as rural and urban, has been taken into account for analysis.

Age wise classification of Widows

In order to find out the change in the socio – economic status of Mudaliar widows over time, age wise classification of

* K.Padmanabhan (2000), Urban Shock, the Processes Urbanisation of Vellore District, I.I.P.A. Tirupattur Local Branch, Tirupattur,

sample widows is become unavoidable. Again the study is about three generation of widows. In the present study, those who are below 40 years are treated as 'young', from 41 to 60 years widows are treated as 'middle' and those widows above 60 years are treated as 'old'. For all future analysis, this classification is kept. The age wise classification of sample widows is presented in table 6.4 below. The same is depicted in fig.

Table - 6.4
Age-wise Classification of Sample Mudaliar Widows

S. No	*Age-wise Classification*	*No. of Widows*		
		Rural	*Urban*	*Total*
1.	Young (Below 40 years)	54 (21.6)	36 (14.4)	90 (18.0)
2.	Middle (41 – 60 years)	118 (47.2)	132 (52.8)	250 (50.0)
3.	Old (Above 60 years)	78 (31.2)	82 (32.8)	160 (32.0)
	Total	250 (100)	250 (100)	500 (100)

Source: Primary Data, (→) Percentage.

As shown in table 6.4 above, there are 90 (18 Percent) widows below 40 years, called as 'Young', 250 widows (50 Percent) called as 'Middle Aged' and 160 widows (32 Percent) called as 'Old'. They are further divided into rural and urban. Accordingly, among the young widows, 54 belonged to rural and 36 belonged to urban, among middle aged widows, 118 belonged to rural and 132 belonged to urban and among old widows , 78 belonged to rural and 82 belonged to urban.

Age of Sample Widows at the Time of Interview

For the purpose of comparison, the present age of sample widows at the time of interview was recorded and the same is provided in table 6.5. They are also classified as rural and urban.

There are only four respondents in the age below 20. there are 17 respondents (3.4 Percent) in the age group between 21 to 30, 69 respondents (13.8 Percent) in the age group of 31 to 40 , 84 respondents (16.8 Percent) in the age group of 41 to 50, 166 respondents in the age group of 51 to 60 and the remaining

Fig : 1. Age-wise Classification of Sample Mudaliar Widows in Rural and Urban Areas

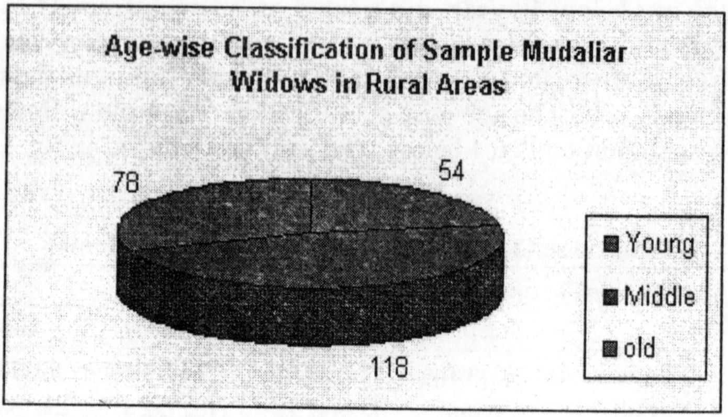

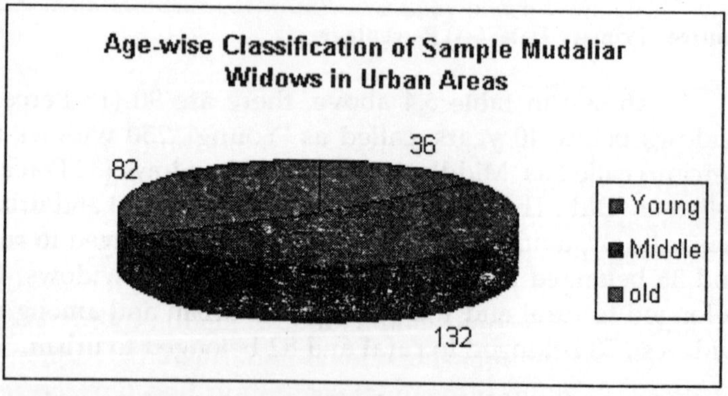

160 respondents are above 60 years of age. As noted in the table above, the number of respondents increase with increase in age up to 60 years of age, the number of respondents fell from 33.2 percent and 32 percent thereafter.

Age at the Time of Marriage

What was the age of the respondents at the time of their marriage? The age, reported by the respondents, is classified and presented in table-6.6.

Table – 6.5
Age of the Respondents at the Time of Interview

S. No.	*Present Age*	*Rural*	*Urban*	*Total*	*Percentage*
1.	Below 20	–	4	4	0.8
2.	21 - 30	10	7	17	3.4
3.	31 - 40	38	31	69	13.8
4.	41 - 50	41	43	84	16.8
5.	51 - 60	82	84	166	33.2
6	Above 60	79	81	160	32.0
	Total	250	250	500	100.0

Source: Primary Data.

Table – 6.6
Age-wise Classification of Widows at the Time of Marriage

S. No	*Age at the Time of Marriage*	*Young*		*Middle*		*Old*		*Total*		*Grand Total*
		R	*U*	*R*	*U*	*R*	*U*	*R*	*U*	
1.	Below 15	7	6	25	37	33	21	65	64	129 (25.8)
2.	16 – 20	20	24	79	68	37	54	136	146	282 (56.4)
3.	21 – 25	22	6	14	23	7	6	43	35	78 (15.6)
4.	26 – 30	5	-	-	4	1	1	6	5	11 (2.02)
	Total	54	36	118	132	78	82	250	250	500 (100)

Source: Primary Data.

As shown in the above table, there are 129 respondents (15.8 Percent) who was below 15 years when they got married, 282 respondents (56.4 Percent) who belonged to 16 – 20 years, 78 respondents (15.5 Percent) who belonged to the age group of 21 to 25 and 11 respondents who were between 26 to 30 while they entered the wedlock. Between rural and urban areas, there is not much difference in the age below 15 years. In the second category there were 146 respondents in the urban areas to 136 respondents in the rural areas in the age group of 21 – 25, there are 43 respondents in rural areas compared to 35 respondents in the urban areas. In the age category of 26 – 30, there were six in rural areas and five respondents in the urban areas.

The mean age of the respondents is calculated and presented in table 6.7.

Table – 6.7
The Mean Age of the Respondent Widows

S. No	Age at the Time of Marriage	Young		Middle		Old		Total		Grand Total
		R	U	R	U	R	U	R	U	
1.	Below 15	7	6	25	37	33	21	65	64	129 (25.8)
2.	16 – 20	20	24	79	68	37	54	136	146	282 (56.4)
3.	21 – 25	22	6	14	23	7	6	43	35	78 (15.6)
4.	26 – 30	5	-	-	4	1	1	6	5	11 (2.02)
	Total	54	36	118	132	78	82	250	250	500(100)
	Mean	13.85	12.0	11.62	11.45	10.76	11.36	11.84	11.69	11.7

It shows that the mean age at marriage of the young respondents was higher 19.1 compared to the middle aged respondents 11.7 and old respondents 10.9. The young respondents are aware of the advantage of higher age than the middle and old respondents. The raising of the marriage age for women has its effect on higher mean age for marriage of younger widows.

The difference in the mean age of the respondents at the time of marriage could be noticed in the rural and urban areas. Among the young respondents, the mean age at marriage of young in the rural areas was higher than the urban areas. The same is the case with regard to middle aged widows and old widows. From the total respondents, the mean age of the widows in rural areas has been estimated as 11.84 as against 11.69 in the urban areas. It is a paradox to note that girls in urban areas are given married earlier compared to the marriage of girls in the rural areas.

Age at Widowhood

The age at widowhood of the sample respondents was recorded for three generations respectively.

Age at Widowhood of the Young Respondents

There are 10 respondents who attained widowhood between 15 to 20 years of age, 16 respondents who attained widowhood between 21 to 25 years of age, 28 respondents attained widowhood between 26 to 30 years of age, 24 respondents who attained widowhood between 31 to 35 years of age and 12 respondents who attained widowhood between 36 to 40 years.

Table – 6.8
Age wise Classification of Widows at the Time of Widowhood (Young Respondents)

S. No	Age at the Time of Widowhood	Area		Total
		Rural	Urban	
1.	15 - 20	5	5	10 (11.11)
2.	21 - 25	12	4	16 (17.77)
3.	26 - 30	16	12	28 (31.11)
4.	31 - 35	13	11	24 (26.66)
5.	36 - 40	8	4	12 (13.33)
	Total	54	36	90 (100.0)

Source: Primary Data, (→) Percentage.

Age at Widowhood of the Middle Aged Respondents

As shown in table 6.9 below, there were 7 respondents (2.8 Percent), who were widowed between 10 to 20 years of age. 41 respondents (16.4 Percent) were widowed while they were between 21 to 30 years. 64 respondents (25.6 Percent) were widowed between the age of 31 to 40 years. 83 respondents

Table - 6.9
Age wise Classification of Widows at the Time of Widowhood (Middle Aged Respondents)

S. No	Age at the Time of Widowhood	Area		Total
		Rural	Urban	
1.	10 - 20	3	4	7 (2.8)
2.	21 - 30	21	20	41 (16.4)
3.	31 - 40	24	40	64 (25.6)
4.	41 - 50	48	35	83 (33.2)
5.	51 - 60	22	33	55 (22.0)
	Total	118	132	250 (100)

Source: Primary Data, (→) Percentage.

(33.2 Percent) were widowed between 41 to 50 years. Lastly 55 respondents (22 Percent) were widowed while they were in the age group of 51 to 60 years. The age at widowhood is also presented at area wise in the table.

Age at Widowhood of the Old Aged Respondents

There were only 5 respondents (3.12 Percent) who attained widowhood between 10 to 20 years of age (Table - 6.10). 10 respondents (6.25 Percent) who attained widowhood between 21 to 30 years of age. 14 respondents (8.75 Percent) who attained widowhood between 31 to 40 years. 23 respondents (14.37 Percent) attained widowhood between 41 to 50 years of age. 42 respondents (26.25 Percent) attained widowhood between 51 to 60 years. 35 respondents attained widowhood between 61 to 70 years. The remaining 31 respondents (19.37 Percent) had attained widowhood between 71 to 80 years of age. Age at widowhood, classified according to area - rural and urban is also presented in the table 6.10.

Table – 6.10
Age at Widowhood of the Old Respondents

S. No	Age at the Time of Widowhood	Area		Total
		Rural	Urban	
1.	10 - 20	3	2	5 (3.12)
2.	21 - 30	5	5	10 (6.25)
3.	31 - 40	4	10	14 (8.75)
4.	41 - 50	13	10	23 (14.37)
5.	51 - 60	19	23	42 (26.25)
6.	61 - 70	17	18	35 (21.87)
7.	71 - 80	17	14	31 (19.37)
	Total	78	82	160 (100)

Source: Primary Data, (→) Percentage.

Duration of Widowhood

How many years the respondents lived as widows till the date of interview? According to each generation the duration of widowhood varies.

Table – 6.11
Duration of Widowhood

Duration in Years	*Young*	*Middle*	*Old*
Below 5	8	7	8
6 - 10	26	6	6
11 - 15	24	10	8
16 - 20	26	28	6
21 - 25	6	33	9
26 - 30	–	41	9
31 - 35	–	59	11
36 - 40	–	60	13
41 - 45	–	6	19
46 - 50	–	–	20
Above 50	–	–	51
Total	90	250	160
Mean	11.80	27.34	37.0

Source: Primary Data.

The mean duration of widowhood for the young respondents was worked out to 11.80 years, for the middle aged respondents it was 27.34 years and for the old respondents, it was 37.0 years. When distribution of respondents to each years of class interval was analysed, it was found 8 respondents below 5 years, 26 respondents 6 to 10 years, 24 respondents in the class interval of 11 to 15 years, another 26 respondents in the age group of 16 to 20 and six respondents in the class interval of 21 to 25 years.

The 250 middle aged respondents are distributed against the duration of widowhood class intervals. As the duration expands, the number of respondents increases till class interval of 36-40, thereafter, the number of respondents has declined to six for the class interval of 41-45.

On the other hand, in the case of old respondents their number increases with the increase in the class interval. There are 51 respondents in the class interval of above 50 years.

The variation in duration of widowhood between generations inter alia establishes the fact that the middle aged and old generation respondents lived longer period compared to the younger generation.

Husband's Age

It is curious to know the husband's age at marriage. Whether the husband's age has got anything to do with the widowhood of the respondents. The husband's age is analysed in terms of his age at marriage and age at death.

Husband's Age at Marriage

As shown in table 6.12 below, there are 11 husbands who was below 15 years at the time of their marriage. All the 11 were belonged to the old respondents. There were none in the age below 15 in the young and middle aged respondents. There are 27 respondents who fall in the age group of 16-20 years. Out of the 27, six belonged to the young, 10 belonged to the middle aged and 11 belonged to old age respondents. In the age group of 21 to 25, there are 181 husband's, out of them 39 belonged to young, 89 belonged to middle aged and 53 belonged to old aged respondents. There were 198 husbands in the age group of 26 to 30 their distribution among various generation of respondents shows 22 among young, 112 among middle aged and 54 among old respondents. 55 husbands belonged to 31 to 35 age group. Their distribution shows 10 among young, 26 among middle aged, 10 among old. There

Table – 6.12
Husbands Age at Marriage

S. No	*Husband's Age*	*Young*		*Middle*		*Old*		*Total*		*Grand Total*
		R	*U*	*R*	*U*	*R*	*U*	*R*	*U*	
1.	Below 15	–	–	–	–	4	7	4	7	11
2.	16 – 20	4	2	4	6	3	8	11	16	27
3.	21 – 25	19	20	41	48	25	28	85	96	181
4.	26 – 30	22	10	61	51	33	21	116	82	198
5.	31 – 35	7	3	10	16	9	10	26	29	55
6.	36 – 40	2	1	2	2	2	7	6	10	16
7.	Above 40	–	–	–	9	2	1	2	10	12
	Total	54	36	118	132	78	82	250	250	500
	Mean	30.81	29.8	30.8	31.0	30.7	30.1	30.8	30.8	30.84

Source: Primary Data.

were 16 husbands fall in the age category of 36-40. Their distribution shows three among young, four among middle and nine among old. The last 12 husbands were with age above 40 at the time of marriage. They belonged to 9 in the middle and three in the old and none in the young category.

The mean age at marriage of the husbands was prepared and presented in the above table. The mean age was calculated separately for rural and urban husbands. It is observed that there is not much difference between generation and between areas. The mean age at marriage for the total husbands was worked out as 30.84. for the young, the mean age at marriage of husbands in urban areas was 29.8 as against 30.81 in the rural areas. For the other generations and areas, the lowest mean was 30.8 and the highest mean was 31.0.

Respondents and Their Husband's Age at Marriage a Comparision

A Correlation analysis has been done with a view to find out the difference in the age at marriage of the respondents and their husbands. The Karl Pearson's Co-efficient of Correlation is calculated to find out the relation between the respondents age at marriage and their husband's age at marriage for all

Table – 6.13
Co-efficient of Correlation of the Respondents Age at Marriage and their Husbands Age at Marriage

Age at Marriage	*No of Respondents*	*No of Husbands*
Below 15	129	11
16-20	282	27
21-25	78	181
26-30	11	198
31-35	–	55
36-40	–	16
Above 40	–	12
Total	500	500
Mean	71.4	71.4
r	-0.19	

Source: Primary Data.

generations. For the purpose of calculating Co-efficient of Correlation the respondents and their husbands are brought under seven class intervals of age. The table below gives the class intervals of age at marriage of the respondents and their husbands.

The calculated 'r' value is -0.19. It shows the respondents age at marriage and their husbands age at marriage are negatively correlated.

Husband's Age at Death

The husbands age at death is presented in table 6.14 below. As indicated in the table, none of the husbands died before the age of 21. But between 21 to 30 years,37 husbands died. Out of them 15 of them belonged to young, 14 belonged to middle and 8 belonged to old. 101 husbands died between the age group of 31 to 40. Distribution of the husbands among various generation shows 47 belonged to young, 46 belonged to middle and eight belonged to old. In the age group of 41 to 50, 16 husbands belonged to young, 70 belonged to middle and nine belonged to old. The 112 husbands died between 51 to 60, of them, five belonged to young, 61 belonged to middle and 46 belonged to old. Out of the 110 respondents, who died

Table - 6.14
Husbands Age at Death

S. No.	*Husbands Age at the Time of Death*	*Young*	*Middle*	*Old*	*Total*	*Percent*
1.	10 - 20	-	-	-	-	-
2.	21 - 30	15	14	8	37	7.4
3.	31 - 40	47	46	8	101	20.2
4.	41 - 50	16	70	9	95	19.0
5.	51 - 60	5	61	46	112	22.4
6.	61 - 70	7	49	54	110	22.0
7.	71 - 80	-	6	22	28	5.6
8.	Above 80	-	4	13	17	3.4
	Total	90	250	160	500	100
	Mean	38.7	49.78	60.45	51.06	

Source: Primary Data.

between the age group of 61 to 70, seven belonged to young, 49 belonged to middle, 54 belonged to old. In the interval of 71 to 80 age group, out of 28 husbands, six belonged to middle and 22 belonged to old category. There were 17 husbands who died abve 80 years of age, of whom, four belonged to middle and 13 belonged to old.

The mean age at death of all husbands was calculated and presented in the above table. The age at death for all the husbands was calculated as 51.06. When it was calculated for each generation, the mean age at death for the husbands of the young generation was 38.7, for husbands of the middle generation, it was 49.78 and for the husbands of the old generation, it was 60.45.

Causes of Husband's Death

It is interesting to find the causes for husband's death. As a result, the causes furnished by the respondents are provided in table 6.15.

Table - 6.15
Causes of Husband's Death

S.No.	*Causes of Husbands Death*	*Young*	*Middle*	*Old*	*Total*
1.	Natural Death	7	34	15	56 (11.2)
2.	Accident	9	19	7	35 (7.0)
3.	Suicide	3	6	-	9 (1.8)
4.	Heart Attack	26	78	68	172 (34.4)
5.	Fever	18	27	16	61 (12.2)
6.	Sugar	7	29	17	53 (10.6)
7.	T.B.	3	12	13	28 (5.6)
8.	Kidney Failure	8	10	13	31 (6.2)
9.	Malaria	4	22	5	31 (6.2)
10.	Jaundice	2	5	3	10 (0.2)
11.	Small Fox	1	3	-	4 (0.8)
12.	Lung Failure	1	2	1	4 (0.8)
13.	Asthma	1	3	2	6 (1.2)
	Total	90	250	160	500 (100)

Source: Primary Data, (→) Percentage.

Heart attack has been indicated as the major cause (34.4 Percent) of husband's death. It was followed by natural illness (11.2 Percent), accident death (7 Percent), suicide (1.8 Percent) and other causes accounted for 45.6 Percent. Other causes include the following: feever (12.2 Percent), sugar (10.6 Percent), T.B. (5.6 Percent), kidney failure (6.21 Percent), malaria (6.2 Percent), jaundice (0.2 Percent), small pox 0.8 Percent), lung failure (0.8 Percent) and Asthma (1.2 Percent).

Husband's Caste

Are the deceased husband's caste same as that of the respondent widows? The answer was 'yes' for the 497 respondents. For the three respondents, their husbands were from other subcaste because of their love marriage. The two elderely widows husbands were from the same sub-caste, though it was a 'love marriage'. It is further classified in the following section.

Nature of Marriage

The nature of marriage implies whether it is an arranged marriage or love marriage. The details are furnished in table 6.16 below.

Table - 6.16
Nature of Marriage

S.No.	Nature of Marriage	Young	Middle	Old	Total Percent
1.	Arranged Marriage	87	249	159	495 (99)
2.	Love Marriage	3	1	1	5 (1)
	Total	90	250	160	500 (100)

Source: Primary Data.

In the young widow category, out of 90 respondents, 87 respondent's marriages were arranged by the families and only 3 respondents were married her lovers.

Among the middle-aged widows, out of 250 respondents, 249 respondents marriages were arranged by the families and only one respondent had married her lover.

Among old generation widows, out of 160 respondents, 159 respondents, marriages were arranged by the families and only one respondent had married her lover.

Marriages Among Kinship

Are the marriage took place with in the caste and among relatives. If marriage took place with in the caste, it can be called as introvert marriage and if the marriage took place among two persons belonging to different castes, it can be called as extrovert. In the case of marriages in Mudaliar community, it is introvert marriages because the marriages took place within the community. Similarly if the marriages took place among persons related each other, it is become kinship marriage.

Table - 6.17
Marriage Among Kinship

S.No.	*Relationship*	*Young*	*Middle*	*Old*	*Total Percent*
1.	No Relationship	53	142	72	267 (53.4)
2.	Relative	37	108	88	233 (46.6)
	Total	90	250	160	500 (100)

Source: Primary Data.

As shown in the table 6.17, 267 respondents (53.4 Percent) had married outside the relationship. 233 (46.6 Percent) respondents had married their relatives.

Among the three generations, more of younger generation respondents (58 Percent) had married out side kinship compared to middle aged (56.8 Percent) and old respondents (45.0 Percent).

Nature of Respondents Families

The nature of families is determined by whether the family is single, nuclear or joint family? Table 6.18 and fig. 2 provide the nature of respondent's families.

Out of the 500 sample respondents, 400 respondents (80 Percent) were belonged to nuclear families compared to 81 respondents (16.2 Percent) belonged to single families or living alone and 19 respondents (3.8 Percent) belonged to joint families. Among the three generation, as the respondents advance in age, their preference for single living is also increasing. The preference for joint families has been vanishing from all generations.

Table - 6.18
Family Status of the Respondents

S.No.	Status	Young	Middle	Old	Total Percent
1.	Single	8	39	34	81 (16.2)
2.	Nuclear	79	204	117	400 (80.0)
3.	Joint	3	7	9	19 (3.8)
	Total	90	250	160	500 (100)

Source: Primary Data.

Fig. 2: Family Status of the Respondents

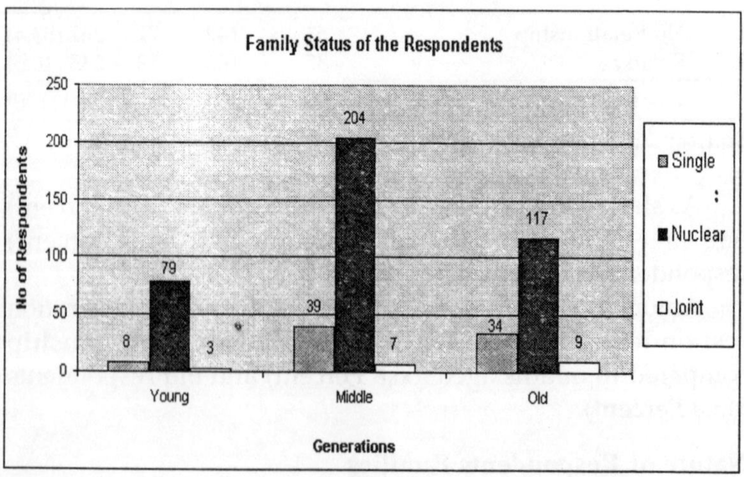

Size of Family of the Respondents

The size of widow's family is determined by her children and the dependents particularly her parents. The size of family of the respondents is given in table 6.19 below.

Table - 6.19
Size of Family of the Sample Respondents

S.No.	Size of Family	Young	Middle	Old	Total Percent
1.	No Children	7	22	16	45 (9.0)
2.	1	25	48	17	90 (18.0)
3.	2	31	49	19	99 (19.8)
4.	3	26	63	25	114 (22.8)
5.	4	1	31	33	65 (13)
6.	5	-	23	21	44 (8.8)
7.	6	-	7	15	22 (4.4)
8.	7	-	6	8	14 (2.8)
9.	Above 7	-	1	6	7 (1.4)
	Total	90	250	160	500 (100)
	Mean	1.95	2.78	3.56	2.86

Source: Primary Data.

There are 45 widows in the sample without any children. They are leading single families. The size of families shows an increase in size of families up to three children, there after it declines.

The average size of all the sample respondents was calculated as 2.86. It was as low as 1.95 for the young generation. 2.75 for middle aged generation and 3.56 for the old generation.

Marital Status of the Children of Widows

The study is about three generation of widows of different age groups, the marital status of children had greater bearing on the life of the widows. As shown in table 6.19, the sample 500 widows had 1380 children, comprising of 739 boys and 641 girls.

Out of the 739 boys, 548 (74.15 Percent) boys got married as against 191 (25.85 Percent) boys remain unmarried. In case of girls, out of 641, 525 (81.90 Percent) were married as against 116 (18.10 Percent) remain unmarried. In the old generation, because of their age, most of their children (both boys and girls) got married (97.9 Percent). In the case of middle and young respondents, the number of unmarried children are more than the married children.

Table - 6.20
Marital Status of Children

S. No	Childrens Classification	Young		Middle		Old		Total		Grand Total
		M	UM	M	UM	M	UM	M	UM	
1.	No.of. Boys	6	59	260	126	282	6	548	191	739
								51.07	62.21	53.55
2.	No.of Girls	17	53	273	58	235	5	525	116	641
								48.92	37.78	46.45
	Total	23	112	533	184	517	11	1073	307	1380
								100	100	100

Source: Primary Data.

SOCIAL STATUS

The social status of the sample widows is analysed in terms of nature of household, level of education, husbands education, pattern of living in relation to dress, use of cosmetics, entertainment, performing customery things like rituals, visiting relatives and friends, writing letters to relatives and friends, going to temples, going to parks and theaters, role in the family (bread winner), cooking, childcare, purchasing, washing and cleaning, looking after business and farming.

Nature of Households

What type of houses in which the respondents do live? It determines their social status. A house is a symbol of protection, security, peace and prosperity. In what type of houses, the respondents have chosen to live is provided in table 6.21.

The table - 6.21 shows the nature of house owned by the respondents. Out of 500 respondents 41.8 Percent of the respondents had lived in R.C.C. roof type of houses, out of this 53 were young, 90 were middle and 66 were old. 41.2 Percent of the respondents have lived in tiled houses. Out of this 26 were young, 110 were middle and 70 were old. 11.2

Table - 6.21
Nature of House Owned

S. No.	*Nature of House Owned*	*Young*	*Middle*	*Old*	*Total*	*Percent*
1.	Hut	8	35	13	56	11.2
2.	Tiled	26	110	70	206	41.2
3.	Thatched	3	15	11	29	5.8
4.	R.C.C. Roof	53	90	66	209	41.8
	Total	90	250	160	500	100

Source: Primary Data.

Percent of the respondents had lived in huts, out of this 8 young, 35 middle and 13 were old. Only 5.8 Percent of the respondents had lived in thatched houses, out of this 3 young, 15 middle and 11 were old.

As the table shows 53 (58.88 Percent) of the young respondents were living in R.C.C. roof building compared to 36 Percent of the middle age respondents and 41.25 percent of the old respondents. It proves inter alia that- young generation respondents are socially better than the respondents belonged to the other generation. (fig. 3)

Education

Education is the process which transforms a human resource into human capital. It changes not only his/her attitude but also it provides an outlook, an aim and strength to accept changes. Education builds up five capabilities in human beings viz., physical, mental, psychological, spiritual and environmental. How far did the respondents acquire education? This question is analysed in three levels like: generation, caste and space-rural and urban. The education of the respondent's husbands is analysed and a comparision between them made.

Classification of Respondents According to Their Education

The respondents are classified according to their education and generation and presented in table - 6.22.

Fig. 3 : Nature of House Owned by the Respondents

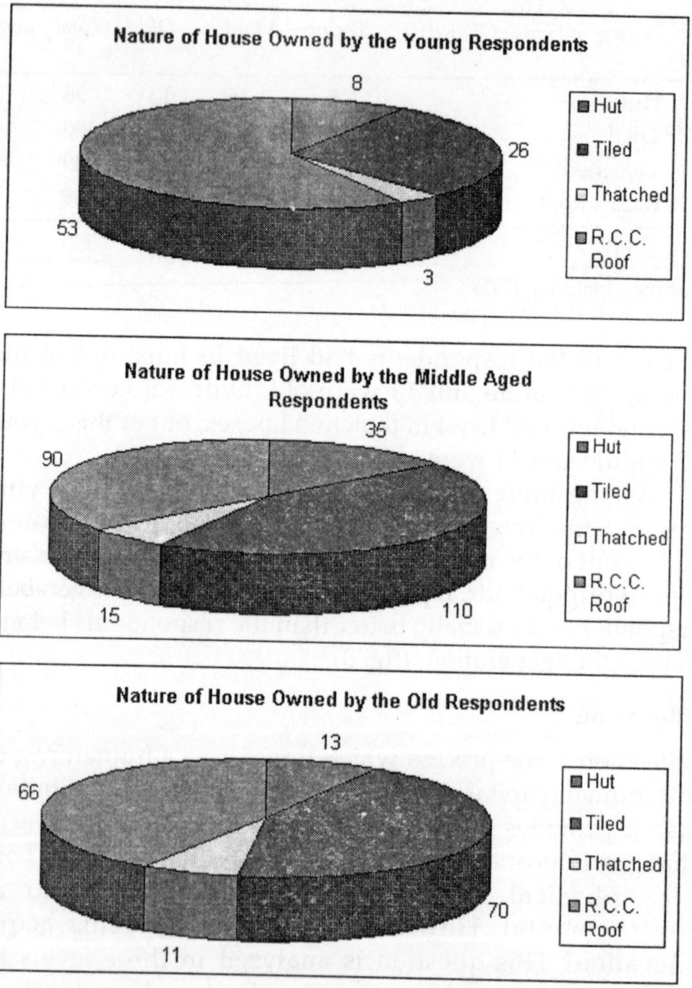

The table shows 256 (51.2 Percent) of the sample respondents were illiterate. Highest incidence of illiteracy (60.63 Percent) is found among old generation respondents compared to middle generation respondents (50.8 Percent) and the younger generation respondents (35.55 Percent). It shows the younger generation respondents are more aware of the importance of education compared to the middle and old

Table - 6.22
Level of Education Sample Respondents

S. No.	*Level of Education Generation*	*Generation*			*Total*	*Percent*
		Young	*Middle*	*Old*		
1.	Illiterate	32	127	97	256	51.2
2.	Primary	21	57	42	120	24.0
3.	Middle	21	32	15	68	13.6
4.	High School	13	27	6	46	9.2
5.	Higher Secondary	1	1	-	2	0.4
6.	Degree	1	3	-	4	0.8
7.	Training	1	3	-	4	0.8
	Total	90	250	160	500	100.00

Source: Primary Data.

generation respondents. Similarly, those who have acquired education in the young and middle generation, have slowly moved upward and few of them had acquired higher secondary, degree and training, which was seldom available to the old generation. Instead of saying 'not availed' it is better to say, educational facilities were not made available to the respondents in old generation. (fig. 4)

Fig. 4 : Educational Level of Sample Respondents

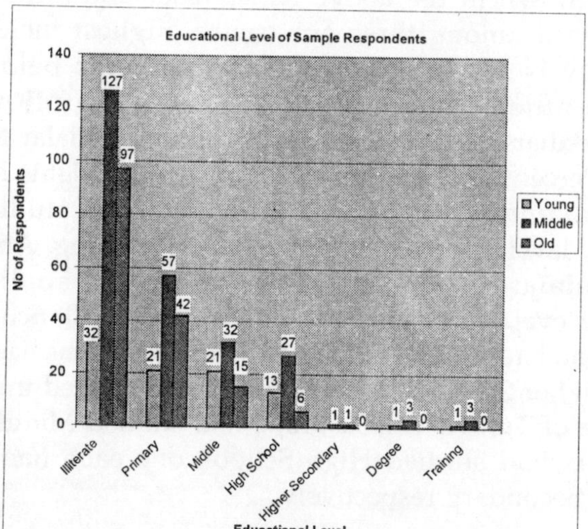

Educational Classification of Respondents According to Caste

How did the respondents belonging to various sub - caste perform in education? The caste-wise educational status of the sample respondents is presented below.

Table - 6.23

Caste-wise Educational Status of the Sample Respondents

S.No.	*Level of Education*	*Caste*			*Total*	*Percent*
		Ch	*Ag*	*Ve*		
1.	Illiterate	73 (55.3)	140 (50.0)	43 (48.31)	256	51.2
2.	Primary	36	56	28	120	24.0
3.	Middle	12	47	9	68	13.6
4.	High School	8	32	6	46	9.2
5.	Higher Secondary	-	1	1	2	0.4
6.	Degree	-	3	1	4	0.8
7.	Training	2	1	1	4	0.8
	Total	131	280	89	500	100.00

Source: Primary Data, Ch: Chenkunther, Ag: Agamudaliar, Ve: Tuluva Vellala.

As shown in the above table, when the illiterates are distributed among three sub-castes, highest incidence of illiteracy is found among the respondents belonged to Chenkunther Mudaliar (55.73 Percent) followed by Agamudaliar (50.00 Percent) and Thuluva Vellalar Mudaliar (48.31 Percent). Among the rest of the respondents belonged to Chenkunther Mudaliar, 36 of them had studied upto primary level, 12 of them had acquired training. Among the Agamudaiar respondents, 56 of them had studied upto Primary level, 47 of them had studied upto Middle School level, 32 of them had studied upto High School level, one had studied upto Higher Secondary level, three had acquired training. In the case of Tuluva Vellalas, nine had studied Middle School level, six had studied High School, one each had studied Higher Secondary respectively.

Educational Classification of Respondents according to Region:

The regional difference in education can be studied from the educational attainment of the respondents in the rural and urban areas. Educational calssification of respondents according to region is presented in table 6.24 below.

Table - 6.24
Educational Classification of Respondents according to Region.

S.No.	*Level of Education*	*Region*		*Total*	*Percent*
		Rural	*Urban*		
1.	Illiterate	155 (62.0)	101 (40.4)	256	51.2
2.	Primary	50 (20.0)	70 (28.0)	120	24.0
3.	Middle	31 (12.4)	37 (14.8)	68	13.6
4.	High School	11 (4.4)	35 (14.0)	46	9.2
5.	Higher Secondary	-	2 (0.8)	2	0.4
6.	Degree	2 (0.8)	2 (0.8)	4	0.8
7.	Training	1 (0.4)	3 (1.2)	4	0.8
	Total	250 (100)	250 (100)	500	100.00

Source: Primary Data.

As shown in the above table, the incidence of illiteracy is highest among the respondents belonging to rural areas (62.0 Percent). The illiteracy of the urban respondents was lower (40.4Percent). Though the Mudaliar caste has been considered as well off the prevalence of high incidence of illiteracy among the respondents reveals their low status of education particularly in the rural areas. In the educational attainment also, the respondents belonging to urban areas had acquired higher level of education compared to their counterparts in the rural areas. For instance, 28 Percent of the respondents in the urban areas had studied Primary School, compared to only 20 Percent of the respondents in the rural areas. 14.8 Percent of the respondents in the urban areas had studied Middle School in the rural areas, 14 Percent of the urban respondents had studied High School against only 4.4 Percent respondents in the rural areas. The Higher Secondary education was completed only by 2 urban respondents. There were two respondents each in the rural and urban areas who had acquired Degree. Similarly, one from the rural areas and three respondents from the urban areas had acquired training. Thus the level of education of the respondents in the rural and urban areas shows that the respondents belonging to urban areas were better educated than the respondents in the rural areas. (fig. 5)

Fig. 5 : Educational Classification of Respondents According to Region

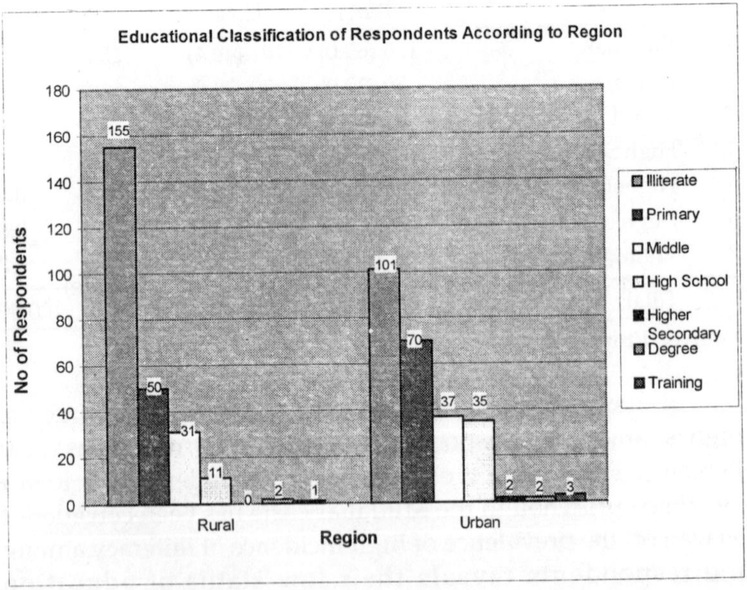

Level of Respondent's Husband's Education

The level of husband's education is an important indicator of the family status of the respondents. The following analysis will show whether the husbands were better educated than the respondents? The answer is presented in table - 6.25.

As the table shows, the incidence of illiteracy was lower among the husbands of the respondents which was 31.4 Percent compared to 51.2 Percent of the respondents who were illiterate. Among the literate husbands 119 (23.8 Percent) had

Table - 6.25
Husband's level of Education

S. No.	*Husbands Education*	*Generation*			*Total*	*Percent*
		Young	*Middle*	*Old*		
1.	Illiterate	39 (43.3)	73 (29.2)	45 (28.12)	157	31.4
2.	Primary	12	53	54	119	23.8
3.	Middle	15	58	31	104	20.8
4.	High School	20	47	22	89	17.8
5.	Higher Secondary	2	8	3	13	2.6
6.	Degree	1	8	4	13	2.6
7.	Training	1	3	1	5	1.0
	Total	90	250	160	500	100.00

Source: Primary Data.

studied Primary School, 104 (20.8 Percent) had studied Middle School, 89 (17.8 Percent) had studied High School, 13 (2.6 Percent) had acquired Degree and five (1.0 Percent) had Training. In acquring literacy also, the husband's status was much higher than the respondents. It indicates the preference being given to male children in the matter of education.

Another disquieting feature could be noticed in the table, that, the husbands of younger respondents are more illiterate than the husbands of the middle and old respondents. While 43.33 Percent of the husbands of young respondents were illiterate, only 29.2 Percent of the middle respondents and 28.12 Percent of the husbands of the old respondents were illiterate. It shows a change in the marriage pattern between literate husbands and the respondents. In the case of middle and old respondents, literate husbands had married more of illiterate respondents. But in the case of young respondents, illiterate husbands had married more of literate respondents. This change in the sociology of marriage between the literate husbands and illiterate wives will have to be analysed further.

Co-efficient of Correlation of Education of the Respondents and their Husbands

The Karl Pearson's Co-efficient of Correlation is calculated to find out the relationship between the respondents education and their husbands education. For the purpose of calculating Co-effieient of Correlation the respondents and their husbands are brought under seven headings of educational qualification. The table below gives the level of education of the respondents and their husbands.

Table - 6.26
Co-efficient of Correlation of the Respondents Education and their Husbands Education.

S. No.	Educational Level	No. of Respondents	No. of Husbands
1.	Illiterate	256	156
2.	Primary	120	119
3.	Middle	68	104
4.	High School	46	89
5.	Higher Secondary	2	13
6.	Degree / Higher Education	4	13
7.	Training	4	5
	Total	500	500
		r = 0.89	

Source: Primary Data, r - Correlation Co-efficient.

The calculated 'r' value is 0.89. It shows the respondents education and their husbands education are highly correlated.

PATTERN OF LIVING

Type of Dress

Dress is meant for covering the bare body and for protecting the body from heat and cold. The pattern of dress varies from community to community and from place to place. Certain dress pattern has been prescribed for widows. After the death of the husbands the widows were forced to wear white saries, which is considered as the symbol of purity. But in the present study, about the dress pattern of the widows of the Mudaliar community, none of the sample respondents were wearing white saries. On the otherhand they had worn colour saries.

Type of Food

Once food restriction was imposed on widows. They should take simple food and they had to live of piety. They should avoid non-vegetarian items of food. How many sample respondents followed this food pattern after their widowhood. The response is presented in table 6.27 below.

Table - 6.27
Type of Food

S. No.	*Husbands Education*	*Young*	*Middle*	*Old*	*Total*	*Percent*
1.	Vegetarian	9 (10.0)	45 (18.0)	32 (20.0)	86	17.2
2.	Non-Vegetarian	81 (90.0)	205 (82.0)	128 (80.0)	414	82.8
	Total	90 (100)	250 (100)	160 (100)	500	100.0

Source: Primary Data.

As shown in the above table, only 17.2 Percent of the respondents preferred vegetarian items of food. On the otherhand, 82.8 Percent of the respondents preferred non-vegetarian items of food. In the young generation, while 90 Percent preferred non-vegetarain items as against 10 Percent preferred vegetarian items.

In case of middle aged respondents, 82 Percent preferred non-vegetarain items as against 18 Percent preferred vegetarian items. Among the old generation, 80 Percent preferred non-vegetarian items as against 20 Percent who preferred vegetarian items. Though highest number of respondents belonging to younger generation prefered non-vegetarian items, the other two generations, the number of respondents, who preferred non-vegetarian items, had been above 80 Percent. Thus the vegetarian type of food imposed on widows has not found favour with the present generation of respondents.

Use of Cosmetics

The cosmetics, generally women use, are talcom powder, lipsticks, nail polish, eye-brow, bindi, kum kum, etc. The use of cosmetics by the sample respondents is presented in table 6.28 below.

Table - 6.28
Use of Cosmetics

S.No.	Use of Cosmetics	Young	Middle	Old	Total	Percent
1.	Use	20 (22.22)	17 (6.8)	7 (4.37)	44	8.8
2.	Do Not Use	70 (77.77)	233 (93.2)	153 (95.63)	456	91.2
	Total	90 (100)	250 (100)	160 (100)	500	100.0

Source: Primary Data.

As shown in the above table, out of the total sample of 500 respondents, 44 (8.8 Percent) respondents were in use of cosmetics and the remaining 456 respondents (91.2) Percent were not in use of cosmetics.

Among the three generation, young generation were in favour of using cosmetics because 20 respondents (20.22 Percent) were using cosmetics compared to 17 respondents (6.8 Percent) belonging to middle age respondents and 7 respondents (4.37 Percent) belonging to old respondents who were using cosmetics. Thus the growing awareness to use cosmetics was felt more by the young generation respondents compared to older generation respondents.

Use of Gold Jewels

Women use jewels to enhance their beauty as well as to provide them security. Gold jewels are highly liquid and it can be pledged or sold easily when ever they need cash. On attaining widowhood, women are forbidden from using anything which will boost their beauty. As could be seen in table 6.29 below, out of the total 500 respondents, 445 respondents (89.0 Percent), were not using jewels as against 55 respondents (11.0 Percent) were using jewels.

Table - 6.29
Use of Jewels

S.No.	Use of Jewels	Young	Middle	Old	Total	Percent
1.	Use	9 (10.0)	22 (8.8)	24 (15.0)	55	11.0
2.	Do Not Use	81 (90.00)	228 (91.2)	136 (85.0)	455	89.0
	Total	90 (100)	250 (100)	160 (100)	500	100.0

Source: Primary Data.

Among the various generations, 24 respondents belonging to old generation were using jewels as against 9 respondents (10 Percent) belonging to young generation and 22 respondents (8.8 Percent) belonging to middle age respondents, who were using jewels.

Entertainment

Entertainment is meant for relaxation of the mind and the body. All the respondents had expressed their opinion against entertainment. But watching television is one form of entertainment, which every body wants to watch. Whether the respondents are allowed to sit along with others to watch television and enjoy it? Even if it is allowed, the respondents were reluctant to sit with others and watch television. Exposure to entertainment will bring down the mental depression among widows. Therefore, the widows will have to be drawn to entertainment in order to save them from mental depression.

PERFORMING CUSTOMARY THINGS

Performing Rituals

Some of the customary rituals performed by women at home are: worshipping at home, making offerings to deceased persons etc. The customary rituals performed by the respondents are depicted in table 6.30 below.

Table - 6.30
Performing Customary Rituals

S. No	*Nature*	*Young*		*Middie*		*Old*		*Total*		*Grand Total*	*Per-cent*
		R	*U*	*R*	*U*	*R*	*U*	*R*	*U*		
1.	Yes	30	26	68	110	52	64	150	200	350	70
2.	No	24	10	50	22	26	18	100	50	150	30
	Total	54	36	118	132	78	82	250	250	500	100

Source: Primary Data.

The above table brings out the opinion of the respondents about performing rituals. Out of 500 respondents, 70 Percent of the respondents were performing rituals and 30 Percent of the respondents were not performing rituals.

In the young widows category, out of 90 respondents, 56 respondents were performing rituals and 34 respondents were not performing rituals. 30 of the young respondents, belonging to rural areas were performing rituals as against 26 respondents in the urban areas. Among those who were not performing rituals, 24 belonged to rural areas only 10 belonged to urban areas.

Among the middle-aged widows, out of 250 respondents, 178 respondents were performing rituals, out of this 68 were rural and 110 were urban. Among those 72 respondents who were not performing rituals, 50 were belonged to rural and 22 belonged to urban areas.

Out of 160 old generation widows, 116 respondents were performing rituals, out of these 52 were rural and 64 were urban. Among the 44 respondents not performing rituals, 26 were rural and 18 were urban.

It could be proved that among those who performed rituals nearly 80 Percent belonged to urban areas compared to 60 Percent belonged to rural areas. In the case of non-performers, 40 Percent belonged to rural areas as against 20 percent belonged to urban areas.

Table - 6.31
Attending Marriage

S. No	*Nature*	*Young*		*Middie*		*Old*		*Total*		*Grand Total*	*Per-cent*
		R	*U*	*R*	*U*	*R*	*U*	*R*	*U*		
1.	Yes	44	33	92	118	70	75	206	226	432	86.4
2.	No	10	3	26	14	8	7	44	24	68	13.6
	Total	54	36	118	132	78	82	250	250	500	100.0

Source: Primary Data.

Attending Marriages

Marriage is an important social function in which 'sumangalis', women who have husbands alive, are expected to participate. Widows are considered 'amangalis' as well as bad oman during the auxpicious occasions like marriages. How the sample respondents perform in attending marriages, is presented in table 6.31 below.

The above table exhibits the respondents opinion regarding attending marriages. Out of 500 respondents 86.4 Percent were attending marriages and only 13.6 Percent were not attending marriages.

In the young widow category, out of 90 respondents, 77 respondents were attending marriages, out of this 44 were rural and 33 were urban. Out of 13 respondents, not attending marriages, 10 were rural and three were urban.

Out of 250 middle-aged widows, 210 respondents were attending marriages, of them 92 were rural and 118 were urban. Among the 40 respondents who were not attending marriages, 26 were rural and 14 were urnan.

Among the old generation widows, 145 respondents were attending marriages, of them 70 were rural and 75 were urban. Only 15 respondents were not attending marriages, of them 8 were rural and 7 were urban.

As it is manifested in the table above, 80 to 90 Percent of the respondents had attended marriage. The remaining 15 Percent of the respondents also should attend the marriages. It depends on the change in attitude of not only others but also the attitude of widows themselves.

Writing Letters to Relatives and Friends

Writing letters requires literacy. Nearly 50 Percent of the sample respondents were illiterate. The remaining respondents were literate. Among them, how many wrote letters to relatives and friends. Through letters, one wants to convey her feelings, renew the relationship and strengthen the fellowship. How many respondents had written letters to relatives and friends? These details are furnished in table 6.32 below.

The above table unfolds the opinion of the respondents about writing letters to relatives and friends. Out of 500 respondents, 68.4 Percent of the respondents were not writing letters to relatives and friends and only 31.6 Percent were writing letters to relatives and friends.

Table - 6.32
Writing Letters to Relatives and Friends

S. No	Nature	Young		Middie		Old		Total		Grand Total	Per-cent
		R	U	R	U	R	U	R	U		
1.	Yes	14	12	28	57	16	31	58	100	158	31.6
2.	No	40	24	90	75	62	51	192	150	342	68.4
	Total	54	36	118	132	78	82	250	250	500	100.0

Source: Primary Data.

In the young widows category, out of 90 respondents, 64 respondents were not writing letters to relatives and friends, out of this 40 rural and 24 urban. Only 26 respondents were writing letters to relatives and friends, out of them 14 were rural and 12 were urban.

Among the middle-aged widows, out of 250 respondents, 165 respondents were not writing letters to relatives and friends, out of this 90 were rural and 75 were urban. Only 85 respondents were writing letters to relatives and friends, out of this 28 were rural and 75 were urban.

Out of 160 old generation respondents, 113 were not writing letters to relatives and friends, out of them 62 were rural and 51 were urban. 47 respondents were writing letters to relatives and friends, out of them 16 were rural and 31 were urban.

Visiting Relatives and Friends

This method of renewing friendship and establishing fellowship could be possible even by those who could not write letters. Are the respondents free to visit their relatives and friends? It could be found from the table 6.33 below.

Out of 500 respondents, 59.2 Percent of the respondents were visiting friends and relatives and only 40.8 Percent of the respondents were not visiting friends and relatives.

In the young widows category, out of 90 respondents 49 respondents were visiting friends and relatives. Of them 38 were rural and 11 were urban. Only 39 respondents were not visiting friends and relatives, of them 14 were rural and 25 were urban.

Table - 6.33
Visiting Relatives and Friends

S. No	Nature	Young		Middie		Old		Total		Grand Total	Per-cent
		R	U	R	U	R	U	R	U		
1.	Yes	38	11	74	82	51	40	163	133	296	59.2
2.	No	14	25	44	50	27	42	87	117	204	40.8
		(26)	(69)	(37)	(37)	(34)	(52)	(34)	(84)		
	Total	54	36	118	132	78	82	250	250	500	100.0

Source: Primary Data.

Among the middle-aged widows, out of 250 respondents, 156 respondents were visiting friends and relatives, of them 74 were rural and 82 were urban. 94 respondents were not visiting friends and relatives, of them 44 were rural and 50 were urban.

Among the old generation widows, 91 respondents were visiting friends and relatives, of them 27 were rural and 42 were urban. 69 respondents were not visiting friends and relatives, of them, 27 were rural and 42 were urban.

One notable feature emerged in the table is that more respondents (84 Percent) belonging to urban areas were not visiting relatives and friends compared to only 34 Percent of the rural respondents who were not visiting relatives and friends. The fear in visiting relatives and friends has been felt more by urban respondents than by the rural respondents.

Going to Temples

The widows were denied the right to go and worship at temples for a long time. But today they are treated equally by law with sumangalis. How many respondents had gone to temples to worship. The answers are given in table 6.34.

As the table shows,75 Percent of the total respondents were giong to temples, but 25 Percent of the respondents were not going to temples.

In the young category, out of 90 respondents, 70 were going to temples, of them 42 were rural and 28 were urban. Only 20 respondents were not going to temples, of them, 12 were rural and 8 were urban.

Table - 6.34
Going to Temples

S. No	Nature	Young		Middie		Old		Total		Grand Total	Per- cent
		R	U	R	U	R	U	R	U		
1.	Yes	42	28	86	105	52	62	180	195	375	75.0
2.	No	12	8	32	27	26	20	70	55	125	25.0
	Total	54	36	118	132	78	82	250	250	500	100.0

Source: Primary Data.

Among the middle-aged widows, 191 were going to temples, of them, 86 were rural and 105 were urban. But 59 respondents were not going to temples, of them 32 were rural and 27 were urban.

In the case of old generation, 114 respondents were going to temples, of them, 52 were rural and 62 were urban and only 46 respondents were not going to temples, of them, 26 were rural and 20 were urban.

The rural urban division of the respondents has brought out certain stark realities. Among those who had gone to temples, urban respondents were more than the rural respondents. On the contrary, among those who had not gone to temples the rural respondents were greater than the urban respondents. This difference is quite visible in all the generations.

Going to Parks and Theatres

People go to parks for relaxation and theatres for entertainment. Commonly, the widows were not encouraged to go to public places particularly parks and theatres. They have to lead a secluded life. How many of the respondents had visited parks and theatres? could be found in table 6.35 below.

Out of 500 respondents 98.6 Percent were not going to parks and theatres and only 1.4 Percent were going to parks and theatres.

In the young widows category, out of 90 respondents, 89 respondents were not going to parks and theatres, out of them 54 were rural and 35 were urban. Only one urban widow was going to parks and theatres.

Table - 6.35
Going to Parks and Theatres

S. No	Nature	Young		Middie		Old		Total		Grand Total	Per-cent
		R	U	R	U	R	U	R	U		
1.	Yes	-	1	2	2	1	1	3	4	7	1.4
2.	No	54	35	116	130	77	81	247	246	493	98.6
	Total	54	36	118	132	78	82	250	250	500	100.0

Source: Primary Data.

Among the middle-aged widows, out of 250 respondents, 246 respondents were not going to parks and theatres. Out of them, 116 were rural and 130 were urban. Only 4 respondents were going to parks and theatres, out of them 2 were rural and 2 were urban.

Among the old-generation widows, out of 160 respondents, 158 respondents were not going to parks and theatres, of them, 77 were rural and 81 were urban. Only 2 respondents were going to parks and theatres, out of them one each was rural and urban.

A very high Percentage of respondents were not going to parks and theatres. This exclusion could be noticed in all the generations. Thus, the widowss had preferred to remain at home rather than going to parks and theatres for relaxation and recreation.

ROLE IN THE FAMILY

Bread Winner

What was the role of the respondents in their families? Whether she is a sole earner, if so, in how many families? If they are not sole earners, what is their contribution to the family? These questions are analysed in table 6.36 below.

Out of 500 respondents, 81 Percent of the respondents were not bread winners, only 19 Percent were bread winners.

In the young widows category, out of 90 respondents, 48 respondents (53 Percent) were bread winners, of them 32 were rural and 16 were urban. Only 42 respondents (47 Percent) were not bread winners, of them 22 were rural and 20 were urban.

Table - 6.36
Role in the Family (Bread Winner)

S. No	Nature	Young		Middie		Old		Total		Grand Total	Per-cent
		R	U	R	U	R	U	R	U		
1.	Yes	32	16	13	24	1	9	46	49	95	19.0
2.	No	22	20	105	108	77	73	204	201	405	81.0
	Total	54	36	118	132	78	82	250	250	500	100.0

Source: Primary Data.

Among the middle-aged widows, out of 250 respondents, 213 respondents (85.20 Percent) were not bread winners, of them, 105 were rural and 108 were urban. Only 37 respondents (14.8 Percent) were bread winners, of them 13 were rural and 24 were urban.

Among the old generation widows, out of 160 respondents, 150 respondents (93.75 Percent) were not bread winners, of them, 77 were rural and 73 were urban. Only 10 respondents (6.25 Percent) were bread winners, of them, one was rural and nine were urban.

Though the bread winners were present in all the generations, in young category, 53 Percent of them were bread winners as against 47 Percent were not bread winners. In the category of middle aged respondents and old generation respondents, 85.20 Percent and 93.75 Percent respondents were not bread winners. Education and training of young respondents had prompted them to take up income earning professions.

Cooking

If the respondents were not engaged in income earning occupation, what else they were doing? The following section would provide answer to the question. How many of them were engaged in cooking? Table 6.37 displays the number of respondents engaged in cooking.

Out of 500 respondents, 72.4 Percent were engaged in cooking in the family and 27.6 Percent were not cooking in the family.

Table - 6.37
Cooking

S. No	Nature	Young		Middie		Old		Total		Grand Total	Per-cent
		R	U	R	U	R	U	R	U		
1.	Yes	49	29	98	98	45	43	192	170	362	72.4
2.	No	5	7	20	34	33	39	58	80	138	27.6
	Total	54	36	118	132	78	82	250	250	500	100.0

Source: Primary Data.

In the young widows category, out of 90 respondents, 78 respondents (86.66 Percent) were cooking, of them, 49 were rural and 29 were urban. Only 12 respondents were not cooking, of them, five were rural and seven were urban.

Among the middle-aged widows, out of 250 respondents, 196 respondents (78.4 Percent) were cooking, of them, 98 were rural and 98 were urban. Only 54 respondents were not cooking. Of them, 20 were rural and 34 were urban.

Among the old generation widows, out of 160 respondents, 72 respondents (45.1 Percent) were not cooking, out of this 33 were rural and 39 were urban. Only 88 respondents (55.0 Percent) were cooking, out of this 45 were rural and 43 were urban.

As expected, a priori, those respondents, who were not earning any income, were engaged in cooking. But the percentage of respondents engaged in cooking varies from generation to generation. In the young generation nearly 86.6 Percent were cooking. But the percentage declined to 78.4 Percent in the case of middle age respondents. Percentage of cooks in the old category had further declined to 55 Percent.

Child Care

Child care is another job suitable to women. But it was performed by only 43.2 Percent of the respondents as against 56.8 Percent of the respondents who performed child care. The intergenerational variation could be found in table 6.38 below.

Out of the 500 respondents, 56.8 Percent were not taking child care. Only 43.2 Percent respondents were taking child care.

Table - 6.38
Child Care

S. No	Nature	Young		Middle		Old		Total		Grand Total	Per-cent
		R	U	R	U	R	U	R	U		
1.	Yes	30	27	54	61	14	30	98	118	216	43.2
2.	No	24	9	64	71	64	52	152	132	284	56.8
	Total	54	36	118	132	78	82	250	250	500	100.0

Source: Primary Data.

In the young widows category, out of 90 respondents, 57 respondents (63.33 Percent) were taking child care activities, of them, 30 were rural and 27 were urban. Only 33 respondents were not taking child care, of them, 24 were rural and nine were urban.

Among the middle aged widows, out of 250 respondents, 135 respondents (54.0 Percent) were not taking child care activities, of them, 64 were rural and 71 were urban. Only 115 respondents (46.0 Percent) were taking child care activities, of them, 54 were rural and 61 were urban.

In the case of old generation widows, 116 respondents (72.5 Percent) were not taking child care activities, of them 64 were rural and 52 were urban. Only 44 respondents (27.5 Percent) were taking child care activities, of them, 14 were rural and 30 were urban.

As it is an established fact, that the young respondents had children so they have to look after them. On the other hand, as the children grow, they do not require child care from their mothers. Therefore, the child care duty has declined as the respondents advance in age. But some of them had undertaken the child care of their grand children of their sons or daughters.

Purchasing

Purchasing is an important function to be performed in the family. How many respondents had enjoyed in purchasing in the family? Table 6.39 demonstrate the fact of purchasing done by the respondents.

Out of 500 respondents, 55.8 Percent were purchasing and only 44.2 Percent were not purchasing.

Table - 6.39
Purchasing

S. No	Nature	Young		Middle		Old		Total		Grand Total	Per-cent
		R	*U*	*R*	*U*	*R*	*U*	*R*	*U*		
1.	Yes	48	22	93	58	36	22	117	102	279	55.8
2.	No	6	14	25	74	42	60	73	148	221	44.2
	Total	54	36	118	132	78	82	250	250	500	100.0

Source: Primary Data.

In the young widows category, out of 90 respondents, 70 respondents (77.77 Percent) were purchasing, out of this 48 were rural and 22 were urban. Only 20 respondents (22.23 Percent) were not purchasing, out of this six were rural and 14 were urban.

Among the middle-aged widows, out of 250 respondents, 127 respondents (50.8 Percent) were purchasing, out of them, 68 were rural and 59 were urban. Only 23 respondents (49.2 Percent) were not purchasing, of them, 50 were rural and 73 were urban.

Among the old generation widows, out of 160 respondents, 54 respondents (33.75 Percent) were purchasing, of them, 28 were rural and 26 were urban. 106 respondents (66.25 Percent) were not purchasing, of them, 50 were rural and 56 were urban.

The above analysis displays the fact that more younger respondents were engaged in purchase compared to the middle aged and old respondents. It is because the younger respondents had enjoyed more liberty than the other two categories of respondents.

Washing and Cleaning

Washing and cleaning are considered to be the domian of women. How for the respondents, after attaining widowhood, have been engaged in washing and cleaning?

Out of 500 respondents, 51 Percent were washing and cleaning and only 49 Percent were not washing and cleaning.

In the young widows category, out of 90 respondents, 64 respondents (71.11 Percent) were washing and cleaning, of them, 39 were rural and 25 were urban. Only 26 respondents were not doing washing and cleaning activities. Of them, 15 were rural and 11 were urban.

Table - 6.40
Washing and Cleaning

S. No	Nature	Young		Middie		Old		Total		Grand Total	Per-cent
		R	U	R	U	R	U	R	U		
1.	Yes	39	25	68	59	28	26	135	110	245	49.0
2.	No	15	11	50	73	50	56	115	140	255	51.0
	Total	54	36	118	132	78	82	250	250	500	100.0

Source: Primary Data.

Among the middle-aged widows, out of 250 respondents, 127 respondents (50.8 Percent) were doing washing and cleaning, of them, 68 were rural and 59 were urban. Only 123 respondents (49.2 Percent) were not doing washing and cleaning, of them, 50 were rural and 73 were urban.

Among the old generation widows, out of 160 respondents, 106 respondents were not doing washing and cleaning, of them, 50 were rural and 56 were urban. Only 54 respondents were doing washing and cleaning activities, of them, 28 were rural and 26 were urban.

Many of the respondents belonging to old generation were very weak as they were above 70 and 75 years of age. With their falling health, they were unable to do this. On the other hand, many of the respondents belonging to young and middle aged were doing washing and cleaning.

Looking After Business

Only nine respondents were looking after business. They continue to carry on the occupation of their husbands. No one else was interested in business. Of the nine respondents looking after business, three of them belonged to rural and six of them belonged to urban centres. Distribution of the nine respondents among various generations shows that two of them belonged to young generation, five of them belonged to middle aged group and two of them belonged to old age group.

Farming

Similarly farming was done by only six respondents (1.2 Percent). Five of them were belonged to rural and one was belonged to urban centre. Distribution of six respondents among various generations shows three of them belonged to young and three of them belonged to middle aged group. None was in the old group. Since most of them in all the generations were engaged in domestic work, they were not engaged in farming.

7
ECONOMIC SPECTRUM OF MUDALIAR WIDOWS

ECONOMIC ATTAINMENT

An economic attainment is an important indicator of the status of an individual, group or community. In order to find out the status of widows, belonging to Mudaliar Community, their economic attainment has been analysed. The economic status of the Hindu Mudaliar Widows is examined in terms of occupation, assets, income, expenditure, savings, investment, and debts.

OCCUPATION

One has to choose an occupation according to his / her capacity or skills for earning income with which one has to live. There are different kinds of occupation one pursues like physical, mental or spiritual. Similarly, the standard of living of a person also depends on the kind of work he / she does and the quantum of income earned from it. What are the occupations pursued by the respondent widows? Accordingly, the respondents were grouped under eight categories as shown in table 7.1 below.

Those eight categories are: coolies, farming, domectic work, teacher, self employed, business, other works and no work. More than half of the respondents (317) 63.4 percent were not doing any work. When they are divided into regions, 159 belonged to rural areas and 158 belonged to urban areas. When they are further divided into generations, larger number of

Table – 7.1
Occupational Status of Widows

S. No	Occupation	Young		Middle		Old		Total		Grand Total
		R	U	R	U	R	U	R	U	
1.	Coolie	19	12	20	35	2	4	41	51	92 (18.4)
2.	Farming	10	1	6	-	-	1	16	2	18 (3.6)
3.	Domestic Work	4	4	5	8	-	4	9	16	25 (5.0)
4.	Teacher	2	2	2	2	-	1	4	5	9 (1.8)
5.	Self Employed	-	-	1	-	-	-	1	-	1 (0.2)
6.	Business	-	2	-	1	2	2	2	5	7 (1.4)
7.	Other Works	4	-	12	6	2	7	18	13	31 (6.2)
8.	No Work	15	15	72	80	72	63	159	158	317 (63.4)
	Total	54	36	118	132	78	82	250	250	500 (100)

Source: Primary Data, ( ) Percentage.

non-workers, 152 out of 250, (60.80 percent) are found among middle aged respondents followed by old generation respondents 135 of 160 (84.37 percent) and lastly by the young generation 30 out of 90 (33.33 percent). In the old generation large number of them were not working because of incapacity due to old age. In the middle and young generation, large number of non- workers were found because they were not sent to work outside.

Among the workers, large number of respondents 92 (18.4 percent) were working as coolies or wage earners. It is followed by other workers 31 (6.2 percent), domestic work 25 (5.0 percent), farming 18 (3.6 percent), teaching 9 (1.8 percent), business 7 (1.4 percent) and one (0.2 percent) was self employed. (fig.1)

The nature of occupation of the respondents points out large number of non-workers and those, who work, are engaged in unskilled work. In the non-working category, some are incapacitated due to old age and sickness but many are prevented from undertaking any other work outside their home/farm.

Fig. 1 : Occupational Status of Widows in Rural and Urban Areas

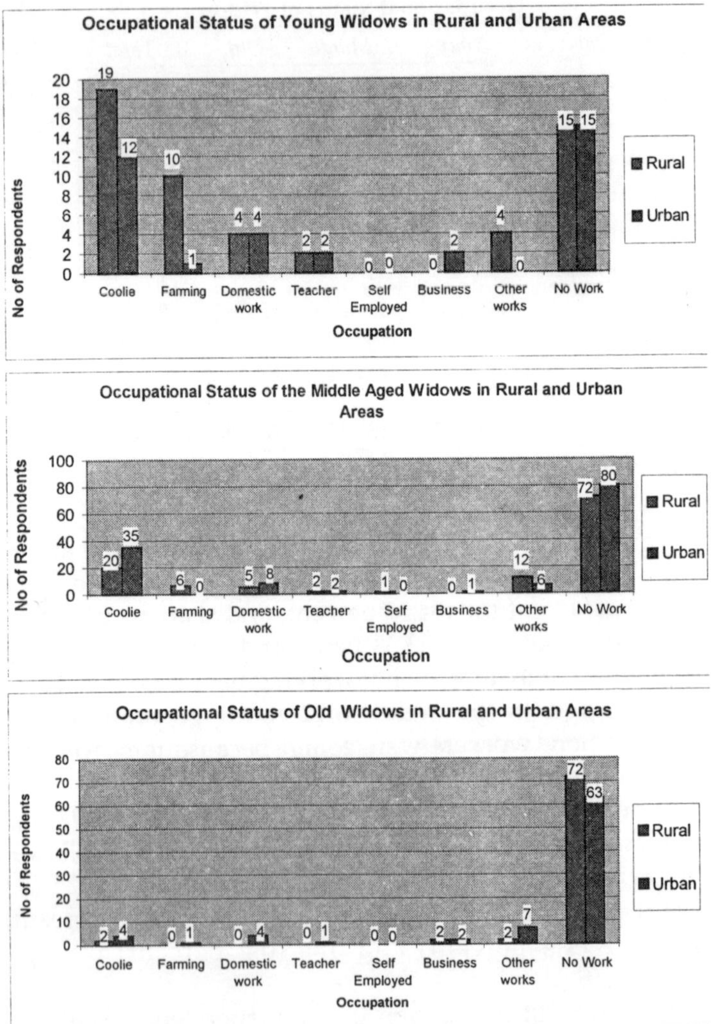

Husbands Occupation

The husband's occupational status was examined and analysed and presented in table 7.2 below.

Unlike the respondents, only four husbands were not doing any work at the time of interview. The husbands of 496

Table – 7.2
Husband's Occupation

S.No.	*Husbands Occupation*	*Young*	*Middle*	*Old*	*Total Percentage*
1.	Coolie	14	64	16	94 (18.8)
2.	Farming	10	33	54	97 (19.4)
3.	Teacher	-	13	8	21 (4.2)
4.	Army	1	3	4	8 (1.6)
5.	Business	8	19	9	36 (7.2)
6.	Tailore	32	38	23	93 (18.6)
7.	Mason	13	43	16	72 (14.4)
8.	Carpenter	3	10	20	33 (6.6)
9.	Conducter	4	4	2	10 (2.0)
10.	Driver	2	6	3	11 (2.2)
11.	Broker (Bus)	-	4	2	6 (1.2)
12.	Commission Agent	1	5	1	7 (1.4)
13.	Accountant	2	5	1	8 (1.6)
14.	No Occupation	-	3	1	4 (0.8)
	Total	90	250	160	500 (100)

Source: Primary Data, ( ) Percentage.

respondents were working before their death. Out of the total, 97 (19.4 percent) husbands were engaged in farming, followd by coolies 94 (18.8 percent), tailoring by 93 (18.6 percent), masons 72 (14.4 percent), business (7.2 percent), 33 of them (6.6 percent) were carpenters, 21 of them (4.2 percent) were teachers, there were 11 (2.2 percent) were drivers, conductors 10 (2.0 percent), eight of them were in army (1.6 percent), eight of them were working as accountants (1.6 percent), seven of them were commission agents (1.4 percent) and six of them were brokers (1.2 percent). The nature of work done by the husbands reveals that more than 80 percent of them were doing skilled works. The remaining of them were doing unskilled work or not doing any work.

RELATIONSHIP BETWEEN THE RESPONDENTS OCCUPATION AND THE OCCUPATION OF THEIR HUSBANDS

The co-efficient of correlation of the respondents and their husbands occupation was calculated and the result is presented in table 7.3 below.

Table – 7.3
Co-efficient of Correlation of the Respondents Occupation and their Husbands Occupation

Occupational Status	*No. of Respondents*	*No. of Husbands*
Coolie	92	94
Farming	18	97
Teacher	9	21
Domestic Work	25	-
Army	-	8
Self Employment	1	-
Business	7	36
Other Works	31	240
No Work / Occupation	317	4
Total	500 -0.12	500

Source: Primary Data.

The Karl Pearson's Co-efficient of Correlation is calculated to find out the relation between respondents occupation and their husbands occupation. For the purpose of calculating co-efficient of correlation the respondents and their husbands occupation were brought under nine categories. The table-7.3 gives the occupational relationship among the respondents and their husbands.

The calculated r value is "0.12. it shows the respondents occupation and their husbands occupation are negatively correlated.

Assets

Ownership of assets is an important source of income. A person's wealth or prosperity is determined by the amount of assets held by him.

The assets are classified into movable, immovable and durable assets. While land and buildings are immovable assets, jewels and vehicles deemed to be movable assets. The bank deposits, stock and shares and national saving certificates etc. are considered as liquid assets.

Movable and Immovable Assets

The movable and immovable assets held by the respondents are presented in table 7.4 below.

Table – 7.4
Widow's Ownership of Assets

S.No.	*Assets*	*Young*	*Middle*	*Old*	*Total*	*Percentage*
1.	Land	7	19	26	52	10.4
2.	House Owned	75	197	146	418	83.6
3.	Jewels	14	60	34	108	21.6
4.	Vehicles	2	4	3	9	1.8

Source: Primary Data, Percentage in column 7 is calculated for total respondents.

As the table shows only 52 (10.4 percent) of the respondents had owned land, 418 (83.6 percent) of them owned houses, 108 (21.6 percent) had owned jewels and 9 (1.8 percent) had owned vehicles. Out of the 500 respondents 82 were staying in rented houses.

Among the generation, seven young respondents had owned land as against 19 belonged to middle generation and 26 belonged to old generation.

In case of buildings, 53 respondents, belonging to middle generation, were living in rented building as against 15 belonging to young generation and 14 belonged to old generation.

Size of Land

Only 52 out of 500 respondents had owned land. What is the size of the land owned by them? The answer to the question is presented in table 7.5 below.

12 respondents owned one acre of land. Another group of 12 respondents owned three acres of land. Two acres of land by nine respondents. Another group of nine respondents owned four acres of land. Five acres of land was owned by two respondents. Six, seven and eight acres were owned by one each respondents. Two respondents owned nine acres each and 10 acres were owned by three respondents. Among the

Table – 7.5
Size of Land Owned by the Respondents

S.No	*Size of land (acres)*	*Young*	*Middle*	*Old*	*Total*	*Percentage*
1.	1	2	2	8	12	23.07
2.	2	1	2	6	9	17.30
3.	3	2	4	6	12	23.07
4.	4	1	5	3	9	17.30
5.	5	1	-	1	2	3.84
6.	6	-	1	-	1	1.92
7.	7	-	1	-	1	1.92
8.	8	-	1	-	1	1.92
9.	9	-	1	1	2	3.84
10.	10	-	2	1	3	5.76
	Total	7(13.46)	19(36.53)	26(50.0)	52(100)	100.00
	Mean	2.71	4.63	2.84	3.48	

Source: Primary Data.

young generation, only seven respondents had owned land, their size was below five acres. Among the middle generation, out of the 19 respondents, 13 respondents owned land below five acres and six respondents had owned land above five acres. In the case of old generation, 24 respondents had owned land below five acres and only two respondents had owned land above five acres. In the ownership and size of land, the middle and old generation respondents had more land compared to the young generation.

Nature of House

The nature of house owned by the respondents, is presented in table 7.6 below. 209 respondents (41.8 percent) had owned R.C.C. roof houses followed by 206 respondents (41.2 percent) had owned tiled houses, 56 respondents (11.2 percent) had owned huts and lastly 29 respondents (5.8 percent) had owned houses thatched with leaves.

Is there any variation in the kinds of houses owned by the respondents belonging to different generations? The above table discloses that more than 50 percent of the young respondents owned R.C.C roof houses compared to only 41.2

Table – 7.6
Nature of House Owned

S. No.	*Nature of House Owned*	*Young*	*Middle*	*Old*	*Total*	*Percentage*
1.	Hut	8	35	13	56	11.2
2.	Tiled	26	110	70	206	41.2
3.	Thatched	3	15	11	29	5.8
4.	R.C.C. Roof	53	90	66	209	41.8
	Total	90	250	160	500	100.0

Source: Primary Data.

percent of the old generation and 36 percent of the middle aged respondents. It proves that young generation respondents are better than the respondents belonging to the other two generation in owning R.C.C. roof houses.

The next type of houses owned by majority of the respondents, was tiled houses. 110 respondents (44.0 percent) of the middle aged respondents, 70 respondents (43.75 percent) of the old generation and 26 respondents (28.88 percent) of the younger generation had owned tiled houses. Of those who owned thatched houses, 15 respondents belonged to middle aged generation, 11 belonged to old generation and three belonged to young generation.

Among the 56 respondents, who owned huts, 35 respondents belonged to middle aged generation, 13 belonged to old generation and eight belonged to young generation.

Husband's Assets

A study of husband's assets is relevant to the study of well-being of the respondents. Though the husbands died long back in the case of middle aged and old respondents, the assets of the deceased husbands are inherited by his wife and children. The ownership of assets by the deceased husbands is presented in table 7.7 below.

As the table shows, only 66 husbands of the respondents (13.2 percent) had no assets. Others owned land (19.4 percent), houses (67.0 percent) shops (0.2 percent) and shares and securities (0.2 percent).

Table – 7.7
Husband's Assets

S.No	Husband's Assets	Young	Middle	Old	Total	Percentage
1.	Land	10	33	54	97	19.4
2.	House Owned	63	181	91	335	67.0
3.	Shops	-	-	1	1	0.2
4.	Shares and Securities	-	1	-	1	0.2
5.	No Asset	17	35	14	66	13.2
	Total	90	250	160	500	100.0

Source: Primary Data.

When the husbands assets are compared with the respondents, husbands had more assets than their widowed wives. As expected, a priori, most of the widows are deprived of their husbands assets.

The distribution of assetless husbands among various generations shows that 17 belonged to young, 35 belonged to middle aged and 14 belonged to old age generation.

CONSUMER DURABLE GOODS

Consumer durable goods are those consumer items used continuously for a longtime. They do not bring any income but gives satisfaction to the user. Most of the items of durable consumer goods, used by the respondents, are of comforts.

Table – 7.8
List of Durable Consumer Goods owned by the Widows

S.No	Durable Consumer Goods	Young	Middle	Old	Total	Percentage
1.	Television	45	146	94	285	57.0
2.	Refrigerator	1	8	9	18	3.6
3.	Washing Machine	-	3	2	5	1.0
4.	Mixie	11	58	49	118	23.6
5.	Grinder	13	42	36	91	18.2
6.	Gas Connection	56	127	91	274	54.8
7.	Telephone	5	15	13	33	6.6

Source: Primary Data, Percentage in column 7 is calculated for total respondents.

As the table demonstrates, 285 respondents (57.0 percent) had Television. Among the various generations, more than 50 percent of the respondents belonging to all generation had owned Television. Similarly 274 respondents (54.8 percent) had liquified gas connections. More than 50 percent of the respondents belonging to all generation had gas connection. Among the other consumer durable goods used by the respondents, refrigerator was used by 18 respondents (3.6 percent), Washing machine was uesd by 5 respondents (1.0 percent), Mixie was used by 118 respondents (23.6 percent), Grinder was used by 91 respondents (18.2 percent), and the Telephone was used by 33 respondents (6.6 percent). The above table further reveals that the respondents from each generation had used more than one durable consumer goods. The value of durable consumer goods used by the respondents is presented in the following section.

VALUE OF DURABLE CONSUMER GOODS OWNED BY THE RESPONDENTS

The value of durable consumer goods, presented in table 7.9 below gives a real picture about the possession of such goods by the respondents.

Table – 7.9
Value of Durable Consumer Goods

S.No	*Value (in Rs)*	*Young*	*Middle*	*Old*	*Total*	*Percentage*
1.	Below 10,000	57	98	68	223	44.6
2.	10,001 - 20,000	15	107	58	180	36.0
3.	20,001 - 30,000	13	35	22	70	14.0
4.	30,001 - 40,000	3	6	6	15	3.0
5.	40,001 - 50,000	2	4	5	11	2.2
6.	Above 50,000	-	-	1	1	0.2
		90	250	160	500	100.0

Source: Primary Data.

As the above table displays, 223 respondents (44.6 percent) had owned durable consumer goods below Rs.10,000. There are 180 respondents (36.0 percent) who owned consumer durable goods between Rs.10,001 to 20,000. 70 respondents

(14.0 percent) owned consumer durable goods between Rs.20,001 to 30,000. 15 respondents (3.0 percent) had owned consumer durable goods between Rs.30,001 to 40,000. 11 respondents had possessed consumer durable goods between Rs.40,001 to 50,000. Only one respondent had owned consumer durable goods above Rs.50000. The overall picture shows that nearly 80 percent of the respondents had possessed consumer durable goods below Rs.20,000. Only 20 percent of the respondents had possessed consumer durable goods above Rs.20,000. It could be observed that most of the respondents had possessed one or two consumer durable goods.

INCOME

Monthly Income of the Respondents

The respondent widow's economic status depends on their income. The monthly income earned by the respondents is provided in table 7.10 below.

Table – 7.10
Monthly Income of the Respondents

S.No	*Monthly Income*	*Young*	*Middle*	*Old*	*Total*	*Percentage*
1.	Below 1000	41	90	20	151	30.2
2.	1001 - 2000	12	4	1	17	3.4
3.	2001 - 3000	2	1	2	5	1.0
4.	3001 - 4000	1	1	1	3	0.6
5.	4001 - 5000	3	1	--	4	0.8
6.	Above 5000	1	1	1	3	0.6
7.	No Income	30	152	135	317	63.4
	Total	90	250	160	500	100.0

Source: Primary Data.

Out of 500 respondents 63.4 percent of the respondents were not earning any income. Among the non-income earners, 30 were belonged to young, 152 were middle and 135 were old. A small group of 183 respondents were earning income. Among them 150 respondents (30.2 percent) income was below Rs.1000, out of this 41 were young, 90 were middle and 20 were old. 17 respondent's (3.4 percent) monthly income was between Rs.1001-2000, out of this 12 were young, 4 were middle, one was old. Those who had monthly income above Rs.2000 were only 15, of them five belonged to income range between Rs.2001-3000, three belonged to income range between 3001-4000, four belonged to income range between Rs.4001-5000 and three who had income above Rs.5000.

Among the income earners between generations, 66.67 percent of the respondents belonging to young generation who had earned monthly income ranging between Rs.1000 to 5000. But in the case of middle age respondents only 39.20 percent respondents had earned monthly income. Only 15.62 percent of the old respondents had earned monthly income. In earning monthly income, the younger generation is better placed compared to the middle aged and old respondents. Prevelance of high illiteracy and old age are the factors which could be attributed to low earning capacity of the majority of the respondents belonged to this generation. (fig.2)

Fig. 2: Monthly Income of the Respondents

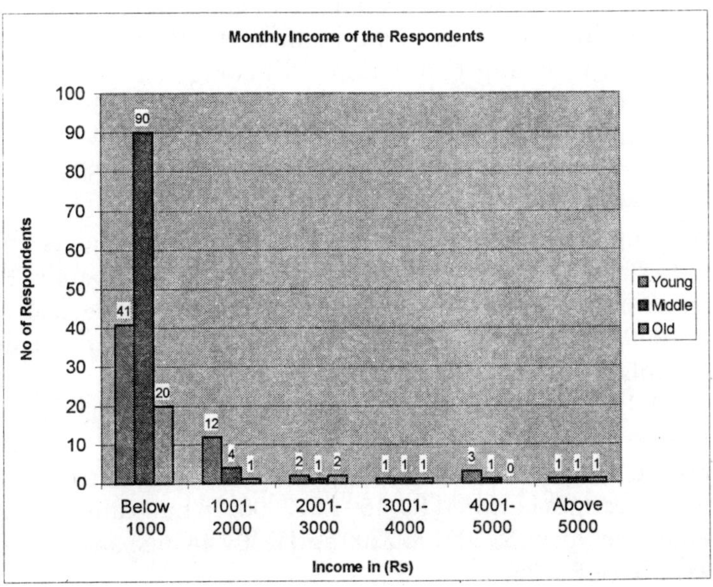

Husband's Monthly Income:

The husband's monthly income at the time of death was collected from the respondents and presented in table 7.11 below.

Table – 7.11
Husband's Income Per Month at the Time of Death

S. No	Husband's Income	Young	Middle	Old	Total (Percentage)
1.	Below 500	42	131	77	250 (50.0)
2.	501 - 1000	26	41	28	95 (19.0)
3.	1001 - 1500	-	7	9	16 (3.2)
4.	1501 - 2000	4	8	4	16 (3.2)
5.	2001 - 2500	3	9	6	18 (3.6)
6.	Above 2500	6	19	19	44 (8.8)
7.	No Income	9	35	17	61 (12.2)
	Total	90	250	160	500 (100)

Source: Primary Data.

As shown in the table above, 61 (12.2 percent) husbands have no income at the time of their death. Of them nine belonged to young generation, 35 belonged to middle age generation and 17 belonged to old generation. It shows inter alia that those husbands without income were dependents.

Among the husbands, who earned income, 250 (50 percent) were earning monthly income, of Rs.500. Of them, 42 belonged to young generation, 131 belonged to middle aged generation and 77 belonged to old generation. Another 95 husbands (19.0 percent) were earning monthly income ranging between Rs.500 to 1000. Thus, nearly 70 percent husbands were earning monthly income below Rs.1000.

Only 94 husbands had earned monthly income ranging between 1001 to 2500. Among them, 16 husband's monthly income ranges between 1001 to 1500, another 16 husband's income ranges between Rs. 1501 to 2000, 18 husband's income ranges between Rs. 2001 to 2500 and lastly 44 husbands income was above Rs. 2500.

It can be concluded that, even though the income of the deceased husbands was not reported correctly, still it appears that the husband's income was very poor lest 'no income'.

FAMILY INCOME

Sources of Family Income

Family income is calculated by pooling the income earned by all members of the family and from all sources. The various sources of income of the respondent's family are presented in table 7.12 below.

Table – 7.12
Sources of Family Income

S. No	*Sources of Income*	*Young*	*Middle*	*Old*	*Total (Percent)*
1.	Old Age Pension	44	128	71	243 (48.60)
2.	Occupation	60	98	25	183 (36.60)
3.	Property	2	4	6	12 (2.40)
4.	Compensation	13	8	2	23 (4.60)

Source: Primary Data.

As shown in column 6 table 7.12, 243 (48.60 percent) of the respondents had received Old Age Pension (OAP). Of them 44 (48.88 percent) belonged to young generation, 128 (51.20 percent) belonged to middle aged generation and 71 (44.37 percent) belonged to old generation. More than 50 percent of the respondents belonged to young and old generation widows had not received old age pension, whereas, nearly 49 percent of the widows belonged to middle age generation had not received old age pension.

Income from occupation as wages was received by 183 respondents (36.60 percent). Distribution among various generation shows that 60 respondents (66.66 percent) belonged to young generation, 98 respondents (39.2 percent) belonged to middle age generation and 25 respondents (15.62 percent) were belonged to old generation. As expected, a priori, more respondents belonged to young generation had earned income from occupation because of their education and literacy compared to middle and old generation respondents.

Only 12 respondents had earned income from property. Of them two belonged to young generation, four respondents belonged to middle generation and six belonged to old generation. Compensation is another source of income earned by the respondent's family. Compensation was received by the respondents when their husbands died by involving in an accident. Out of the 23 respondents who received compensation, 13 belonged to young generation, eight belonged to middle generation and two respondents belonged to old generation.

Another observation could be made from the above table that the respondents, who belonged to young generation could receive income from more than one source. It is because more than 50 percent of them could receive income from occupation and compensation. These sources of income had placed the younger generation respondents in a better position compared to the other two generation respondents. The size of family income is given in the following section.

Size of Family Income

For calculating family income only 397 respondents were taken into account, the remaining 103 respondents were living independently.

Table – 7.13
Size of Family Income

S.No	Family Income	Young	Middle	Old	Total	Percentage
1.	Below 500	30	40	14	84	21.16
2.	501 - 1000	18	56	36	110	27.70
3.	1001 - 1500	2	14	9	25	6.30
4.	1501 - 2000	9	32	17	58	14.61
5.	2001 - 2500	–	29	39	68	17.13
6.	2501 - 3000	1	23	24	48	12.10
7.	3001 - 3500	–	3	1	4	1.00
	Total	60	197	140	397	100

Source: Primary Data.

Size of family income depends on the income, property, business, sale of crops, livestock, rent from buildings and wages and salaries earned by the members of the family. Out of the total respondents, only 397 respondents had family income. Of them, 60 belonged to young generation, 197 belonged to middle generation and 140 belonged to old generation.

The distribution of respondents among various family income group shows that there were 84 (21.15 percent) below Rs.500 per month, 110 respondents (27.70 percent) in family income range between Rs.500 to 1000, 25 respondents in the income range of Rs.1001 to 1500, 58 respondents (14.61 percent) in the income range of 1501 to 2000, 68 respondents (17.13 percent) in the income range between Rs.2001 to 2500, 48 respondents (12.10 percent) in the income range between Rs.2501 to 3000 and there were four respondents in the income range between Rs.3001 to 3500.

There were more number of respondents beyond monthly income range above Rs.2000 in middle generation and old generation because they were grown up and their sons and daughters were working and earning.

EXPENDITURE

Expenditure is a prism through which one could visualise the level of living. All the respondents undertake monthly expenditure. Their monthly volume of expenditure is presented in table 7.14 below.

As shown in the table above, 255 respondents (51.0 percent) had spent less than Rs.1000 per month. Distribution of the respondents among various generations shows that 53 respondents belonged to young generation, 116 respondents belonged to middle age generation and 86 respondents were belonged to old generation. In the second slab of expenditure, there were 163 respondents (32.6 percent). Putting the first and second slabs together, there are 418 respondents (83.6 percent). The remaining 82 respondents are distributed among various expenditure slabs as follows. There are 44 respondents (8.8 percent) in the expenditure range between Rs.2001 to 3000. 18

Table – 7.14
Monthly Expenditure of Widows

S. No.	Monthly Expenditure (in Rs)	Young	Middle	Old	Total	Percentage
1.	Below 1000	53	116	86	255	51.0
2.	1001 - 2000	31	95	37	163	32.6
3.	2001 - 3000	2	22	20	44	8.8
4.	3001 - 4000	-	10	8	18	3.6
5.	4001 - 5000	2	3	6	11	2.2
6.	Above 5000	2	4	3	9	1.8
	Total	90	250	160	500	100

Source: Primary Data.

respondents are in the fourth range of expenditure between Rs.3001 to 4000 per month. 11 respondents fall in the expenditure slab of Rs.4001 to 5000 and nine respondents fall in the expenditure above Rs.5000 per month. The size of expenditure demonstrates that majority of the respondents are poor because they had spent less than Rs.2000 per month. Only very few, who had spent more than Rs.2000 per month, appeared to be better off.

Disaggregation of Expenditure

Having analysed the monthly gross expenditure of the respondents, monthly expenditure on each item or disaggregation of monthly expenditure is made.

Expenditure on Food

Expenditure on food is an important item. Below Rs.500 expenditure per month was incurred by 194 respondents (38.8 percent). Of them 49 belonged to young generation, 86 belonged to middle generation and 59 belonged to old generation.

274 respondents (54.8 percent) had spent between Rs. 501 to 1000 per month on food. Of them 38 belonged to young generation, 139 belonged to middle generation and 97 belonged to old generation. When both the categories are added, the percentage would go up to 93.6 percent. Those who spent

Table - 7.15
Monthly Expenditure on Food

S. No.	*Expenditure in (Rs)*	*Young*	*Middle*	*Old*	*Total*	*Percentage*
1.	Below 500	49	86	59	194	38.8
2.	501 - 1000	38	139	97	274	54.8
3.	1001 - 1500	3	21	4	28	5.6
4.	1501 - 2000	-	4	-	4	0.8
	Total	90	250	160	500	100

Source: Primary Data.

between Rs.1001 to 1500 was 28 (5.6 percent). Of them, three belonged to young generation, 21 belonged to middle generation and four belonged to old generation. Only eight respondents had spent between Rs.1501 to 2000 on food. They belonged to middle generation. The pattern of expenditure on food shows very meagre sum allotted for food, it proves inter alia that the respondents had been taking only cereals and they had not given importance to nutritive food.

Expenditure on Rent

Those respondents who did not own house, had to live in rented houses. There were 82 respondents who lived in rented buildings.

Table – 7.16
Monthly Expenditure on Rent

S.No	*Expenditure in (Rs)*	*Young*	*Middle*	*Old*	*Total*	*Percentage*
1.	Below 500	12	39	9	60	73.17
2.	501 – 1000	2	12	3	17	20.73
3.	1001 – 1500	1	2	2	5	6.09
	Total	15	53	14	82	100

Source: Primary Data.

As the Table shows, 60 respondents had paid monthly rent below Rs.500. Of them, 12 belonged to young generation, 39 belonged to middle generation and nine belonged to old generation. There were 17 respondents (20.73 percent) had paid a monthly rent of Rs.501 to 1000. Of them, two belonged to young generation, 12 belonged to middle generation and three belonged to old generation. There were five respondents who paid monthly rent ranging between Rs.1001 to 1500, of them, one belonged to middle generation and three belonged to old generation.

Expenditure on Clothes

Cloth is an essential item next to food for human survival. As clothes are purchased during festivals, annual expenditure on cloths was recorded.

Table – 7.17
Annual Expenditure on Clothes

S.No	*Annual Expenditure on Clothes*	*Young*	*Middle*	*Old*	*Total*	*Percentage*
1.	Below 500	53	158	112	323	64.6
2.	501 - 1000	35	88	46	169	33.8
3.	1001 - 1500	2	3	2	7	1.4
4.	1501 - 2000	–	1	–	1	0.2
	Total	90	250	160	500	100

Source: Primary Data.

As the above table shows, 323 respondents had spent below Rs. 500 annually for clothes. Of them, 53 belonged to young generation, 158 belonged to middle generation and 112 belonged to old generation. There were 169 respondents (33.8 percent) who spent annually between Rs.501 to 1000 on clothes. Of them, 35 belonged to young generation, 88 belonged to middle generation and 46 belonged to old generation. There were seven respondents (1.4 percent) had spent between 1001 to 1500 per annum on clothes. Of them, two belonged to young generation, three belonged to middle generation and two belonged to old generation. Only one respondent had spent between Rs.1501 to 2000 clothes, who belonged to middle generation.

The expenditure on clothes shows that the respondents had spent minimum on clothes.

Expenditure on Medicine

The expenditure incurred by all the respondents inter alia proves that the respondents had given importance to health. The monthly expenditure incurred by the respondents on medicine is presented in table 7.18 below.

Table – 7.18
Monthly Expenditure on Medicine

S.No	*Expenditure in (Rs)*	*Young*	*Middle*	*Old*	*Total*	*Percentage*
1.	Below 500	82	99	59	240	48.0
2.	501 – 1000	5	57	43	105	21.0
3.	1001 – 1500	3	52	37	92	18.4
4.	1501 – 2000	–	27	19	46	9.2
5.	2001 – 2500	–	13	2	15	3.0
	Above 2500	–	2	–	2	0.4
	Total	90	250	160	500	100

Source: Primary Data.

As the table shows, 240 respondents (48.0 percent) had spent less than Rs.500 on medicine. Of them, 82 belonged to young generation, 99 belonged to middle generation and 59 belonged to old generation. 105 respondents (21.0 percent) had spent between Rs.501 to 1000 on medicine. Of them, five belonged to young generation, 57 belonged to middle generation and 43 belonged to old generation. 92 respondents (18.4 percent) had spent between Rs. 1001 to 1500 on medicine. Of them, 52 belonged to middle generation, 37 belonged to old generation and three belonged to young generation. The remaining respondents belonged to middle and old generation, whose expenditure on medicine ranges between Rs.1501 to 2500 per month. The expenditure of the middle and old generation respondents was higher compared to young generation because the former fell sick very often due to age factor.

Expenditure on Education

Though quite a number of respondents were illiterate, they realised the importance of education, and all of them had incurred expenditure on education of their children. Table 7.19 below gives the annual expenditure incurred by the respondents on education.

Table – 7.19

Annual Expenditure on Education

S.No	*Annual Expenditure on Education in (Rs)*	*Young*	*Middle*	*Old*	*Total*	*Percentage*
1.	Below 500	59	45	10	114	22.8
2.	501 - 1000	11	87	35	133	26.6
3.	1001 - 1500	5	49	62	116	23.2
4.	1501 - 2000	12	27	32	71	14.2
5.	2001 - 2500	1	38	21	60	12.0
6.	Above 2500	2	4	-	6	1.2
	Total	90	250	160	500	100

Source: Primary Data.

As the table shows, 114 respondents (22.8 percent) had spent below Rs.500 on education. 133 respondents (26.6 percent) had spent Rs.501 to1000 on education. 116 respondents (23.2 percent) had spent between Rs.1001 to 1500 per annum on education. 71 respondents (14.2 percent) had spent between Rs.1501 to 2000 on education annually. 60 respondents (12.0 percent) had spent between Rs.2001 to 2500 annually on education. Six respondents (1.2 percent) had spent above Rs. 2500 annually on education. All the respondents, belonging to all the generation, had incurred expenditure on education. It shows their awareness about the importance of education. This awareness will definitely improve the status of next generation which will pave the way for progress.

Expenditure on Fuel

Fuel comprises of electricity for lighting and gas for cooking. How much each respondents had spent on fuel? Table 7.20 below gives the monthly fuel expenditure of the respondents.

Table – 7.20
Monthly Expenditure on Fuel

S.No	*Monthly Expenditure on Fuel*	*Young*	*Middle*	*Old*	*Total*	*Percentage*
1.	Below 500	79	178	141	398	79.6
2.	501 - 1000	9	59	16	84	16.8
3.	1001 - 1500	2	12	3	17	3.4
4.	1501 - 2000	-	1	-	1	0.2
	Total	90	250	160	500	100

Source: Primary Data.

As the table shows, 398 (79.6 percent) had spent less than Rs.500 on fuel every month. In the next slab of Rs.501 to 1000, there were 84 respondents (16.8 percent). Of them nine belonged to young generation, 59 respondents belonged to middle generation and 16 respondents belonged to old generation. There are 17 respondents (3.4 percent) who had spent between Rs.1001 to 1500 monthly on fuel. Of them two belonged to young generation, 12 belonged to middle generation and three belonged to old generation. The remaining one respondent, who belonged to middle generation, had spent between Rs.1501 to 2000.

Expenditure on Cosmetics

Among the total respondents, 44 respondents had used cosmetics. Of them, 20 belonged to young generation, 17 respondents belonged to middle generation and seven respondents belonged to old generation. It shows younger

Table – 7.21
Monthly Expenditure on Cosmetics

S.No	*Monthly Expenditure on Cosmetics*	*Young*	*Middle*	*Old*	*Total*	*Percentage*
1.	Below 500	17	16	6	39	88.64
2.	501 - 1000	3	1	1	5	11.36
	Total	20	17	7	44	100

Source: Primary Data.

generation respondents were bold enough to use cosmetics compared to other two generation respondents.

The above table furnishes the details of monthly expenditure incurred by the respondents on cosmetics. Out of the 44 respondents, 33 (88.63 percent) had spent below Rs.500 per month on cosmetics. Of them, 17 belonged to young generation, 16 belonged to middle generation and six belonged to old generation. There were five respondents who had spent between Rs.501 to 1000 per month. Of them, three belonged to young generation, one each belonged to middle and old generations.

Expenditure on Travel

Travel makes the people move from one place to another. Movement is one of the progressive dimensions of human resource development because it enhances knowledge, promote relationship and expand one's vision. How many respondents had undertaken travels and how much they had spent on travels. All these details are furnished in table 7.22 below.

Table – 7.22
Monthly Expenditure on Travel

S.No	*Monthly Expenditure*	*Young*	*Middle*	*Old*	*Total*	*Percentage*
1.	Below 100	13	26	31	70	14.0
2.	101 - 200	5	7	12	24	4.8
3.	201 - 300	2	6	11	19	3.8
4.	301 - 400	1	5	2	8	1.6
5.	401 - 500	1	2	2	5	1.0
6.	Not Spending	68	204	102	374	74.8
	Total	90	250	160	500	100

Source: Primary Data.

As shown in the above table, 374 respondents (74.80 percent) had not undertaken any travel during the year of interview. Only a small minority of 126 respondents had travelled. Their expenditure varies from Rs.100 to 500.

The highest incidents of non-travellers are found in young generation followed by middle and old generation. The young generation respondents felt the rigours of imposed immobility much more than the two old generations.

INVESTMENT

Expenditure may be either consumption expenditure or investment. The consumption expenditure has been witnessed in the previous section. In this section, investment expenditure incurred by the respondents are analysed. Table 7.23 below furnishes the number of respondents who made investment and quantum of their investment.

Table – 7.23
Quantum of Investment

S.No	*Quantum of Investment*	*Young*	*Middle*	*Old*	*Total*	*Percentage*
1.	Below 25,000	2	5	5	12	54.54
2.	25,001 – 50,000	1	1	1	3	13.63
3.	50,001 – 75,000	1	–	1	2	9.09
4.	75,001 – 1,00,000	1	–	1	2	9.09
5.	Above 1,00,000	–	2	1	3	13.63
	Total	5	8	9	22	100

Source: Primary Data.

Out of 500 respondents, only 22 respondents (4.4 Percent) could make investment. Five of them belonged to young generation, 8 of them belonged to middle aged generation and nine of them belonged to old generation.

Their quantum of investment varies from Rs.25,000 to more than Rs. One lac (table 7.16). Out of the 22 respondents, 12 (54.54 percent) had invested below Rs.25000. Out of them, two belonged to young, five each belonged to middle and old age respondents. There were three respondents who had invested between Rs.25,001 to 50,000. Two of the respondents had invested between Rs.50,001 to 75,000 and another two respondents had invested between Rs.75,001 to 1,00,000. There were two respondents who had invested more than Rs.1,00,000. Though a miniscule of the respondents could make investment but it was substantial. It would be interesting to note the sources of investment made by the respondents, which forms the next section.

SOURCES OF INVESTMENT

Table 7.24 provides the sources of investment made by the respondents. Land was the preferred investment of the 10 respondents. Of them six belonged to old generation and two each belonged to young and middle generations. Next priority for investment was livestock for nine respondents. Of them, five belonged to middle generation and two each belonged to young and old generations. For others, two respondents had invested in buildings and one had invested in jewels.

Table 7.24
Sources of Investment

S.No	*Sources of Investment*	*Young*	*Middle*	*Old*	*Total*	*Percentage*
1.	Land	2	2	6	10	45.45
2.	Building	–	1	1	2	9.09
3.	Livestock	2	5	2	9	40.90
4.	Jewels	1	–	–	1	4.54
	Total	5	8	9	22	100

Source: Primary Data.

The choice of investment made on land, building and livestock was productive while the investment made on jewels was not productive, which was made by only one respondent.

SAVINGS

Saving is an economic function of income and consumption expenditure. As we have already noticed, majority of the respondents had poor income but all of them were incurring expenditure. In this situation, it is beyond the capacity of the respondents to save. Even then, two of the respondents had reported to have saved, who formed only 0.4 percent of the total respondents. Other respondents had no strength to save. It was found their sources of savings was banks.

DEBTS

It is paradoxical to note that the respondents had nothing to save but they had spent more than their known source of income. Then the question arises, how did they meet the expenditure? The answer to the question is debt. How many respondents were in debts, how much they had borrowed and what were the sources of borrowing, these are analysed in the following sections.

Widows in Debts

Table 7.25 shows how many respondents were in debts and how many were not in debts?

Table – 7.25
Widows in Debt

S.No	*Debt*	*Young*	*Middle*	*Old*	*Total*	*Percentage*
1.	Yes	41	123	36	200	40.0
2.	No	49	127	124	300	60.0
	Total	90	250	160	500	100

Source: Primary Data.

Of`the total respondents, 200 respondents (40.0 percent) had borrowed while 300 respondents (60.0 percent) had not borrowed. Among those who borrowed, 41 belonged to young generation, 123 respondents belonged to middle age generation and 36 respondents belonged to old generation. Among three generations, smallest borrowers belonged to old generation 22.5 percent, followed by young generation 45 percent and lastly 49.2 percent of the middle generation.

Quantum of Debt

The quantum of bet incurred by the 200 respondents is presented in table 7.26 below.

There are 113 respondents (56.5 percent) who had borrowed below Rs.25,000. Of them, 27 belonged to young generation, 67 belonged to middle generation and 19 belonged to old generation. In the next table, 41 of the respondents had borrowed between Rs.25,001 to 50,000, of them, nine belonged

Table – 7.26
Quantum of Debt

S.No	Amount of Debt	Young	Middle	Old	Total	Percentage
1.	Below 25,000	27	67	19	113	56.5
2.	25,001 - 50,000	9	25	7	41	20.5
3.	50,001 - 75,000	–	6	4	10	5.0
4.	75,001 - 1,00,000	4	11	2	17	8.5
5.	Above 1,00,000	1	14	4	19	9.5
	Total	41	123	36	200	100

Source: Primary Data.

to young generation, 25 belonged to middle generation and seven belonged to old generation. There were 10 respondents who borrowed between Rs.50,001 to 75,000, of them, six belonged to middle generation and four belonged to old generation. There were 17 respondents who borrowed between Rs.75,001 to 1,00,000, of them, four belonged to young generation, 11 belonged to middle generation and two belonged to old generation. There were 19 respondents who had borrowed above Rs.1,00,000, of them, one belonged to young generation, 14 respondents belonged to middle generation and four respondents belonged to old generation.

Purpose of Borrowing

What was the purpose of their borrowing? The response of the respondents was recorded and presented in table 7.27 below.

Table – 7.27
Purpose of Borrowing:

S.No	Purpose of Borrowing	Young	Middle	Old	Total	Percentage
1.	Marriage	4	44	12	60	30.0
2.	Education	7	15	2	24	12.0
3.	Medical	8	25	3	36	18.0
4.	Day to Day Expense	11	13	5	29	14.5
5.	Business	6	5	3	14	7.0
6.	House Building	4	15	9	28	14.0
7.	Others	1	6	2	9	4.5
	Total	41	123	36	200	100

Source: Primary Data.

Out of the 200 respondents, 60 (30 percent) had used the borrowed money for meeting marriage expenses. Of them, 44 belonged to middle generation, 12 belonged to old generation and four belonged to young generation. 36 respondents had borrowed to meet medical expenses, of them, 25 belonged to middle generation, eight belonged to young generation and three belonged to old generation. 29 respondents had borrowed to meet day to day expenses, of them, 13 belonged to middle generation, 11 belonged to young generation and five belonged to old generation–for construction of houses, 28 respondents had borrowed, of them, 15 belonged to middle generation, nine belonged to old generation and four belonged to young generation.

Education was the priority for borrowing for 24 respondents, of them, 15 belonged to middle generation, seven belonged to young generation and two belonged to old generation. 14 respondents had borrowed for the purpose of business, of them, six belonged to young generation, five belonged to middle generation and three belonged to old generation. Nine of the respondents had borrowed for miscellaneous purpose, of them, six belonged to middle generation, two belonged to old generation and one belonged to young generation.

Except marriage, medical and day to day expenses, borrowing for other purposes was productive. While marriage expense was customary, expenditure on medicine was unavoidable but the borrowing for day to day expense was for survival.

Sources of Borrowings

From where the respondents had borrowed is more important than the quantum of borrowing. The institutional sources of borrowing would help the borrower to develop, whereas, the traditional non-institutional sources of borrowing would cripple the initiative of the borrower. The sources of borrowing is presented in table 7.28 below.

Among the borrowers, majority of them 142 (71.0 percent), had borrowed from money lenders, of them, 31 respondents

Table – 7.28
Sources of Borrowings

S.No	*Sources of Borrowing*	*Young*	*Middle*	*Old*	*Total*	*Percentage*
1.	Bank	3	14	7	24	12.0
2.	Financial Institution	1	1	1	3	1.5
3.	Money Lenders	31	91	20	142	71.0
4.	Relatives	6	17	8	31	15.5
	Total	41	123	36	200	100

Source: Primary Data.

belonged to young generation, 91 respondents belonged to middle generation and 20 belonged to old generation. It was followed by 31 respondents (15.5 percent), who borrowed from relatives, of them, 17 belonged to middle generation, eight belonged to old generation and six belonged to young generation.

On the other hand , 24 respondents (12 percent) had borrowed from banks, of them, 14 belonged to middle generation, seven belonged to old generation and three respondents belonged to young generation. A small number of three respondents had borrowed from financial institutions like Land Development Bank and Tamil Nadu Small Industries Corporation. Of the three, one each belonged to young, middle and old generations respectively.

The flaggering question is, why majority of the respondents had borrowed from traditional moneylenders and relatives? One need not go a long way to find answer to this question. Lack of awareness about the banks, more understanding with the local moneylenders and relatives etc., are the forces which propel the respondents to approach moneylenders and relatives for advances rather than banks and financial institutions.

8
THE CAPACITY OF MUDALIAR WIDOWS TO TAKE DECISIONS

INTRODUCTION

Decision making in a family depends on the nature of family. In the joint family, decision making is centred in the hands of the eldest male person. But in the nuclear family, decision making is dispersed and women are also supposed to take part in it. In the extended family system, women tend to participate more in the family decision-making[1]. How far a widowed women is empowered to take decision, which would affect the family or it would relate to day to day affairs of the family. K. Malathi, in her study on the Naidu Widows Capacity to take decision, has shown that less than 50 percent of the sample widows could take independent decision while the rest of the respondents had depended on others to take decisions[2].

The present study is concerned with the question how far the Hindu Mudaliar Widows have taken independent decisions? If they could not take independent decisions, on whom they were depending to take decision?

These question are analysed in relation to purchase of assets, marriage of sons and daughters, celebration of festivals, ceremonies, investments, borrowings, savings, health and management of business. If the respondents fail to take independent decision, on whom they were depending and to what extent they were depending. These things were analysed with the help of primary data collected from the respondents.

DECISION ON PURCHASE OF ASSETS

As already pointed out assets denote movable or immovable and perishable or durable consumer goods. The answers of the respondents are edited and presented in table 8.1 below.

Table- 8.1
Decision on Purchase of Assets

S. No.	Decision	Young		Middle		Old		Total		Grand Total	Percentage
		R	U	R	U	R	U	R	U		
1.	Own	1	2	12	19	8	5	21	26	47	9.4
2.	Others	11	4	22	16	29	11	62	31	93	18.6
3.	Not Applicable	42	30	84	97	41	66	167	193	360	72.8
	Total	54	36	118	132	78	82	250	250	500	100.0

Source: Primary Data.

As shown in the table, only 47 respondents (9.4 percent) could take independent decision in the matter of purchase of assets. When they are divided between regions, 21 belonged to rural areas and 26 belonged to urban areas. Thus it shows that more widows belonging to urban areas are able to take decision on matters of purchase of assets compared to the widows belonging to rural areas.

Among the generations, 31 widows, belonging to middle generation, could take independent decision compared to three from young generation and 13 belonged to old generation.

93 respondents (18.6 percent) had reported that the decisions were taken by others. Of them, 62 belonged to rural areas and 31 belonged to urban areas. It could be observed that more rural respondents depend on others to take decision compared to urban respondents.

In between generations, 15 were belonged to young generation, 38 belonged to middle aged generation. Out of the total respondents, 360 (72.8 percent) had reported that it is not applicable to them. It is because these respondents are neither consulted or concerned about them.

DECISION ON MARRIAGE OF SONS AND DAUGHTERS

The parents have to take decision on the marriage of their sons and daughters. After attaining widowhood, who take decision on the marriage of sons and daughters? The respondent's responses are presented in table 8.2 below.

Table – 8.2

Decision Making on Marriage of Sons and Daughters

S. No.	*Decision*	*Young*		*Middle*		*Old*		*Total*		*Grand Total*	*Percentage*
		R	*U*	*R*	*U*	*R*	*U*	*R*	*U*		
1.	Own	13	10	31	55	9	23	53	88	141	28.2
2.	Others	30	16	59	42	22	40	111	98	209	41.8
3.	Not Applicable	11	10	28	35	47	19	86	64	150	30.0
	Total	54	36	118	132	78	82	250	250	500	100.0

Source: Primary Data.

As could be seen in the above table, 141 respondents (28.2 percent) could take independent decision on the marriage of sons and daughters, urban respondents are more than the rural respondents. While 88 urban respondents could take independent decision as against 53 rural respondents. Among various generations, 86 respondents belonging to middle generation could take independent decision as against 32 respondents belonging to old generation and 23 respondents belonging to young generation.

As regards others take decision, there are 209 (41.8percent) respondents. Of them 111 belonged to rural and 98 belonged to urban showing more respondents belonging to rural areas depending on others for taking decision.

It is not applicable to 150 respondents (30.0 percent) as they were young, or others who live independently.

DECISION ON CELEBRATION OF FESTIVALS

The religious festivals normally celebrated by the Hindu Mudaliar are: Pongal, Mahashivaratri, Ram Navami, Reksha Bandhan, Durga Puja, Diwali, Ayutha Pooja etc. How many respondent widows had taken decision to celebrate festivals could be found in table 8.3 below.

Table – 8.3
Decision Making on Celebration of Festivals

S. No.	Decision	Young		Middle		Old		Total		Grand Total	Percentage
		R	U	R	U	R	U	R	U		
1.	Own	19	8	39	52	22	12	80	72	152	30.5
2.	Others	29	18	67	47	35	32	131	97	228	45.6
3.	Not Applicable	6	10	12	33	21	38	39	81	120	24.0
	Total	54	36	118	132	78	82	250	250	500	100.0

Source: Primary Data.

Out of total respondents, 152 (30.4 percent) respondents could take independent decision on festivals. Of them, 80 belonged to rural areas and 72 belonged to urban areas. In taking decisioon for celebrating festivals, there were more rural respondents compared to urban respondents. Disrtibution of respondents among various generations shows that there are 27 belonging to young generation, 91 belonged to middle age generation and 34 respondents belonging to old generation. Only in the middle age generation, there were more urban respondents compared to rural respondents.

For 228 respondents (45.6 percent), decision to celebrate festivals was taken by others. Of them 131 were belonged to rural areas and 97 belonged to urban areas.

There are 120 respondents for whom this question is not applicable because they were not participating in these festivals. Among them 59 belonged to old generation, 54 belonged to middle age generation, and 16 belonged to young generation. It reveals that the respondents belonging to middle and old generation are less participative compared to young generation respondents.

DECISION ON CEREMONIES

Ceremonies are organised at family level during auspicious and anxious occasions like marriage, birth days, ear-boring, removing hair, attainment of puberty, seemandam, death, remembrance days, arrivals and departures etc. In these ceremonies, how far the respondent widows had taken decision? It is analysed in table 8.4 below.

Table – 8.4
Decision Making on Ceremonies

S. No.	Decision	Young		Middle		Old		Total		Grand Total	Percentage
		R	U	R	U	R	U	R	U		
1.	Own	13	9	46	24	13	14	72	47	119	23.8
2.	Others	25	13	47	49	47	28	119	90	209	41.8
3.	Not Applicable	16	14	25	59	18	40	59	113	172	34.4
	Total	54	36	118	132	78	82	250	250	500	100.0

Source: Primary Data.

As shown in table above, 119 respondents (23.8 percent) had taken independent decision on ceremonies as against 209 respondents (41.8 percent) the decision was taken by others. 172 respondents (34.4 percent) had reported that it is not applicable to them. In the rural and urban areas, more respondents belonged to rural areas had taken independent decision as against only 47 respondents belonging to urban areas who could take decision. Among others who took decision, 119 respondents belonged to rural areas as against 90 respondents belong to urban areas.

In the case of non-applicable respondents, there are 113 respondents belonged to urban areas as against only 59 respondents belonged to rural areas.

DECISION ON INVESTMENT

Investment is made on immovable property or movable property or durable consumer goods. Purchasers used to consult others before purchasing these items. How many of the respondents had exercised their capacity to take decision on investments. Table 8.5 provides the details.

As shown in table, 41 (8.2 percent) respondents had excercised their capacity on investment. Of them, 23 belonged to urban centres and 18 belonged to rural areas.

Table – 8.5
Decision Making on Investments

S. No.	Decision	Young		Middle		Old		Total		Grand Total	Percentage
		R	U	R	U	R	U	R	U		
1.	Own	3	6	11	11	4	6	18	23	41	8.2
2.	Others	9	3	18	12	22	10	49	25	74	14.8
3.	Not Applicable	42	27	89	109	52	66	183	202	385	77.0
	Total	54	36	118	132	78	82	250	250	500	100.0

Source: Primary Data.

The distribution of respondents among various generations shows that 22 belonged to middle aged generation, nine belonged to young generation and 10 belonged to old generation.

There were 74 respondents (14.8 percent) who dependent on others for taking decision on investments. Of them, 49 belonged to rural areas and 25 belonged to urban areas. Distribution of respondents among various generations shows that 32 belonged to old generation, 30 belonged to middle generation and 12 belonged to young generation.

385 respondents (77.0 percent) had reported that it was not applicable to them. It shows that they had not made any investments.

DECISION ON BORROWINGS

Decision on borrowings relates to : from whom to borrow? how much to borrow? And on what conditions to be borrowed? Borrowers have to take decision on these matters. The details furnished by the respondents are provided in table 8.6 below.

Out of 59 respondents who borrowed, 21 respondents (4.2 percent) had excrcised their decision. Of them, 12 respondents belonged to urban centres and nine belonged to rural areas. Distribution of respondents among various generation shows that two belonged to young generation, 10 belonged to middle generation and nine belonged to old generation.

Among others who had taken decision for borrowing, 22 belonged to urban centres and 16 belonged to rural areas.

Table – 8.6
Decision on Borrowing

S. No.	*Decision*	*Young*		*Middle*		*Old*		*Total*		*Grand Total*	*Percentage*
		R	*U*	*R*	*U*	*R*	*U*	*R*	*U*		
1.	Own	1	1	4	6	4	5	9	12	21	4.2
2.	Others	2	4	5	8	9	10	16	22	38	7.6
3.	Not Applicable	51	31	109	118	65	67	225	216	441	88.2
	Total	54	36	118	132	78	82	250	250	500	100.0

Source: Primary Data.

Distribution of respondents among various generation shows that 19 belonged to old generation, 13 belonged to middle generation and six belonged to young generation. For 441 respondents, it is not applicable because they have not borrowed.

DECISION ON SAVINGS

Saving depends on the decision taken on quantum, period of saving, sources of saving etc. Those who save will have to analyse these factors and arrive at a conclusion. Table 8.7 gives the decision taken by the respondents.

Table – 8.7
Decision on Saving

S. No.	*Decision*	*Young*		*Middle*		*Old*		*Total*		*Grand Total*	*Percentage*
		R	*U*	*R*	*U*	*R*	*U*	*R*	*U*		
1.	Own	–	–	1	3	3	3	4	6	10	2.0
2.	Others	2	1	6	4	7	6	15	11	26	5.2
3.	Not Applicable	52	35	111	125	68	73	231	233	464	92.8
	Total	54	36	118	132	78	82	250	250	500	100.0

Source: Primary Data.

Out of those who saved, 26 respondents, ten respondents have taken their own decision. Of this, six respondents belonged to urban areas and four respondents belonged to rural areas. The distribution of respondents among various generation shows that six of them belonged to old generation and four belonged to middle generation.

Among the 26 respondents who depended on others for saving, 15 belonged to rural areas and 11 belonged to urban areas. Distribution of respondents among various generation shows that 13 respondents belonged to old generation, 10 respondents belonged to middle generation and three respondents belonged to young generation. It is not applicable to 464 respondents as they had not saved at the time of interview.

DECISION ON HEALTH

Health is an important indicator of well-being. How many respondents had consulted medical personnel in case of ill-health? The answer to the question can be found in table 8.8 below.

Table – 8.8
Decision on Healths

S. No.	Decision	Young		Middle		Old		Total		Grand Total	Percentage
		R	U	R	U	R	U	R	U		
1.	Own	–	1	2	3	3	2	5	6	11	2.2
2.	Others	1	2	3	3	2	5	6	10	16	3.2
3.	Not Applicable	53	33	113	126	73	75	239	234	473	94.6
	Total	54	36	118	132	78	82	250	250	500	100.0

Source: Primary Data.

As the table reveals, 473 respondents (94.6 percent) had not availed medical care, for, they did not take care of their health after the attainment of widowhood.

Only 27 respondents had availed medical facilities either on their own or on the advice of others. As the table indicates, only 11 respondents (2.2 percent) had used their discretion to avoid medical facilities. Of them, six belonged to urban centres and five belonged to rural areas. The distribution of the respondents among various generations shows that five each belonged to old and middle generation, one belonged to young generation.

There were 16 respondents who depended on others to take decision in order to avail health services. Of them, 10 belonged to urban centres and six belonged to rural areas. The distribution of respondents among various generation shows that seven respondents belonged to old generation, six respondents belonged to middle generation and three respondents belonged to young generation.

DECISION ON MANAGEMENT OF BUSINESS

After attaining widowhood, how many respondents had engaged in the management of business and how many of them had taken their decisions. Table 8.9 provides answer to the above question.

Table – 8.9
Decision on Management of Business

S. No.	Decision	Young		Middle		Old		Total		Grand Total	Percentage
		R	U	R	U	R	U	R	U		
1.	Own	–	–	–	1	–	1	–	2	2	0.4
2.	Others	–	3	1	5	2	5	3	13	16	3.2
3.	Not Applicable	54	33	117	126	76	76	247	235	482	96.4
	Total	54	36	118	132	78	82	250	250	500	100.0

Source: Primary Data.

482 (96.4 percent) had not engaged in management of business. So they refrained themselves from taking any decision. Of the 18 respondents, who had engaged themselves in management of business, two respondents could take independent decision and 16 respondents had to depend on others for taking decision. The two respondents, who had taken their own decision, were belonged to one each to middle age generation and old generation. Both of them belonged to urban areas.

Among those who depended on others to take decision, 13 belonged to urban centres and three belonged to rural centres. The distribution of these respondents to various generation shows that seven belonged to old generation, six belonged to middle generation and three belonged to young generation.

REGRESSION ANALYSIS ON DECISION MAKING

Regression analysis was done to predict the variable, which influence the decision-making capacity of widows. Those variables which had correlation with the decision making were chosen and used in the model. The stepwise model in the regression was used in the analysis to arrive at the regression equation. The following table presents the details of analysis.

Table – 8.10
Regression Analysis for the Dependent Variable Decision Making

S.No.	*Variable*	*Beta*	*'t' value*	*Sig.*
1.	Present Age	.138	3.111	.002
2.	Education	-.138	-.015	.988
3.	Income	.061	1.378	.169
4.	Occupation	.028	.621	.535

Source: Primary Data.
Constant = .722 t = 7.868 P0.05 Sig.
F = 9.677 DF = 500 P.05 Sig. R square .019

The variable introduced in the regression model are Age, Education, Income and Occupation. The initial screening procedure under stepwise regression method has eliminated education, income and occupation from the regression model since their 't' value were not significant.

The remaining variables were fitted into a regression model. Decision making capacity of widows was considered as the dependent variable present age was used in the model to predict the independent variable.

The present age of widows plays a predominant role in predicting the decision making capacity of widows. The 't' value is * 3.111 and the Beta value is * .138 both the values are higher. So age is the strong predictor of the four variables introduced. Hence, widows in higher age group take their own decision while, widows in lower age group depend on others for decision making.

The 'F' value is Significant (F = 9.677 DF = 500, P0.05) and this indicates that the regression equation predicts the dependent variable at greater level. The constant value .722 is also statistically Significant. (t = 7.868, P0.05).

DECISION MAKING AND INCOME

How far the decision making is related to their income? A Chi-Square Test was conducted to find out the relationship between the decision making and the income of the widows, the results are presented in table 8.11. below.

Table – 8.11
Chi-Square Test on Decision Making

Test	*Value*	*DF*	*Sig.*
Pearson Chi-Square	272.2	1	.000

From the result it could be observed that the significant level value is less than 0.05, therefore, there is a significant relationship between decision-making capacity of widows and their income. Hence, the proposed hypothesis is proved.

NOTES

1. Lalitha Srinath (2000), An Indian Book Review, Vol. 3 (4), Sage Publications, New Delhi, p. 27.
2. K. Malathi (2001), Socio Economic Status of Hindu Naidu Widows in Walajapet Taluk, Vellore District, An Published Ph.D Thesis Sacred Heart College, Tirupattur, p. 19.

9

IMPACT OF WOMEN WELFARE PROGRAMMES ON THE STATUS OF MUDALIAR WIDOWS

INTRODUCTION

Women and children, who represent 67.7 Percent of the country's total population should constitute the most important target groups in the present-day context of developmental planning. Therefore, their concerns are placed on the priority list of the country's development agenda.

EMPOWERMENT OF WOMEN

Empowerment of Women Year

The year 2001 is very significant for women in India as the government made a major policy initiative of declaring the year 2001 as the Women's Empowerment Year. This was to intensify the efforts of both governmental and non-governmental organisations towards fulfilling the Ninth Plan commitment of empowering women. Also, the government has adopted a National Policy for Empowerment of Women in 2001 to provide an enabling environment for women to exercise their rights freely both within and outside their homes at par with men. Further, a Task Force on Women and Children was also setup in 2000 under the chairpersonship of Shri K.C. Pant, Deputy Chairman, Planning Commission to review all the existing legislations and the on-going programmes for women and also to draw up an year-long thematic calender of activities to celebrate Women's Empowerment Year[1].

Strategies to Empower Women

1. Setting up of a National Commission for Women (NCW) in 1992 to safeguard the interests of women.
2. Setting up of a Rashtriya Mahila Kosh (RMK) in 1993 for women to meet the credit needs of poor and assetless women.
3. Adoption of the National Nutrition Policy (NNP) in 1993 to fulfil the constitutional commitment to ensure adequate nutritional standard to its people especially to women and children.
4. Launching of Indira Mahila Yojana (IMY) in 1995-96 on pilot basis recast and ratifield in 2000 as Integrated Women's Empowerment Programme (IWEP)
5. Launching of Stree-Swa-Shakti project in 1999 which was earlier known as Rural Women's Development and Empowerment Project (RWDEP).
6. Distance Education Programme for Women's Self-Help Group etc.

NINTH FIVE YEAR PLAN STRATEGIES TO EMPOWER WOMEN

Stree Shakti Puraskars

For the first time in the history of the Department of Women and Child Development, Five National Awards, known as, 'Stree Shakti Puraskars, were instituted in 1999, each one carrying a cash prize of Rs. 1,00,000 and a Citation, to be given annually in the name of five eminent women in the Indian history viz; Kannaki, Matha Jijabai, Devi Ahilya Bai Holkar, Rani Lakshmi Bai and Rani Gaidinliu. These will be conferred to honour and recognise the achievements of individual women who have triumphed under difficult circumstances and have fought for and established the rights of women in various areas such as education, health, agriculture, rural-industry, protection of forest and environmrnt, awareness generation and consciousness on women's issues through art and media.

Support to Training-cum-Employment Programme (STEP)

The programme of STEP, was launched in 1987, aims to upgrade the skills of poor and assetless women through training-cum-employment-cum-income generation activities, credit and market linkages in the traditional sectors of agriculture, animal husbandry, dairying, fisheries, handlooms, handicrafts, khadi and village industries, sericulture, and wasteland development etc. Under this programme a comprehensive package of services, such as, extension inputs, market linkages etc. are provided besides linkage with credit for transfer of assets. During 2000-2001, this programme has received a significant boost. 12 new projects benefiting around 48,550 women in eight states were sanctioned. Of the Ninth Plan outlay of Rs. 88.32 crores, an expenditure od Rs. 58.27 crores was incurred during 1997-2001.

Socio Economic Programme

The Socio-Economic Programme (SEP) endeavours to provide employment opportunities on full/part time basis to destitute women, widows, deserted women and the Physically handicapped to supplement their meagre family income. This programme is being implemented by the Central Social Welfare Board (CSWB). The scheme of SEP has been reviewed and modified to expand the scope of the programme. Now organisations, working for the handicapped, women's co-operative organisations and institutions like Jails, Nari Niketans etc. are also made eligible to receive grants under this programme. Grants to the extent of 85 Percent of the Project Cost are provided by the Board, the balance being the matching contribution from the NGOs. During the year 2000-2001, grants amounting to Rs. 33.70 lakhs benefiting 5,819 women have been sanctioned under this scheme.

Condensed Courses of Education and Vocational Training Programme (CCE&VT)

The scheme of Condensed Courses of Education and Vocational Training Programme (CCE&VT) was started in 1958 with the objectives of providing basic education and skills to needy women viz., widows, destitutes, deserted and also those belonging to economically backward classes. A vocational training programmes extends training for young girls / women in employment-oriented trades such as dress designing computer courses, type setting, batik, handloom weaving, nursery teachers training, stenography etc. to enable them to get employment in government public sector undertakings, corporations, autonomous bodies, private sector, etc. The voluntary organisations are given grants to conduct courses of 2 year duration to enable 15+ to pass Middle and Matric level examinations. The Ninth plan outlay for this programme was Rs. 45.60 crores.

Working Women's Hostels

To extend safe and inexpensive accommodation for working women of lower income groups, financial assistance is extended to voluntary and other autonomous organisations to the extent of 75 Percent of the cost of the construction of the hostel building and 50 Percent of the cost of the land. The income ceiling for eligibility of hostel accommodation has been raised from Rs. 5000 to Rs. 16000 per month in metropolitan cities and from Rs. 4500 to Rs. 15000 per month in other cities and towns w.e.f. 14th July 1998. A resident is allowed to stay in these hostels for a maximum period of 5 years. Women undergoing employment oriented education/professional courses are also eligible for accommodation in these hostels. During the year 2000-2001 grants amounting to Rs. 7.89 lakhs have been sanctioned for the maintenance of 34 Working Womens Hostels, which benifitted 810 women.

Short Stay Homes for Women and Girls

The scheme for Short Stay Homes which takes care of the women and girls in social/moral danger, is now being implemented by the CSWB. The schemes provides temporary shelter to women and girls who are;

1. Being forced into prostitution.
2. Made to leave their homes without any means of subsistence and have no social protection from

exploitation or are facing litigation on account of marital disputes.

3. Victims of mental, maladjustment, emotional disturbances and social ostracism.
4. Escaped from their homes due to family problems, mental or physical torture and need shelter, psychiatric treatment and counselling for their rehabilitation and re-adjustment in family or society. During 2000-2001, 120 new short stay homes have been sanctioned to raise the total number of short stay homes to 272 . For the Annual Plan 2001-2002, the approved outlay was Rs. 10.00 crore, of this, Rs. 1.00 crore for the North Eastern Region.

Indira Mahila Yojana (IMY)

During 2000-2001, the government approved restructuring of Indira Mahila Yojana (1995), into 'Integrated Women's Empowerment Programme (IWEP) to empower women through;

1. Generating awareness by disseminating information / knowledge to bring about an attitudinal change.
2. Help women achieve economic strength through micro-level income generating activities.

More than 42,000 Self-Help Women's groups have been formed under the scheme, of which, about 2000 groups were formed during 2000-2001. The Ninth Plan outlay for IWEP was Rs. 165.00 crores. For the Annual Plan 2001-2002, the approved outlay was Rs. 19.50 crores.

National Commission for Women

The National Commission for Women (NCW), is a statutory body constituted under the National Commission for Women Act 1990 to protect or promote the interests and safeguard the rights of women. The Commission maintains a complaint cell as one of the core units to process both written and oral complaints and takes suo-moto action in matters relating to:

(i) Deprivation of women's rights, (ii) non-implementation of laws, (iii) non-compliance of policy decisions, (iv) guidelines or instructions aimed at mitigating hardships to women, (v) takingup issues arising out of such matters with appropriate authorities. The Commission received a total of 5286 complaints during the year 2000 which include dowry deaths (527), murder (235), rape (277), molestation (11), dowry harassment (963), sexual harassment (267) and other type of harassment (2747). For the Annual Plan 2001-2002, a sum of Rs.5.00 crore has been provided[2].

Rehabilitation of Widows at Virndavan

For the rehabilitation of marganilised women of Virndavan and to monitor flow of benefits of central schemes to the target group, a central committee under the chairperson of the Minister of State for Women and Chid Development was set up. The Committee consists of the Chairpersons of the National Commission for Women and of the Central Social Welfare Board; Secretaries of the Ministry of Social Justice and Empowerment and Department of Youth Affairs and Sports, the Secretary and Joint Secretary of the Nodal Department of Women and Child Development, representatives of Voluntary organisations and women's activists in the field.[2]

WOMEN EMPOWERMENT IN TAMIL NADU

Women Slavery Condemned

Tamil Nadu is one of the states, which have played a leading role in the empowerment and development of women. 'Empowerment of Women' has become a fashionable term nowadays. But long before the term became vogue, and feminine movement came into existance, Periyar E.V. Ramasami, a great social revolutionary of the 20th century worked for the improvement of the status of women and their rights. He gave equal priority for raising the status of women, abolition of untouchability and discrimination based on caste. He regretted that nearly 50 Percent of the manpower of the country was wasted because of the slavery of women.

Periyar encouraged widow remarriage. He firmly believed that the right to divorce for women was most essential safeguard for them. Thus, Periyar suggested many things for the empowerment of women. The Dravidian Parties, which have been in power in Tamil Nadu since 1967, have implemented a number of schemes/programmes for the welfare and empowerment of women.

Property Rights for Women

Based on the resolution passed in 1929 at Self-Respect Conference, Tamil Nadu, as a forerunner , passed a legislation on the 6th May, 1989 providing property rights for women in ancestral property. Not only that, in many schemes e.g., Samathuvapurams (Equality Villages), Patta (title deed) is given only to women, even in households with male member as head of the family.

TAMIL NADU GOVERNMENT SCHEMES TO PROMOTE THE WELFARE OF WOMEN

Marriage Assistance Schemes

Moovalur Ramamirtham Ammaiyar Memorial Marriage Financial Assistance Scheme

At the time, the scheme was introduced in 1989, only Rs. 5000 were given as marriage assistance. The criteria adopted included (i) the bride must have appeared for 10th standard examination. In case of SC/ST, the bride should have studied upto 5th standard. (ii) annual income should not exceed Rs.12,000. (iii) bride should have completed 18 years of age (iv) only one daughter in a family is eligible. In 1996 the assistance was increased to Rs. 10,000. Since 1996, a sum of Rs.22,85,93,000 was given as assistance to 2,28,593 poor girls.

Anjugam Ammaiyar Inter-Caste Marriage Assistance Scheme

In 1989, Rs.5000 was given as assistance under this scheme. In 1996, it was increased to Rs.10,000, not only that, if any one of the couple was Adidravida, since October 2, 1997, the assistance has been increased to Rs.20,000.

Dr. Dharmambal Ammaiyar Memorial Widow Re-marriage Scheme

The assistance under the scheme, which was introduced in 1975, was increased to Rs.5000 in 1989, Rs.7000 in 1997-98 and Rs.10,000 in 1999-2000.

Mother Teresa Memorial Destitute Women Marriage Assistance Scheme

The financial assistance under the scheme was Rs.2000 in 1996-97. Gradually, it was increased to Rs.3000 in 1997-1998, Rs.5000 in 1998-1999 and Rs.7000 in 1999-2000.

OTHER SCHEMES

E.V.R. Nagammai Memorial Girls Free Graduate Education Scheme

In 1989-90, free education upto degree level was given to girls from families whose annual income was less than Rs.12,000. In 1996, the income ceiling limit was increased to Rs.24,000 per annum.

E.V.R. Mani Ammai Memorial Poor Widow's Daughters Marriage Scheme

The assistance under the scheme was Rs.1000 in 1990. in 1999, it was increased to Rs.7,000.

Dr. Muthulakshmi Reddy Memorial Maternity Financial Assistance Scheme

This scheme was introduced with object of providing nutritious meal to women who become pregnant. The assistance is sanctioned for a period of four months (for 2 months before delivery and 2 months after delivery). Rs.28,74,70,000 were sanctioned from 1996 to December 2000. More than seven lakhs women benefited from the scheme.

Sathya Ammaiyar Creches for Children Scheme

In order to look after the children of working women and those affected by sickness, since 1996, 175 creches have been set up and 17,700 children benefit from it.

Sathiyavani Muthu Free Sewing Machines Distribution Scheme

Since 1996, sewing machines have been distributed to 14,365 destitute women at a cost of Rs.23,03,000.

Sivakami Ammaiyar Girls Children Protection Scheme

The government introduced the scheme in 1997. If a women below the age of 40, with only two female children (and without a male child) undergoes tubectomy, Rs.1500 will be deposited in the name of each child for a period of five years in the Tamil Nadu Finance Corporation, renewed every five years, and when the girls reach the age of 20, they can get the amount along with interest. If a woman undergoes tubectomy with only one female child Rs.3000 will be deposited for a period of five years, renewed every five years and the girl when she attains the age of 20 can get the amount with interest. For 1,17,136 girl children, a sum of Rs.19,00,20,000 has been created as deposit fund. This scheme is of crucial importance, especially for reducing infant mortality of girl children, and as a measure of population control.

Bangaru Ammaiyar Women (Self-Help Groups Schemes)

The scheme was introduced in November 1989, with financial assistance from International Agricultural Development Fund, with the object of promoting self-help groups among socially and economically disadvantaged women. Since 1996, this scheme has been reformulated and merged with the newly formulated women's scheme. Under this scheme, nearly 8,07,000 women have become members of 45,719 self-help groups.

Pension for Weaker Sections

A sum of Rs.200 is given as financial assistance for old women, weavers, fisherwomen, landless agricultural labourers, destitute widows, physically handicapped and deserted women. For widows and deserted women, even if there is a son above the age of 18, a G.O. was passed on 2-6-1998 to provide old age financial assistance.

Free Distribution of Books and Note Books to Children of Widows

Books and note books are distributed freely for the children of widows whose annual income is less than Rs.12,000.

Financial Assistance for Women Entrepreneurs

A scheme was introduced in 1996 under which 250 first generation women entrepreneurs received a grant upto Rs.50,000 per head.

Priority for Women in the Allotment of Industrial Sites

Since 1996, priority has been given for women entrepreneurs in the allotment of sites in industrial sites.

Assistance for Fisher Women

25 mechanised boats have been freely given to fisher women co-operative societies.

33 Percent Reservation for Women in Local Body Elections

Tamil Nadu is the first state in India to have introduced 33 Percent reservation for women in Local Body Elections. There are 44,143 women holding positions in Tamil Nadu Local Bodies.

Fair Price Shops Run by Women

The scheme was first introduced in 1998 in Madurai and now there are 230 shops in different districts.

Women Micro-Credit Schemes

This scheme was introduced in Chennai on January 1, 1999 and from may 2, 1999, it was extended to all Municipalities and Panchayat Unions. It provides Micro-Credit to Self-Help Groups of women in villages. Under this scheme, upto October 2000, 535 Self-Help women have received credit upto Rs.2.33 crores. The credit, that is, given every day, ranges from Rs.100 to Rs.5000. So far, 1,44,913, women have been benefited from the scheme. Women's savings under the scheme is Rs.11.54 crores.

Women Teachers in Primary Schools

As a result of various G.O.s issued by the Tamil Nadu government, opportunities have been created for the appiontment of women teachers in large numbers in schools. Of the total number of 1,66,187 teachers, women teachers number 98,291. As per the government orders, 30 Percent of the government jobs are reserved for women.

Women in Police Department

A decision was taken in 1973 by the government to appoint women in Police Department. As a result, 4570 women have got job opportunities in the department.

Financial Assistance for Destitute Widows/Deserted Women

Under this scheme, which was started on June 1, 1975, all widows without limit are given financial assiatance. Since 1996, 3,86,149 widows and 63,566 deserted women were benefited from this scheme.

Dr. M.G.R. Nutritious Meal Scheme

In Nutritious Meal Scheme alone, about 2 Lakh women's are employed[3].

Tamil Nadu government has implemented the above schemes which have gone a long way in the development and empowerment of women.

WOMEN EMPOWERMENT AND THE HINDU MUDALIAR WIDOWS

Having realised the plight of the voiceless women, particularly the widows, both the Central and State Governments have announced various policy measures and adopted several strategies to ameliorate the living condition of the women. Whether these declared polices have achieved their objectives? And whether the target group has received benefits under these programmes and schemes of the Government.

State Shakti Puraskars is a prize instituted to honour those women who excelled in social and women welfare.

There are number of talented women in the society, honouring them amount to honouring the women gender as a whole, from the sample respondents no one had an opportunity to secure this rare honour.

The programme on support to training-cum-employment is aimed at upgrading the skills of the poor and assetless women. There are number of widows belonging to the Hindu Mudaliar Community but none of them was benifitted from this programme.

The Socio-Economic Programme (SEP) also aims at generating employment to destitute women and widows. How many of the sample respondents were benefitted? There was none from the sample respondents.

The Central Scheme, Condensed Courses of Education and Vocational Training Programme (CCE&VT) aims at providing education and vocational training to widows, destitutes and deserted women. Even the young respondents, anxious to learn, were not benifitted from this programme, for , they were not aware of it.

The other programmes like Working Women Hostels and Short Stay Homes are not beneficial to the respondent widows as they were not working as well as they were not allowed to move out from their villages. Many of them were not allowed to visit relatives and friends.

Out of nearly 23 programmes, the respondents had not received any benefit from them except the Old Age Pension. Nearly 50 percent of the respondents had received old age pension of Rs.200 per month. The remaining 50 percent respondents were denied old age pension or they were made to wait endlessly. Another pathetic situation is that all the respondents expressed during interview that they were not aware of any of these programmes. The information does not reach them, in this information age, either due to their illiteracy and ignorance or other members of the family successfully prevent the information from reaching the respondents.

It is, therefore, not enough to adopt policies, pass legislations and programmes and schemes for the benefit of widows, it should be seen that the deserving widows really receive benefits. The most important requirement is the change in the attitude of widows as well as others attitude towards widows. It will inter alia empower widows and it will enable the widows to secure the rightful place in the society.

BENEFICIARIES OF OLD AGE PENSION

How many of the respondents had received old age pension given by the state Government? Out of the total sample of 500, only 243 respondents had received old age pension. The scope of old age pension was expanded so as to include the destitute widows irrespective of their age. The classification of the beneficiaries of the old age pension is presented in table 9.1 below.

Table –9.1
Beneficiaries of Old Age Pension

S. No.	Area	Young		Middle		Old		Total		Grand Total	Percentage
		R	U	R	U	R	U	R	U		
1.	Tirupattur	2	7	25	11	10	9	37	27	64	26.3
2.	Vaniyambadi	3	-	9	2	1	8	13	10	23	9.4
3.	Ambur	2	2	6	3	2	1	10	6	16	6.5
4.	Gudiyattam	2	2	4	16	3	2	9	20	29	11.9
5.	Vellore	5	9	14	20	6	10	25	39	64	26.3
6.	Walajapet	3	2	3	-	1	2	8	11	19	7.8
7.	Ranipet	4	-	2	4	2	5	8	9	17	6.9
8.	Arcot	1	-	5	4	2	7	7	4	11	4.5
	Total	22	22	68	60	27	44	117	126	243	100

Source: Primary Data.

Out of the 243 beneficiaries, 126 respondents belonged to urban areas as against 117 respondents belonged to rural areas. Distribution of beneficiaries among various taluks shows that 64 beneficiaries (26 percent) each belonged to Tirupattur and Vellore. There are 29 beneficiaries belonged to Gudiattam taluk, 23 beneficiaries belonged to Vaniyambadi taluk, followed by 19 beneficiaries belonged to Walajapet taluk, 17 beneficiaries belonged to Ranipet taluk, 16 beneficiaries belonged to Ambur taluk, and 11 beneficiaries belonged to Arcot taluk.

It could also be seen the distribution of benificiaries among the three generations. 44 out of 90 (48.88 percent) young respondents could receive benefit under old age pension scheme. In the case of middle aged respondents, 128 out of 250 (51.2 percent) could receive benefits. The number of beneficiaries belonging to old age respondents were 71 out of 160 (44.37 percent). Thus the young and old respondents who received benefits were below 50 percent but the beneficiaries belonged to middle age were just above 50 percent.

Those non-beneficiaries, who looked to the Government, were destined to wait without knowing how long? Therefore, the old age pension should be extended to all widows without discrimination.

REFERENCE

Mid Term Appraisal of 9th Five Year Plan (1997-2002), (2000), Government of India, Planning Commission, New Delhi, October, pp. 215-227.

Annual Plan 2001-2002, (2001), Government of India, Planning Commission, New Delhi, pp. 282-287.

A. Ranga Reddy, (2002), "Empowerment of Women and Ecological Development", Serials Publications, New Delhi, pp. 334-343.

10
PROBLEMS AND SUGGESTIONS

PROBLEMS OF THE HINDU MUDALIAR WIDOWS

The problems of the Hindu Mudaliar Widows have been analysed under five sub-sections: (i) attitude of widows towards their activities or their involvement in certain organisations, (ii) other's attitude towards widows, (iii) Re-marriage attempts, (iv) problems reported by the sample widows and (v) their suggestions to solve the problems.

Attitude of the Respondent Widows

Attitude, as defined by Thurston (1946), is the degree of positive or negative effects associated with some psychological objects. By taking Thurston's definition as the base, change in attitude of widows towards remarriage, employment, participation in politics, participation in women's organisation, participation in panchayats and municipalities, education after widowhood, receiving help from male members and adoption of children, have been analysed.

Attitude Towards Re-marriage

One's attitude is formed by the social, cultural and anthropological influences prevailing in a particular place. The Hindu widows attitude towards re-marriage has been negative for a long time. A women, after marriage, has become one with her husband, prefer to die with the deceased husbands, so that, their oneness remain inseparable even after death. A woman, who, survives after the death of her husband, considered as a curse, therefore, number of prohibitions have been imposed on her. Even after passage of time, the practice of sati, wife self immolating herself after the death of their husbands, has been forcefully imposed and many unwilling young widows were forced to end their life by jumping into their husband's pyre. A man, after the death of his wife, merrily lives by marrying another women, that right to life has been denied to widows. The crusader of the Hindu Religious revivalism have questioned the abnoxious practice and organised various movements to abolish it and to save the young women from destruction. It has led to the passing of the Abolition of the Sati Act.

The age old practice of 'Sati', though prohibited by law, has been in vogue in various forms. Ill-treatment of widows, who lost her husband in various forms, even by her own family members, had inflicted deep wounds in their minds. Therefore, it is not an easy thing to clean the dreaded memories from the heart of a widow.

So, the throught of remarriage is being abandoned by the fear of condemnation, maltreatment and ostricism in a society, which had looked at widows with a coloured glass. The rationalist movement and thinking on the one side and the activities of forward thinking and activities of men and women on the other and the liberal education, scientific advancement, the growing tendency to unentangle oneself from the clutches of superstition and obscuranticism had penetrated iron hearts and fill it with humanism and compassion for the sisters who had undergone endless miseries for centuries. It results in the occurance of slow but visible change in the attitude of widows about themselves. Or, they started realising the change in the society which slowly expresses its acceptance of widows.

How much the widows attitude towards remarriage has changed? This question is analysed in the table given below.

As shown in the table above, 81 respondent widows (16.2 percent of the total) had agreed for remarriage. Of them, 37 belonged to rural areas and 44 belonged to urban areas. Between rural and urban areas, more urban respondents had agreed to remarriage copmared to rural respondents. Among

Table – 10.1
Attitude of Widows Towards Re-Marriage

S. No.	*Attitude*	*Young*		*Middle*		*Old*		*Total*		*Grand Total*	*Percen-tage*
		R	*U*	*R*	*U*	*R*	*U*	*R*	*U*		
1.	Agree	5	8	21	22	11	14	37	44	81	16.2
2.	Disagree	48	23	93	104	63	64	204	191	395	79.0
3.	Neutral	1	5	4	6	4	4	9	15	24	4.8
	Total	54	36	118	132	78	82	250	250	500	100.0

Source: Primary Data.

various generations, 13 respondents belonged to young generation, 43 respondents belonged to middle generation and 25 respondents belonged to old generation. In all the generation, the number of urban respondents, who argued for remarriage was more than the rural respondents. It is also included in fig. 1.

Fig. 1: Attitude of Widows Towards Re-Marriage

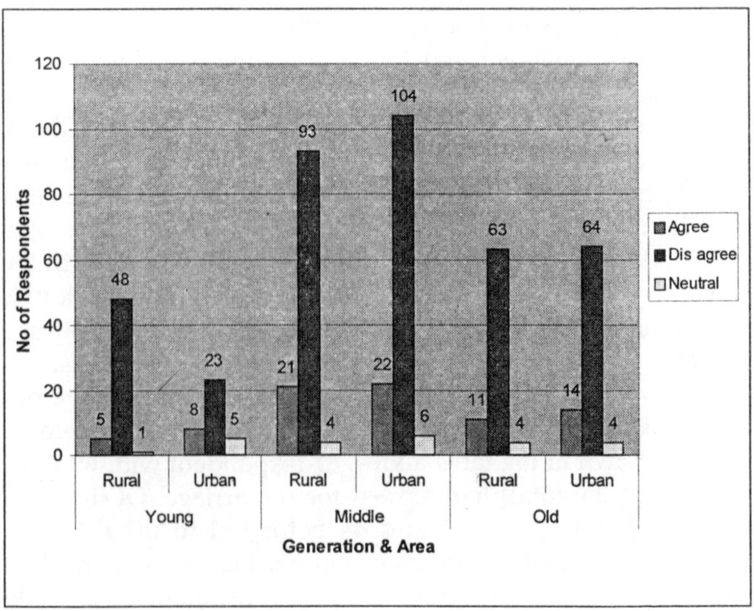

395 respondents (79.0 percent) had disagreed for re-marriage. Of them, 204 respondents were belonged to rural areas and 191 respondents were belonged to urban areas. It could be observed that there were more respondents disagreed for remarriage, who belonged to rural areas compared to urban respondents.

There were 24 respondents who maintained neutrality with rergard to re-marriage. Of them, nine belonged to rural areas and 15 belonged to urban areas. Among various generations, six belonged to young generation, 10 belonged to middle generation and eight belonged to old generatrion.

The above analysis shows gradual change in the attitude of widows belonging to all generation towards re-marriage. This change in the widow's attitudinal change should be strengthend by arranging more and more widow re-marriages. Shri Phule in Maharashtra showed the way by marrying a widow by himself as well as allowing his sons to marry widows some 75 years back. Such stalwarts, in large numbers, should come forward to marry widows. They would be an example to others who will be bold enough to follow their path.

Attitude towards Employment after Widowhood

Employment is an essential avocation for one who is willing to earn income and to lead a good standard of living. How many widows in the sample were willing to take up employment after widowhood? Table 10.2 presents the attitude of sample respondents towards employment after widowhood. The same is illustrated in fig.2.

Table – 10.2
Attitude of Widows Towards Employment After Widowhood

S. No.	*Attitude*	*Young*		*Middle*		*Old*		*Total*		*Grand Total*	*Percentage*
		R	*U*	*R*	*U*	*R*	*U*	*R*	*U*		
1.	Agree	50	26	82	103	56	56	188	185	373	74.6
2.	Dis Agree	4	10	26	27	21	23	51	60	111	22.2
3.	Neutral	-	-	10	2	1	3	11	5	16	3.2
	Total	54	36	118	132	78	82	250	250	500	100.0

Source: Primary Data.

Fig. 10 : Attitude of Widows towards Employment after Widowhood

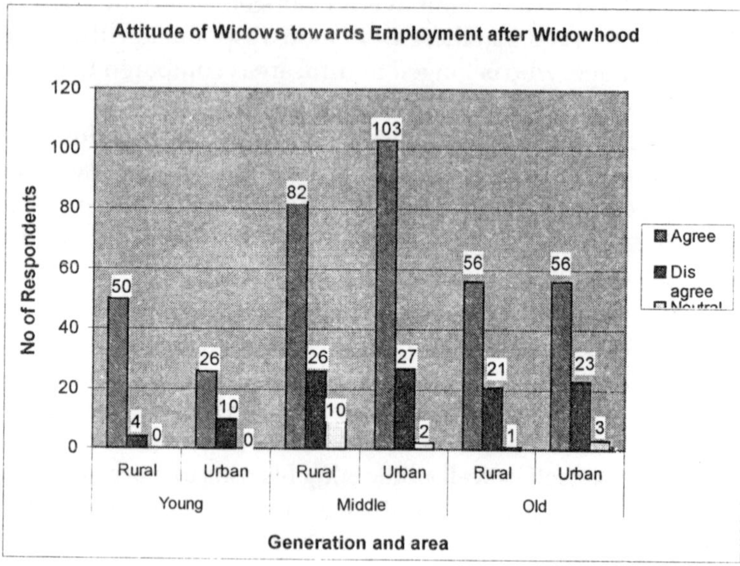

Out of the total sample, 373 (74.6 percent) respondents had agreed to take up employment after widowhood. Of them, 188 respondents were belonged to rural areas and 185 respondents were belonged to urban areas. The percentage of respondents who agreed to take up employment after widowhood varies from generation to generation. In the young generation 76 (84.44 percent) respondents were in favour of taking up employment after widowhood. In the case of middle generation, 185 (74 percent) respondents and in the case of old generation, 112 (70 percent) respondents were in favour of employment. As it is observed, highest percentage of respondents belonged to young generation who were in favour of employment after widowhood compared to the middle and old generation respondents.

Among those who disagreed to take up employment after widowhood, 51 belonged to rural areas and 60 belonged to urban areas. Highest number of respondents (53) who disagreed to employment had belonged to middle generation, followed by 44 respondents belonged to old generation and 14 respondents belonged to young generation.

There were 16 (3.2 percent) respondents, who were neutral with regard to employment after widowhood. Of them, 11 belonged to rural areas and five belonged to urban areas. Generation wise, there were none in the young generation, but there were 12 respondents in the middle generation and four belonged to old generation.

Attitude of Widows Towards Participation in Politics

We are living in a democratic society. Every citizen is empowered to rule their country. Representative system of governance has been adopted for the sake of convenience. The law does not prohibit any citizen from participating in politics. In this circumstance what is the attitude of the sample Hindu Mudaliar widows in participation in politics. The replies gathered from the respondents are presented in table 10.3 below.

Table – 10.3
Attitude of Widows towards Participation in Politics

S. No.	Attitude	Young		Middle		Old		Total		Grand Total	Percentage
		R	U	R	U	R	U	R	U		
1.	Agree	11	3	13	15	7	4	31	22	53	10.6
2.	Dis Agree	41	32	101	114	67	76	209	222	431	86.2
3.	Neutral	2	1	4	3	4	2	10	6	16	3.2
	Total	54	36	118	132	78	82	250	250	500	100.0

Source: Primary Data.

As shown in the above table, 53 respondents (10.6 percent) were in favour of participation in politics. 431 respondents (86.2 percent) were against participation in politics. There were 16 respondents (3.2 percent) who were neutral with regard to participation in politics. The participants belonging to rural areas were more in number, 31, who agreed to participate in politics after widowhood compared to 22 respondents belonging to urban areas.

Table – 10.4
Attitude of Widows towards Participation in Women Organisation

S. No.	Attitude	Young		Middle		Old		Total		Grand Total	Percentage
		R	U	R	U	R	U	R	U		
1.	Agree	2	1	7	4	2	1	11	6	17	3.4
2.	Dis Agree	51	35	108	124	75	79	234	238	472	94.4
3.	Neutral	1	-	3	4	1	2	5	6	11	2.2
	Total	54	36	118	132	78	82	250	250	500	100.0

Source: Primary Data.

Attitude towards Participation in Women Organisation

The table 10.4 indicates that the attitude of widows towards participation in women's organisation. Out of 500 respondents, 94.4 percent were disagreed with participation in womens organisation, out of this, 86 were young, 232 were middle and 154 were old. 3.4 percent had agreed to participate in womens organisation, out of this three were young, 11 were middle and three were old. Only 2.2 percent were neutral, out of this, one belonged to young generation, seven and three were belonged to middle and old generation respectively.

Attitude of Widows Towards Participation in Local Bodies

As it is in the case of widows attitude towards participation in politics, only few respondents had agreed to participate in local bodies like panchayats and municipalities.

Table – 10.5
Attitude of Widows towards Participation in Local Bodies

S. No.	Attitude	Young		Middle		Old		Total		Grand Total	Percentage
		R	U	R	U	R	U	R	U		
1.	Agree	3	4	8	3	2	2	13	9	22	4.4
2.	Dis Agree	50	31	107	127	72	77	229	235	464	92.8
3.	Neutral	1	1	3	2	4	3	8	6	14	2.8
	Total	54	36	118	132	78	82	250	250	500	100.0

Source: Primary Data.

92.8 percent respondents had disagreed to participate in local administration. Out of this 81 were belonged to young generation, 234 were middle and 149 were old generation. 4.4 percent were agreed towards participation in panchayats and municipalities, out of this, seven were young, 11 were middle and four were old. Only 2.8 percent were neutral towards participation in panchayats and municipalities, out of this 2 were young, five were middle and seven were old.

Thus, the respondents were not aware of their rights regarding their role in politics and local administration like panchayats and municipalities.

Education after Widowhood

Education is a continuing life long process. It is a powerful weapon, empowers every one who acquires it. Though, more than 50 percent of the respondent widows were illiterate, they have not possesed the required information about the importance of education. Education takes place in three stages viz., litercay, studying and education. At literacy stage, one learns the language, at the studying stage, one studies for job and at the education stage, one learns for life or it can be called as life-long education.

What is the attitude of the respondents towards education after widowhood? The answers are presented in table 10.6 below.

Table - 10.6
Attitude of Widows towards Education after Widowhood

S. No.	*Attitude*	*Young*		*Middle*		*Old*		*Total*		*Grand Total*	*Percentage*
		R	*U*	*R*	*U*	*R*	*U*	*R*	*U*		
1.	Agree	9	10	7	9	4	7	20	26	46	9.2
2.	Disagree	45	24	109	120	72	70	226	214	440	88.0
3.	Neutral	-	2	2	3	2	5	4	10	14	2.8
	Total	54	36	118	132	78	82	250	250	500	100.0

Source: Primary Data.

Out of 500 respondents, 88 percent had disagreed with education after widowhood, out of this 69 were young, 229 were middle and 142 were old. 9.2 percent had agreed with education after widowhood, out of this, 19 were young, 16 were middle and 11 were old. Only 2.8 percent were neutral towards education after widowhood, out of this, two were young five were middle and seven were old.

As it is observed, out of the 46 respondents, who agreed for education after widowhood, 26 were belonged to urban centres compared to 20 blonged to rural areas.

Among various generations there were more young respondents who expressed their desire to continue education after widowhood. 21.11 percent of the young respondents were for education after widowhood as against only 6.4 percent belonged to middle generation and 6.8 percent belonged to old generation. In between generations, younger generation widows manifest more awareness towards education compared to the middle and old generation respondents.

In general, the low attitude of the respondents towards education after widowhood calls for more extention education among women particularly widows.

Attitude Towards Receiving Help from Male Members

Gender conflict is very common between male members and widows. As a result, widows look male members with suspicions and they hate the male members. Consequently a widow's attitude towards male members has been negative. How did the respondent widows look upon male members for help? Table 10.7 provide answer to the above question.

Table – 10.7

Attitude of Widows towards Receiving Help from Male Members

S. No.	Attitude	Young		Middle		Old		Total		Grand Total	Percentage
		R	U	R	U	R	U	R	U		
1.	Agree	3	5	6	11	2	4	11	20	31	6.2
2.	Disagree	51	30	110	118	73	75	234	223	457	91.4
3.	Neutral	–	1	2	3	3	3	5	7	12	2.4
	Total	54	36	118	132	78	82	250	250	500	100.0

Source: Primary Data.

As expresed, a priori, the above table shows 457 (91.4 percent) of the respondents had disagreed to receive help from male members. Out of this 81 were young, 228 were middle and 148 were old. 6.2 percent of the respondents were agreed to receive the help from male members, out of this, eight were young, 17 were middle and six were old. Only 2.4 percent were neutral to receive the help from male members, out of this, one was young urban widow, five were middle and six were old generation widows.

Between regions, more urban respondents had agreed to receive help from male members compared to the rural respondents. Therefore, it is become necessary to resolve the gender conflict through proper understanding and through neutral accommodation.

Attitude towards Adoption of Children

Adoption is a method of legalising a heir. Widows, without children, could adopt a child for the sake of security and to look after the property after the death of the widow. How many respondents had agreed to adoption of children? It is analysed in table 10.8 below.

Table – 10.8
Attitude of Widows towards Adoption of Children

S. No.	Attitude	Young		Middle		Old		Total		Grand Total	Percentage
		R	U	R	U	R	U	R	U		
1.	Agree	2	3	2	8	2	3	6	14	20	4.0
2.	Disagree	52	31	116	123	75	77	243	231	474	94.8
3.	Neutral	-	2	-	1	1	2	1	5	6	1.2
	Total	54	36	118	132	78	82	250	250	500	100.0

Source: Primary Data.

Out of 500 widows, 94.8 percent of widows had disagreed to adopt children. Out of this, 83 were young, 139 were middle and 152 were old. 4 percent of the widows had agreed to adopt children, out of this, five were young, ten were middle and five were old. Only 1.2 percent of the widows were neutral to adopt children, out of this, two were young urban widows, one was middle urban widow and three were old generation widows.

It could be observed that there were more respondents who had agreed to adoption compared to rural respondents. Further, there were number of independent respondents in the sample in the study area. They too had disagreed to adoption of children. Perhaps, they might not have the means to look after a child. Further, they have been threatened by the in-laws family not to adopt, for fear of losing the property and income of the deceased person. It is the duty of the society to give legal protection to those widows who come forward for adoption.

ATTITUDE OF OTHERS TOWARDS WIDOWS

What do others think of widows? Was there any change in their attitude towards widows? For the purpose of the present study, others include parents, brothers, sisters, parents-in-law, brother-in-law, sister-in-law, sons, daughters, co-workers, shopkeepers, women and men. The attitude of these people towards widows has been recorded in five point scale viz., affectionate, considerate, helping, resentful and helpful. The results of the analysis is presented in the following sections.

Attitude of Parents towards Widows

Parents are the first and last resort to widows. They are also the cushion to meet the emotional and psychological tension of the widowed daughters. What is the attitude of the parents of the respondent widows?, is presented in table 10.9.

As shown in the table, 315 parents (63.0 percent) of the respondents were affectionate towards them, of them, 170 respondents were belonged to rural and 145 respondents were urban. It shows that rural parents were more affectionate towards their widowed daughters compared to the parents of urban areas. Among the remaining parents, 67 (13.4 percent) were considerate, 85 parents (17.0 percent) were helping and no response was recorded by 31 parents (6.2 percent). No parent, rural or urban, was resentful.

Between generations, 160 parents (64.0 percent) of the middle respondents had shown affection to their widowed

Table – 10.9
Attitude of Parents towards Widow

S. No.	Attitude	Young		Middle		Old		Total		Grand Total	Percentage
		R	U	R	U	R	U	R	U		
1.	Affectionate	30	25	80	80	60	40	170	145	315	63.0
2.	Considerate	7	3	22	8	10	17	39	28	67	13.4
3.	Helping	15	8	5	34	3	20	23	62	85	17.0
4.	Resentful	–	–	–	2	–	–	–	2	2	0.4
5.	No Response	2	–	11	8	5	5	18	13	31	6.2
	Total	54	36	118	132	78	82	250	250	500	100

Source: Primary Data.

daughters compared to 55 parents (61.4 percent) of the young respondents and 100 parents (62.5 percent) of the old generation. Similarly, the parents, who were condiderate, helping and non responsc could be found between generations. Among the non-response, highest number is found in the middle generation followed by old generation and young generation. 'Blood is thicker than Water', statement is proved by the parents of the widow respondents.

Attitude of Brothers towards Widows

On the death of the parents, a widow has to move closer to her brother inorder to draw support in various forms like emotional support, financial support etc. Table 10.10 shows the support received by the respondents from their brothers.

Table – 10.10
Attitude of Brothers towards Widows

S. No.	Attitude	Young		Middle		Old		Total		Grand Total	Percentage
		R	U	R	U	R	U	R	U		
1.	Affectionate	4	2	1	7	–	3	5	12	17	3.4
2.	Considerate	–	1	–	1	–	–	–	2	2	0.4
3.	Helping	10	8	54	48	32	29	96	85	181	36.2
4.	Resentful	–	–	–	–	–	–	–	–	–	–
5.	No Response	40	25	63	76	41	50	149	151	300	60.0
	Total	54	36	118	132	78	82	250	250	500	100

Source: Primary Data.

17 respondents (3.4 percent) had expressed that the attitude of brothers towards them was affectionate. On the other hand, 181 respondents (36.0 percent) had reported that they had received help from brothers. Of them, 96 respondents belonged to rural areas and 85 respondents were belonged to urban areas. There were more rural respondents who received help from brothers than the urban respondents. 300 respondents (60 percent) had reported 'no response' regarding brothers attitude towards widows.

Attitude of Sisters Towards Widows

Like brothers, the widows may fall confidently upon sisters, whose help is real and stable. The attitude of sisters towards widows is presented in table 10.11 below.

Table – 10.11
Attitude of Sisters towards Widow

S. No.	Attitude	Young		Middle		Old		Total		Grand Total	Percentage
		R	U	R	U	R	U	R	U		
1.	Affectionate	38	23	78	66	30	22	146	111	257	51.4
2.	Considerate	7	8	20	19	27	24	54	51	105	21.0
3.	Helping	9	4	15	20	16	16	40	40	80	16.0
4.	Resentful	-	-	-	-	-	-	-	-	-	-
5.	No Response	-	1	5	27	5	20	10	48	58	11.06
	Total	54	36	118	132	78	82	250	250	500	100

Source: Primary Data.

Out of the total respondents 257 (51.4 percent) of the respondents had found their sisters affectionate, 105 (21.00 percent) sisters were considerate, 80 (16.0 percent) sisters were found to be helping. Only 58 respondents (11.6 percent) had no response. Between rural and urban areas, there were more sisters to be affectionate, considerate, and helping in rural areas than in the urban areas. Among the resentful sisters, there were more in urban areas than in the rural areas.

Between generations, 67.7 percent of the yopung respondents had found their sisters affectionate and the rest were considerate, helping and none was resentful. In the case of middle generation 57.6 percent of the respondents had found their sisters affectionate and the rest were found to be considerate and helpful. Among the old generation, only 32.3 percent of the respondents had found their sisters affectionate and the rest were considerate and helping.

Attitude of Parents-in-Law towards Widows

Generally husband's relative's attitude towards widowed daughters-in-laws has been negative because of their too much affection towards their deceased sons. They accuse and blame the daughter-in-law as they were the cause of their son's death. Therefore, they considered the widow as a bad oman. How did the parents-in-law in the study area look upon their daughters-in-law? The answers are presented in table 10.12 below.

Table – 10.12
Attitude of Parents-in-law towards Widow

S. No.	Attitude	Young		Middle		Old		Total		Grand Total	Percentage
		R	U	R	U	R	U	R	U		
1.	Affectionate	7	9	18	13	1	2	26	24	50	10.0
2.	Considerate	2	3	5	7	1	2	8	12	20	4.0
3.	Helping	3	3	4	2	2	1	9	6	15	3.0
4.	Resentful	30	20	84	102	6	8	120	130	250	50.0
5.	No Response	12	1	7	8	68	69	87	78	165	33.0
	Total	54	36	118	132	78	82	250	250	500	100

Source: Primary Data.

Quite contrary to the expectation, the parents-in-law of 50 respondents (10 percent) had shown affection towards their daughters-in-law, of them, 26 belonged to rural areas and 24 belonged to urban areas. 20 (4.0 percent) of the respondents had reported that their parents-in-law were considerate. 15 (3.0 percent) respondents had reported that their parents-in-law were helpful to them. 250 (50.0 percent) of the respondents had reported that their parents-in-law were resentful for extending any help. 165 (33.0 percent) respondents had expressed no response.

Attitude of Brothers-in-Law towards Widows

Similar to the Parents-in-law, the attitude of brothres-in-law towards widows has been one of ogling, flirtation, molestation and debauchment. But there were few cases of helpful also. As shown in table 10.13.

Table – 10.13
Attitude of Brothers-in-Law towards Widow

S. No.	Attitude	Young		Middle		Old		Total		Grand Total	Percentage
		R	U	R	U	R	U	R	U		
1.	Affectionate	3	2	4	5	1	1	8	8	16	3.2
2.	Considerate	2	2	4	2	-	-	6	4	10	2.0
3.	Helping	1	1	2	1	-	-	3	2	5	1.0
4.	Resentful	45	27	57	79	50	42	152	148	300	60.0
5.	No Response	3	4	51	45	27	39	91	88	169	33.8
	Total	54	36	118	132	78	82	250	250	500	100

Source: Primary Data.

16 (3.2 percent) respondents had reported that their brothers-in-law were affectionate. 10 (2.0 percent) respondents had reported that the attitude of brothers-in-law was considerate. To five respondents, the attitude of their brothres-in-law was helpful.

But 300 respondents (60.0 percent) had reported that the attitude of their brothers-in-law was resentful. 169 respondents (33.8 percent) had not responded to the question.

Attitude of Sisters-in-law towards Widows

Paripasu with the attitude of brothers-in-law, the attitude of sisters-in-law towards widows has been hostile, belligerent, cruel and unfriendly. It is against undue attachment towards deceased brothers which has resulted in developing opposition to widows. Table 10.14 gives the attitude of sisters-in-law towards widows.

As could be seen in the above table, 12 respondents (2.4 percent) reported that their sisters-in-law were affectionate. Five respondents reported that their sisters-in-law were

Table – 10.14
Attitude of Sister-in-law towards Widow

S. No.	Attitude	Young		Middle		Old		Total		Grand Total	Percentage
		R	U	R	U	R	U	R	U		
1.	Affectionate	2	2	4	3	1	--	7	5	12	2.4
2.	Considerate	1	1	1	2	–	--	2	3	5	1.0
3.	Helping	1	--	1	1	–	--	2	1	3	0.6
4.	Resentful	43	27	76	82	43	64	162	173	335	67.0
5.	No Response	7	6	36	44	34	18	77	68	145	29.0
	Total	54	36	118	132	78	82	250	250	500	100

Source: Primary Data.

considerate. Only three respondents reported their sister-in-law were helpful. On the other hand, 335 respondents (67.9 percent) reported resentful nature of their sisters-in-law. Of them, 162 respondents belonged to rural areas and 173 respondents belonged to urban areas. 145 respondents (29.0 percent) had expressed no response.

Attitude of Son towards Widows

The widows who had son and daughters were in an advantageous position because they could rely on sons and daughters for safety, security and stability. Table 10.15 gives the attitude of sons towards widows.

Table – 10.15
Attitude of Sons towards Widow

S. No.	Attitude	Young		Middle		Old		Total		Grand Total	Percentage
		R	U	R	U	R	U	R	U		
1.	Affectionate	27	22	90	94	55	62	172	178	350	70.0
2.	Considerate	2	5	15	12	10	6	27	23	50	10.0
3.	Helping	3	3	4	5	5	5	12	13	25	5.0
4.	Resentful	3	2	–	7	1	2	4	11	15	3.0
5.	No Response	19	4	9	14	7	7	35	25	60	12.0
	Total	54	36	118	132	78	82	250	250	500	100

Source: Primary Data.

As expected, a priori, 350 (70 percent) of the sample respondents reported that their sons were affectionate. 50 (10 percent) respondents reported their sons were considerate. Helpful nature of sons were reported by 25 respondents (5 percent). Another 15 respondents reported the resentful nature of their sons. 60 respondents (30.0 percent) had not responded. The middle and old respondents had grown up children. So the respondents could very well depend on their sons for fulfilling their needs. The young widows had sons who were young. So the young widows had little scope for depending on their sons.

Attitude of Daughters towards Widows

Next to sons, daughters are the strong source on whom the widows could depend confidently and trustfully. An air of fearlessness and dauntlessness prevails between widowed mother and daughters. Table 10.16 gives the attitude of daughters towards widows.

Table – 10.16
Attitude of Daughters towards Widow

S. No.	Attitude	Young		Middle		Old		Total		Grand Total	Percentage
		R	U	R	U	R	U	R	U		
1.	Affectionate	44	36	118	104	78	77	240	217	457	91.4
2.	Considerate	3	-	-	5	-	2	3	7	10	2.0
3.	Helping	2	-	-	10	-	3	2	13	15	3.0
4.	Resentful	-	-	-	-	-	-	-	-	-	-
5.	No Response	5	-	-	13	-	-	5	13	18	3.6
	Total	54	36	118	132	78	82	250	250	500	100

Source: Primary Data.

To 457 respondents (91.4 percent) daughters were affectionate. Of them, 240 respondents were rural and 217 respondents were urban. Of the remaining respondents, 10 respondents (2.0 percent) had agreed that their daughters were considerate. 15 respondents (3.0 percent) reported their daughters were helpful. 18 respondents had not responded. None was resentful. Therefore, the daughters attitude towards widows was favourable, friendly and accomodative.

Attitude of Co-Workers towards Widow

How did the co-workers look at widows? The answer provided by the rerspondents are presented in tablee 10.17 below.

Table – 10.17
Attitude of Co-Workers towards Widow

S. No.	Attitude	Young		Middle		Old		Total		Grand Total	Percentage
		R	U	R	U	R	U	R	U		
1.	Affectionate	24	22	70	48	33	47	127	117	244	48.8
2.	Considerate	19	2	21	30	26	2	66	34	100	20.0
3.	Helping	11	8	25	23	4	4	40	35	75	15.0
4.	Resentful	-	4	2	13	4	2	6	19	25	5.0
5.	No Response	-	-	-	13	11	27	11	45	56	11.2
	Total	54	36	118	132	78	82	250	250	500	100

Source: Primary Data.

As could be seen in the above table, 244 (48.8 percent) respondents reported that the co-workers were affectionate. Co-workers are those colleagues who work with the widows and the daily wage earners who are employed in the family or in the farm. 100 respondents considered co-workers as considerate. To 75 respondents, the co-workers were helpful. 25 respondents (five percent) reported that the co-workers were resentful. 56 respondents had expressed no response.

Attitude of Shopkeepers towards Widows

Shopkeepers are those people whom the housewives meet daily to purchase household requirements. How the shopkeepers look at the widows? Is there any change in their attitude towards widows? These questions are analysed in table 10.18 below.

As displayed in the above table, 400 (80.0 percent) respondents are reported to be affectionate towards widows as against only 10 respondents (2 percent) who reported the shopkeepers as resentful. For 50 respondents, the shopkeepers were considerate and for another 15 (3 percent) respondents the shopkeepers were helpful. 25 respondents had expressed no response.

Table – 10.18
Attitude of Shopkeepers towards Widow

S. No.	Attitude	Young		Middle		Old		Total		Grand Total	Percentage
		R	U	R	U	R	U	R	U		
1.	Affectionate	44	36	78	108	58	76	180	220	400	80.0
2.	Considerate	10	-	14	21	2	3	26	24	50	10.0
3.	Helping	-	-	8	2	2	3	10	5	15	3.0
4.	Resentful	-	-	4	1	5	-	9	1	10	2.0
5.	No Response	-	-	14	-	11	-	25	-	25	5.0
	Total	54	36	118	132	78	82	250	250	500	100

Source: Primary Data.

As majority of the shopkeepers are reported to be affectionate, it can be considered as a change in their attitude towards widows.

Attitude of Women towards Widows

Only a woman may know the problem of another woman. So a question is asked to find out the attitude of women towards widows. Table 10.19 presents the attitude of women towards widows.

Table – 10.19
Attitude of Women towards Widow

S. No.	Attitude	Young		Middle		Old		Total		Grand Total	Percentage
		R	U	R	U	R	U	R	U		
1.	Affectionate	40	31	108	112	35	49	183	192	375	75.0
2.	Considerate	10	3	10	18	7	2	27	23	50	10.0
3.	Helping	2	1	-	1	9	12	11	14	25	5.0
4.	Resentful	2	1	-	1	4	7	6	9	15	3.0
5.	No Response	-	-	-	-	23	12	23	12	35	7.0
	Total	54	36	118	132	78	82	250	250	500	100

Source: Primary Data.

375 respondents (75 percent) had reported that women are generally affectionate towards them, as against 50 respondents

(10 percent) reported that women were considerate and 25 respondents (5 percent) had reported that the women were helpful to them. only 15 respondents (3 percent) had reported that the women were resentful towards them. No response was made by 35 respondents (7 percent).

Attitude of Men towards Widows

How the men look at widows? Table 10.20 gives men's views on widows.

Table – 10.20
Attitude of Men towards Widow

S. No.	*Attitude*	*Young*		*Middle*		*Old*		*Total*		*Grand Total*	*Percen-tage*
		R	*U*	*R*	*U*	*R*	*U*	*R*	*U*		
1.	Affectionate	39	26	97	94	48	76	184	196	380	76.0
2.	Considerate	13	5	10	11	-	1	23	17	40	8.0
3.	Helping	2	5	10	22	9	2	21	29	50	10.0
4.	Resentful	-	-	1	5	6	3	7	8	15	3.0
5.	No Response	-	-	-	-	15	-	15	-	15	3.0
	Total	54	36	118	132	78	82	250	250	500	100

Source: Primary Data.

380 respondents (76 percent) had reported that 'men were affectionate'. 'Men were considerate' was reported by 40 respondents (8 percent). 'Men were helpful' was reported by 50 respondents (10 percent). Three respondents reported that men were resentful and three respondents had chosen not to express response.

The above analysis demonstrates inter alia the attitude of a cross section of the society representing parents, parents-in-law, sisters, sisters-in-law, brothers, brothers-in-law, co-workers, shopkeepers, women and men. Each section reveals different attitude towards respondents in the study area.

REGRESSION ANALYSIS

Multiple Regression Analysis on Attitude of Widows

Multiple Regression analysis was done to predict the attitude of widows. Those variables, which had correlation with the attitude of widows were chosen and introduced in the model. The stepwise method in multiple regression was used in the analysis to arrive at the regression equation. The following table presents the details of analysis.

Table – 10.21
Multiple Regression Analysis for the Dependent Variable Attitude of Widows

S.No	*Variable*	*Beta*	*'t' Value*	*Sig*
1.	Income	.108	2.304	.022
2.	Education	.020	.442	.659
3.	Age	-.034	-.757	.449
4.	Occupation	-.015	-.259	.795

Source: Primary Data.

Constant = 1.828 t = 80.762 P. 05 Sig.
F = 5.308 DF = 499 P. 05 Sig. R Square = .011

The variables introduced in the regression model are income, education, occupation and present age of the respondents. The initial screening procedure under stepwise regression method has eliminated education, occupation and age from the regression model since their 't' value were not significant.

The remaining variables were fitted into a regression model. Attitude of widows was considered as the dependent variable. The independent variable, income was used in the model to predict the dependent variable.

Income plays a predominant role in predicting the attitude of widows. The 't' value is 2.304 and Beta value is .108 both the values are higher. So income is the strongest predictor of the four variables introduced. Hence, widows with higher income have positive attitude and widows with lower income have negative attitude.

The 'F' value is significant (F = 5.308 DF = 499, P. 0.05) and this indicates that the regression equation predicts the dependent variable at greater level. The constant value 1.828 is also statistically significant (t = 80.762, P. 0.05).

Regression Analysis on Attitude of Others:

Regression Analysis was done to study the attitude of others (Parents, Brothers, Sisters, in-laws, Sons, Daughters, Co-workers, Shopkeepers, Men and Women in general) towards widows.

Those variables, which had correlation with the attitude of others viz., Income, Education, Occupation and Age were chosen and introduced in the model. The stepwise method in regression was used in the analysis to arrive at the regression equation. The following table present the details of analysis.

Table – 10.22
Regression Analysis for the Dependent Variable Attitude of Others

S.No	*Variable*	*Beta*	*'t' Value*	*Sig*
1.	Income	.147	3.322	.001
2.	Education	.083	1.885	.061
3.	Age	.078	1.375	.170
4.	Occupation	-.063	-1.415	.158

Source: Primary Data.

Constant = 20.062 t = 101.616 P. 05 Sig.

F = 11.033 DF = 500 P. 05 Sig. R Square = .022

In the initial screening procedure under stepwise regression method has eliminated Education, Occupation, and Age from the regression model since the 't' values were not significant.

The remaining variables were fitted into a regression model. Attitude of others towards widows as considered as the dependent variable. The independent variable, income was used in the model to predict the dependent variable.

Income plays a predominant role in predicting the attitude of others towards widows. The 't' value is 3.322 and Beta value is .147 both the values are higher. So income is the strongest predictor of the four variables introduced. Hence, the attitude of others towards widows is depending on the income status of widows. It also proves the hypothesis.

The F value is significant (F = 11.033, DF = 500, P. 0.05) and this indicates that the regression equation predicts the dependent variable at greater level. The constant value 20.062 is also statistically significant (t = 101.616, P. 0.05).

Correlation Matrix of Socio-Economic Variables

A correlation matrix was done to describe the relationship among the variables education, income, occupation, attitude of widows and attitude of others toward widows. The results of the matrix is provided in the table 10.23 below.

Table–10.23
Correlation Matrix of Variable

S.No	*Variables*	*Education*	*Income*	*Occupation*	*Attitude of widows*	*Attitude of others*
1.	Education	1.00	.065	.088*	.026	.099*
2.	Income		1.000	.625**	.102*	.047*
3.	Occupation			1.000	0.57	.113*
4.	Attitude of Widows				1.000	.016*
5.	Attitude of Others					1.000

Source: Primary Data.
* Correlation is significant at the 0.05 level.
* Correlation is significant at the 0.01 level.

As displayed in the above table education is positively correlated with occupation. The correlation is significant. When the level of education increases, the level of occupation also increases or higher the level of occupation. The variable education is also correlated with the attitude of others towards widows. The correlation is significant. The attitude of others towards widows depending on the level of education of widows. The widows with higher level education receive positive attitude from others and vice versa.

The variable income positively correlated with occupation. The correlation is highly significant. Higher the level of occupation, higher the level of income. Income is also positively correlated with attitude of widows and the attitude of others. Widows with higher income have got positive attitude and the attitude of others towards widow is also positive.

The variable 'occupation' is positively correlated with the attitude of others towards widows and the correlation is significant. The attitude of others depending on the occupational status. Widows with higher level of occupation receive positive attitude from others while it is not so in the case of widows who have got low level occupation.

In general it is understood that the attitude of widows depending on their level of income and the attitude of others towards widows depending on the variable education, occupation and income.

LEVELS OF DEPRIVATION

An attempt was made to estimate the level of deprivation based on possessions at the household level of some basic social and physical amenities of life using the data collected. The proposition is that if a it should possess at least three of the six necessities of a family. They are 1. literate or not 2. pucca house or not 3. availability of land 4. availability of TV/radio/bicycle 5. whether the household has got electricity 6. rented home / own house.

A household which does not have any of the above six possessions is considered to be in 'Abject Deprivation' / AD; those which have one or two of the possessions is 'Moderate Deprivation' / MD; The four as in 'Just Above the Deprivation (JAD) and 5 or 6 items in 'Well Above Deprivation' (WAD). the two categories AD and MD are considered together constituting the deprived sections of the population.

For each household each variable is given a score of 1 or 0 indicating their presence or absence in the household. As an explanation of the utility of each of the variable, first we perceive that the presence of literate member in a household makes a difference in determining the quality of life. If the respondent is literate a score of 1 is assigned and otherwise 0, similarly, the presence of electricity, and presence of at least one of the amenities such as radio or bicycle or television is assigned a score of 1 each and otherwise zero.

The type of house and nature of house is a reflection on the living standard of a family. It was assigned a score of 0 for kutcha house and rent house and 1 for pucca house and own home. It is considered land as the prime determinant of economic well-being in rural India. Accordingly, it is assigned and otherwise 0. The description of the variables is shown in Table-10.24.

Table –10.24
Variables Used in Computing Deprivation Score (DS)

S. No	*Variable used*	*Description*	*Categorisation of House hold on Deprivation Based on Total Score*
1.	Literacy	0 = Illiterate 1 = Literate	0 : 'Abject Deprivation' (AD) 1-2: 'Moderate Deprivation' (MD)
2.	Type of Home	0 = Kuohha home 1 = Pucca home	3-4: 'Just above Deprivation'(JAD) 5-6: 'Well above Deprivation' (WAD)
3.	Nature of Home	0 = Rent home 1 = Own home	
4.	Electricity	0 = Not Electrified 1 = Electrified	
5.	Radio/TV/ Vehicle	0 = None of there 1 = At least on of there	
6.	Land Holding	0 = No land 1 = Have one acre land	

Source: Primary Data.

Table –10.25
Distribution of Deprivation Score

Composite Score	*Frequency*	*Percentage*
1 - 2	41	8.2
3 - 4	313	62.3
5 - 6	146	29.2
Total	500	100.0

Source: Primary Data.

The above table provides data on the distribution of household with composite scores ranging from 2 to 6 as defined above. The table reveals only three levels of deprivation viz., Moderate Deprivation (MD), Just Above Deprivation (JAD) and Well Above Deprivation (WAD). Among the total respondents 62.6 percent of widows are in just above deprivation (JAD) level, 19.2 are in well above Deprivation (WAD) level. The deprived sections of the population constitute 8.2 percent. They fall in the category of Moderate Deprivation.

The above analysis proves the first hypothesis that the widows of the Mudaliar community continue to face deprivation, though the level of deprivation varies from "Moderate" to "Well above deprivation".

REMARRIAGE ATTEMPTS

In a growing and changing society, human beings have to fulfil their aspiration. Any customs and conventions, blocking the way or progress, will have to be abated inorder to achieve the full growth of all the members of society. As a result, widows, whom remarriage denied, are made to relent their attitude towards remarriage. When men and women are declared equal, why men alone could remarry after the death of his wife, the same right denied to a women whose hosband is no more. The efforts made by social activists, rationalists and social legislation guaranteeing equal rights to men and women have awaken the conscience of the society to see the reason and to do its best to restore equality, which have been forbidden for a long time.

In the present study, a question is asked whether any re-marriage attempt has been made by the respondents or by her relatives. The answers are presented in table 10.26 below.

Table – 10.26
Re-marriage Attempt

S.No	*Re-marriage Attempt*	*Young*	*Middle*	*Old*	*Total*	*Percentage*
1.	Yes (Made)	4	6	2	12	2.4
2.	No (Not Made)	86	244	158	488	97.6
	Total	90	250	160	500	100

Source: Primary Data.

Only 12 respondents (2.4 percent) had reported attempt of re-marriage was made. Of them four belonged to young generation, six belonged to middle generation and two belonged to old generation. It shows only a miniscule of respondents had reported re-marriage attempts. Majority of the respondents found themselves in a quandry without making any re-marriage attempt. Even those, who made remarriage attempts, the marriage did not take place mainly because of in-laws, parents and relatives.

PROBLEMS OF WIDOWS

The innumerable problems faced by the respondent widows were classified as economic, emotional, physical, mental and psychological. The problems faced by the respondent widows are recorded, classified as above and presented in table 10.27 and in fig.3.

Table – 10.27
Problems faced by the Widows

S.No	*Problems faced*	*Young*	*Middle*	*Old*	*Total*	*Percentage*
1.	Economic Problems	85	229	134	448	89.6
2.	Emotional Problems	63	148	78	289	57.8
3.	Physical Problems	5	17	7	29	5.8
4.	Mental Problems	8	26	9	43	8.6
5.	Psychological Problems	3	8	2	13	2.6

Source: Primary Data, Percentage is calculated for total respondents.

Out of the total respondents, 448 respondents (89.6 percent) had economic problems like employment, income, debts, borrowings, source of investment and looking after the assets. Of this, 85 respondents belonged to young generation, 229 respondents belonged to middle generation and 134 respondents belonged to old generation. The highest percent of young respondents had faced economic problems because the sudden death of their bread winner has put the young widows in a spot. The loss of income, loneliness and burden of the family had inflicted severe strain on her compared to the other two generation widows.

Fig. 3 : Problems faced by the Widows

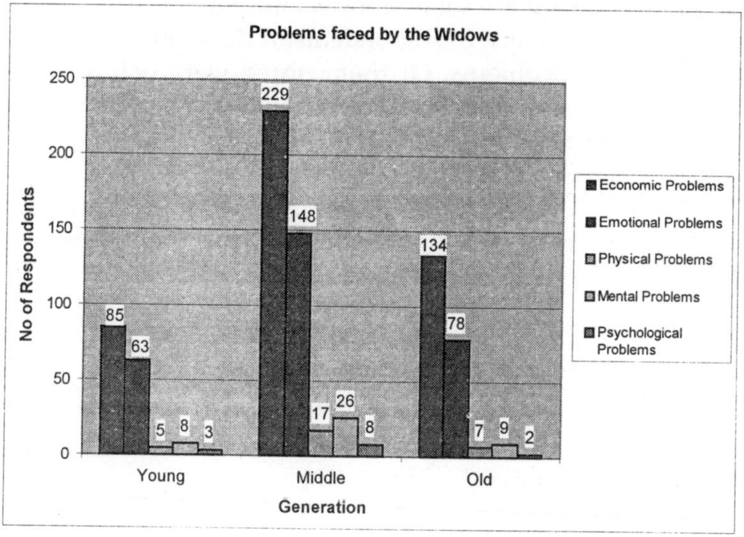

The emotional problems were faced by 289 respondents (57.8 percent), of them, 62 respondents belonged to young generation, 148 respondents belonged to middle generation and 78 respondents belonged to old generation. The memory of the deceased person and the sentiments were the emotional problems faced more by the young respondents compared to the middle and old generation respondents.

Physical problems are the direct result of emotional problems and economic problems. Failure to take adequate food, and non-availability sufficient income to purchase essential item are the reasons for the failure of health. Such physical problems are faced by 29 respondents (5.8 percent). Of them, five respondents belonged to young generation, 17 respondents belonged to middle generation and seven belonged to old generation.

43 (8.6 percent) respondents had faced mental problems. Mental problems are associated with insanity, nursing, forgetfulness, feeble mindedness etc. Of them, eight belonged to young generation, 26 respondents belonged to middle generation and nine belonged to old generation.

Alivation, neurotic, sadxistic, introvert, extrovert, nervous disorder, traumatic are some of the symptoms of psychological problems. There were 13 respondents in the sample who had psychological problems. Of them, three were belonged to young generation, eight belonged to middle generation and two belonged to old generation.

SUGGESTIONS

The suggestions provided by the respondents themselves are recorded and presented in table 10.28 below.

Table – 10.28
Suggestions to Remove the Problems

S.No	Suggestions	Young	Middle	Old	Total	Percentage
1.	Education	36	91	82	209	41.8
2.	Self-Employment	18	61	43	122	24.4
3.	Self-Confidence	4	25	7	36	7.2
4.	Hard work	2	6	-	8	1.6
5.	Courage	27	53	22	102	20.4
6.	Talent	2	8	2	12	2.4
7.	No Suggestions	1	6	4	11	2.2
	Total	90	250	160	500	100

Source: Primary Data.

As could be seen in the above table, 209 respondents (41.8 percent) had given first priority to education. Among them, 36 respondents belonged to young generation, 91 respondents belonged to middle generation and 82 respondents belonged to old generation. Second priority of the respondents had gone to self-employment, as it was suggested by 122 respondents (24.4 percent). It was followed by the suggestion of acquiring courage by 102 respondents (20.4 percent). Development of self-confidence was suggested by 36 respondents (7.2 percent). The other suggestions like talent by 12 (2.4 percent) respondents and hardwork by 8 (1.6 percent) respondents and 11 respondents (2.2 percent) had not made any suggestions.

As majority of the respondents had suggested education as the panaetia for all their problems, the uplifement of the respondent widows depends on provision of compulsory education for all girls. For, education provides knowledge and knowledge is power.

DEPENDENCY OF WIDOWS

It was hypothesised that the respondent widows continue to depend on the parents or in-laws. The dependency ratio was calculated and presented in table 10.29.

Table–10.29
Dependency Ratio

Generation	*Area*	*Siblings*	*In-laws*	*Parents*	*Independent*
Young	Rural	1	15	7.5	3.5
	Urban	1	8	4	5
	Total	1	24	11.5	8.5
Middle	Rural	1	26.7	6.7	5
	Urban	1	15	5	12
	Total	1	20	5.7	9
Old	Rural	1	11.6	1.2	1.8
	Urban	1	3.5	1	2
	Total	1	6	1	1.3

The dependency ratio has been calculated for three generation separately. For young generation in rural area, the ratio of dependency between Siblings, In-laws, parents, and Independent is 1:15:7:3 and in urban areas the dependency ratio is 1:8:4:5. It shows that more number of widows depend on in-laws rather than others in the case of both rural and urban widows.

With regard to middle generation, the dependency ratio is between siblings, in-laws, parents, and independent is 1:26:6:5 in rural area and 1:15:5:12 in urban area. The dependency ratio is higher for in-laws in both rural and urban widows.

In the case of old generation, the dependency ratio between siblings, in-laws, parents and independent is 1:11:1:2 in rural area and 1:3:1:2 in urban areas. The dependency ratio is higher for in-laws in the case of both rural and urban widows. But the ratio of rural widows for in-laws is quite higher than the ratio of urban widows.

While comparing all three generation, the dependency ratio is higher for in-laws in all generation widows. It shows that more number of widows prefer either to stay with in-laws or want to depend on them. It also proves the second hypothesis that the widows continue to depend on the earnings of her family or in-laws families.

SAMPLE WIDOW'S VISION

As normal human beings, who undergone the immeasurable misery due to the death of their husband, the widows had reason to expect not only to protect themselves from the social humiliation but also to secure their rightful place from the various constituents of her families and relatives. The expectations of the respondent widows are recorded and presented in table 10.30 below.

Table – 10.30
Respondent Widows Expectations

S.No	*Expectations from*	*Young*	*Middle*	*Old*	*Total*	*Percentage*
1.	From Married Sons	8	120	122	250	50.0
2.	From Government	51	56	14	121	24.2
3.	From Parents	16	13	3	32	6.4
4.	From Married Daughters	1	17	10	28	5.6
5.	From other Relatives	3	14	8	25	5.0
6.	From Society	1	10	1	12	2.4
7.	Husbands Family	4	2	1	7	1.4
8.	No Expectations	6	18	1	25	5.0
	Total	90	250	160	500	100

Source: Primary Data.

250 respondents (50.0 percent) expectation had gone to married sons. According to these respondents, they had brought up their sons by giving everything, therefore, it is the son's turn to look after their widowed mother. Though the claim of the respondents is justifiable, how far the sons are going to fulfil the aspirations of their widowed mothers. Aid

from the government is the expectations of 121 respondents (24.3 percent). For 32 respondents (6.4 percent) parents are the main source of help.

Married daughters are the source of help for 28 respondents (5.6 percent). 25 respondents (5.0 percent) had lot of expectation from the relatives followed by 12 respondents (2.4 percent) who had expectation from the society. Expectations from husband's families are expressed only by 7 respondents (1.4 percent) thus by showing very little priority to them.

25 respondents (5.0 percent) had not expressed any expectations. The expectations of the majority of the respondent widows had imposed severe burden on their sons from whom they expected a lot.

11
SUMMARY OF FINDINGS AND CONCLUSIONS

THE FOCUS

Women, the better half of men, play an important role in the family as a mother, wife, daughter-in-law, sister-in-law. The developing nations have utilised women force to the optimum level and realised that women possess potential, knowledge and skills that are assets to the family and society. Though women were plaeed in a highly esteemed position during the vedic period, avaricious men degraded and debased them. When a woman becomes a widow, she is considered as a curse and all the basic rights are denied to her. She has to live like an outlaw. Though christianity, Islam and Buddhism allow re-marriage of widows, the Hindu religious customs did not allow re-marriage of widows even after the Hindu Law of 1856 had permitted the same. Though re-marriage of widows among lower Hindu castes is common, the remarriage of widows among high castes is a taboo.

Several crusders fought for the rights of widows. Social reform movements, started in various parts of India, particularly in Maharashtra and Tamil Nadu, have led to the adoption of various legislative measures, including the Abolition of Sati Act, and the Hindu Widows Re-marriage Act. Various welfare schemes for the betterment of widows have been introduced in Tamil Nadu since the launching of the five year plans. Several women's welfare organisations have come forward to work for the upliftment of widows. How far have these legislations, reforms, social activism, and welfare schemes brought about a transformation among the Hindu Mudaliar Widows, a community chosen for the present study, is the topic of this research.

OBJECTIVES

The overall objective of the study is to analyse the socio - economic status of Mudaliar Community widows in three generations and to find out the change in their status and to suggest measures for their improvement. The specific objectives of the study are: 1. To find out the social status of widows in the Mudliar Community. The social status relates to the nature of house-holds, singles, nuclear or joint families, pattern of living in terms of dresses, food, entertainment, performing rituals, attending ,marriage, visiting relatives and friends, going to theatres and parks, role in the family - bread winner, cooking, childcare, washing and cleaning. 2. To study the economic condition of widows in the Mudaliar Community. The economic status will be analysed in terms of family income, source of income, expenditure on food, non - food items like rent, cloths, education, entertainment, travel, saving and investment, debt incurred, sources of borrowing etc. 3. To ascertain the role of widows in the decision making in the family. The decision making relates to buying and selling of daily requirements, purchase and sale of movable and immovable items including land, building, marriage of daughters, sons and other relatives, celebration of festivals, ceremonies, investments, from whom to borrow, where to save, whom to approach for health assistance etc. 4. To examine the impact of women welfare programmes on the status of widows belonging to Mudaliar community in Tamil Nadu. 5. To find out the problems faced by Mudaliar Community widows in Tamil Nadu. The problems relate to the economic, emotional, physical, mental and cultural etc. 6. To suggest measures to empower widows socially and economically.

HYPOTHESIS

The above objectives are based on the following hypotheses.

1. The widows in the Mudaliar Community continue to face deprivation, exclusion and social stigma in spite of the social movements and social legislations protecting their rights.
2. The widows continue to depend on the earnings of the male members of her family either on sons, father, or father-in-laws.
3. The decisions concerning widows are taken by other members of the family as her decision to have negative effect.
4. The attitude of others towards widows has not changed in spite of passage of time.

THEORETICAL BASIS

The following concepts and past studies are reviewed and used in the present study.

- Widow
- Widowhood
- Household
- Dependency
- Decision-Making
- Attitude
- Social Stigma
- Social Exclusion
- Social Status
- Economic Status
- Generation
- Investment
- Saving
- Remarriage
- Caste

THE APPROACH

Hindu Mudaliar Community

The social status of the Hindu Mudaliar widows is the subject matter for the present study. They were living in large numbers in Vellore district. They belong to 'socially and economically advanced community' according to the Government of Tamil Nadu.

Selection of the Study Area

The Vellore district of Tamil Nadu forms the area of the study. Vellore district emerged as a district with highest population of the Mudaliar community. Therefore, Vellore district is chosen for the present study.

Three Generation of Widows

Widows undergo innumerable miseries after attaining widowhood. Their Sufferings attracted the attention of the researcher and to take up the problem of widows for deeper analysis. Studies have been made on the status of widows drawn from different communities. So they have failed to identify the plight of widows of particular community. The social and economic perception of widows varies from community to community. Hence, the present study is an attempt to identify the problems of widows in different age groups, they are classified as young (below 40 years), middle (40-60 years) and old (above 60 years).

Identification of Hindu Mudaliar Widows Households

From the selected villages/wards all the Mudaliar widows households were identified and from among them, 25 widows households chosen by means of simple random sampling method. The ultimate sample size consists of 500 widows households, divided into villages (rural) – 250 and municipal towns (urban 250) The selected Mudaliar widows were post-stratified into young (below 40 years), middle (40-60 years) and old generation (above 60 years of age).

Collection of Data

Pre-tested structured interview schedule was used to collect the required information from the widows. The data was collected during the year 2002-2003.

Tools of Analysis

The collected data was analysed with the help of the following statistical tools like percentages, averages, standard deviation, chi-square test and correlation analysis, correlation matrix, regression analysis, deprivation analysis and dependency ratio.

THE RESULTS

The results of the analysis of the collected data from the respondent widows are given in a summary form below.

Social Status of Mudaliar Widows

There were 131 widows belonged to Chenkunther sub-castes, 280 widows belonged to Agamudiyar sub-castes and 89 widows belonged to Tuluva Vellala sub-castes.

90 (18 Percent) widows were below 40 years, called as 'Young', 250 widows (50 Percent) called as 'Middle Aged' and 160 widows (32 Percent) called as 'Old'. They are further divided into rural and urban. Accordingly, among the young widows, 54 belonged to rural and 36 belonged to urban, among middle aged widows, 118 belonged to rural and 132 belonged to urban and among old widows , 78 belonged to rural and 82 belonged to urban.

129 respondents (15.8 Percent), who was below 15 years, got married, 282 respondents (56.4 Percent), who belonged to 16 - 20 years, 78 respondents (15.5 Percent) who belonged to the age group of 21 to 25 and 11 respondents who were between 26 to 30 while they entered the wedlock. Between rural and urban areas, there is not much difference in the age below 15 years. In the second category there were 146 respondents in the urban areas to 136 respondents in the rural areas in the age group of 21 - 25, there are 43 respondents in rural areas compared to 35 respondents in the urban areas. In the age category of 26 - 30, there were six in rural areas and five respondents in the urban areas.

The mean age at marriage of the young respondents was higher at 19.1 compared to the middle aged respondents 11.7 and old respondents 10.9. The young respondents are aware of the advantage of higher age than the middle and old respondents. The raising of the marriage age for women has its effect on higher mean age for marriage of younger widows.

The mean age of the widows in rural areas has been estimated as 11.84 as against 11.69 in the urban areas.

In the young widows category 10 respondents who attained widowhood between 15 to 20 years of age, 16 respondents who attained widowhood between 21 to 25 years of age, 28 respondents attained widowhood between 26 to 30 years of age, 24 respondents who attained widowhood between 31 to 35 years of age and 12 respondents who attained widowhood between 36 to 40 years.

In the middle aged widows, 7 respondents (2.8 Percent), who were widowed between 10 to 20 years of age. 41 respondents (16.4 Percent) were widowed while they were between 21 to 30 years. 64 respondents (25.6 Percent) were widowed between the age of 31 to 40 years. 83 respondents (33.2 Percent) were widowed between 41 to 50 years. Lastly 55 respondents (22 Percent) were widowed while they were in the age group of 51 to 60 years.

Only 5 respondents (3.12 Percent) who attained widowhood between 10 to 20 years of age. 10 respondents (6.25 Percent) who attained widowhood between 21 to 30 years of age. 14 respondents (8.75 Percent) who attained widowhood between 31 to 40 years. 23 respondents (14.37 Percent) attained widowhood between 41 to 50 years of age. 42 respondents (26.25 Percent) attained widowhood between 51 to 60 years. 35 respondents attained widowhood between 61 to 70 years. The remaining 31 respondents (19.37 Percent) had attained widowhood between 71 to 80 years of age.

The mean age at marriage for all the husbands was worked out as 30.84 for the young, the mean age at marriage of husbands in urban areas was 29.8 as against 30.81 in the rural areas. For the other generations and areas, the lowest mean was 30.8 and the highest mean was 31.0.

The mean duration of widowhood for the young respondents was worked out to 11.80 years, for the middle aged respondents it was 27.34 years and for the old respondents, it was 37.0 years.

The respondent's age at marriage and their husband's age at marriage are negatively correlated.

The mean age at death of all husbands was calculated as 51.06. The mean age at death of the husbands of the young generation was 38.7, for husbands of the middle generation, it was 49.78 and for the husbands of the old generation, it was 60.45.

Heart attack has been indicated as the major cause (34.4 Percent) of husband's death. Other causes reported were natural illness (11.2 Percent), accident death (7 Percent), suicide (1.8 Percent) and others accounted for 45.6 Percent. Other causes include the following: fever (12.2 Percent), Diabetes (10.6 Percent), T.B. (5.6 Percent), kidney failure (6.21 Percent), malaria (6.2 Percent), jaundice (0.2 Percent), small pox 0.8 Percent), lung failure (0.8 Percent) and Asthma (1.2 Percent).

495 respondents marriages were arranged by the families and only five respondents husbands were from other sub-caste because of their love marriage.

267 respondents (53.4 Percent) had married outside the relationship. 233 (46.6 Percent) respondents had married their relatives.

400 respondents (80 Percent) were belonged to nuclear families compared to 81 respondents (16.2 Percent) belonged to single families or living alone and 19 respondents (3.8 Percent) belonged to joint families.

The average size of all the sample respondents was calculated as 2.86. It was as low as 1.95 for the young generation. 2.75 for middle aged generation and 3.56 for the old generation.

The total sample widows households had 1380 children, comprising of 739 boys and 641 girls. Out of 739 boys, 548 (74.15 Percent) boys got married as against 191 (25.85 Percent) boys remain unmarried. In case of girls, out of 641, 525 (81.90 Percent) were married as against 116 (18.10 Percent) remain unmarried.

Out of 500 respondents 41.8 Percent of the respondents had lived in R.C.C. roof type of houses, 41.2 Percent of the respondents had lived in tiled houses. 11.2 Percent of the respondents had lived in huts, and only 5.8 Percent of the respondents had lived in thatched houses.

Illiteracy is highest among the respondents belonging to rural areas (62.0 Percent). The illiteracy of the urban respondents was lower (40.4Percent). The respondents education and their husbands education are highly correlated.

All the sample respondents were wearing colour saries, none of the sample respondents were wearing white saries.

17.2 Percent of the respondents preferred vegetarian items of food and 82.8 Percent of the respondents preferred non-vegetarian items of food.

Out of the total sample of 500 respondents, 44 (8.8 Percent) respondents were in use of cosmetics and the remaining 456 respondents (91.2) Percent were not in use of cosmetics.

445 respondents (89.0 Percent), were not using jewels as against 55 respondents (11.0 Percent) were using jewels.

Entertainment is meant for relaxation of the mind and the body. All the respondents had expressed their opinion against entertainment.

Out of 500 respondents, 70 Percent of the respondents were performing rituals and 30 Percent of the respondents were not performing rituals.

Marriage is an important social function in which 'Sumangalis', women who have husbands alive, are expected to participate. Of the total respondents, 86.4 Percent were attending marriages and only 13.6 Percent were not attending marriages.

68.4 Percent of the respondents were not writing letters to relatives and friends and only 31.6 Percent were writing letters to relatives and friends. In the young widows category, out of 90 respondents, 64 respondents were not writing letters to relatives and friends and 26 respondents were writing letters to relatives and friends. Among the middle-aged widows, out of 250 respondents, 165 respondents were not writing letters to relatives and friends. In the old generation widows, 113 were not writing letters to relatives and friends, out of them 62 were rural and 51 were urban. 47 respondents were writing letters to relatives and friends.

59.2 Percent of the respondents were visiting friends and relatives and only 40.8 Percent of the respondents were not visiting friends and relatives.

75 Percent of the total respondents were giong to temples, but 25 Percent of the respondents were not going to temples.

Out of 500 respondents 98.6 Percent were not going to parks and theatres and only 1.4 Percent were going to parks and theatres.

The bread winners were present in all the generations, in young category, 53 Percent of them were bread winners as against 47 Percent were not bread winners. In the category of middle aged respondents and old generation respondents, 85.20 Percent and 93.75 Percent respondents were not bread winners. Education and training of young respondents had prompted them to take up income earning professions.

In the young generation, nearly 86.6 Percent were cooking. But the percentage declined to 78.4 Percent in the case of middle age respondents. Percentage of cooks in the old category had further declined to 55 Percent .

Child care is another job suitable to women. But it was performed only by 43.2 Percent of the respondents as against 56.8 Percent of the respondents who performed child care.

Purchasing is an important function to be performed in the family. Out of 500 respondents, 55.8 Percent were purchasing and 44.2 Percent were not purchasing.

Washing and cleaning are considered to be the domian of women. Out of 500 respondents, 51 Percent were washing and cleaning and 49 Percent were not washing and cleaning.

Only nine respondents were looking after business. They continue to carry on the occupation of their husbands. Distribution of the nine respondents among various generations shows that two of them belonged to young generation, five of them belonged to middle aged group and two of them belonged to old age group.

Farming was done by only six respondents (1.2 Percent). Five of them were belonged to rural and one was belonged to urban centre.

An Economic Spectrum of Mudaliar Widows

More than half of the respondents (317) 63.4 percent were not doing any work. Among the workers, large number of respondents 92 (18.4 percent) were working as coolies or wage earners. It is followed by other workers 31 (6.2 percent), domestic work 25 (5.0 percent), farming 18 (3.6 percent), teaching 9 (1.8 percent), business 7 (1.4 percent) and one (0.2 percent) was self employed.

Unlike the respondents, only four husbands were not doing any work at the time of interview. The husbands of 496 respondents were working before their death. Out of the total, 97 (19.4 percent) husbands were engaged in farming, followed by coolies 94 (18.8 percent), tailoring by 93 (18.6 percent), masons 72 (14.4 percent), business (7.2 percent), 33 of them (6.6 percent) were carpenters, 21 of them (4.2 percent) were teachers, there were 11 (2.2 percent) were drivers, conductors 10 (2.0 percent), eight of them were in army (1.6 percent), eight of them were working as accountants (1.6 percent), seven of them were commission agents (1.4 percent) and six of them were brokers (1.2 percent).

52 (10.4 percent) of the respondents had owned land, 418 (83.6 percent) of them owned houses, 108 (21.6 percent) had owned jewels and 9 (1.8 percent) had owned vehicles. Out of the 500 respondents 82 were staying in rented houses. Among those who owned land, 12 respondents owned one acre of land. Another group of 12 respondents owned three acres of land. Two acres of land by nine respondents. Another group of nine respondents owned four acres of land. Five acres of land was owned by two respondents. Six, seven and eight acres were owned by one each respondents. Two respondents had owned nine acres each and 10 acres were owned by three respondents. In the ownership and size of land, the middle and old generation respondents had more land compared to the young generation.

209 respondents (41.8 percent) had owned R.C.C. roof houses followed by 206 respondents (41.2 percent) had owned tiled houses, 56 respondents (11.2 percent) had owned huts and lastly 29 respondents (5.8 percent) had owned houses thatched with leaves.

Only 66 husbands of the respondents (13.2 percent) had no assets. Others owned land (19.4 percent), houses (67.0

percent) shops (0.2 percent) and shares and securities (0.2 percent).

285 respondents (57.0 percent) had Television. 274 respondents (54.8 percent) had liquefied gas connections. More than 50 percent of the respondents belonging to all generation had gas connection. 18 respondents (3.6 percent), bad refrigerator. Washing machine was used by 5 respondents (1.0 percent), Mixie was used by 118 respondents (23.6 percent), Grinder was used by 91 respondents (18.2 percent), and the Telephone was used by 33 respondents (6.6 percent).

223 respondents (44.6 percent) had owned durable consumer goods below Rs.10,000. There are 180 respondents (36.0 percent) who owned consumer durable goods between Rs.10,001 to 20,000. 70 respondents (14.0 percent) owned consumer durable goods between Rs.20,001 to 30,000. 15 respondents (3.0 percent) had owned consumer durable goods between Rs.30,001 to 40,000. 11 respondents had possessed consumer durable goods between Rs.40,001 to 50,000. Only one respondent had owned consumer durable goods above Rs.50000.

Out of 500 respondents 63.4 percent of the respondents were not earning any income. Among the non-income earners, 30 were belonged to young, 152 were middle and 135 were old. A small group of 183 respondents were earning income. Among them 150 respondents (30.2 percent) income was below Rs.1000, out of this 41 were young, 90 were middle and 20 were old. 17 respondent's (3.4 percent) monthly income was between Rs.1001-2000, out of this 12 were young, 4 were middle, one was old. Those who had monthly income above Rs.2000 were only 15, of them five belonged to income range between Rs.2001-3000, three belonged to income range between 3001-4000, four belonged to income range between Rs.4001-5000 and three who had income above Rs.5000.

61 (12.2 percent) husbands have no income at the time of their death. Among the husbands, who earned income, 250 (50 percent) were earning monthly income, of Rs.500. Another 95 husbands (19.0 percent) were earning monthly income ranging between Rs.500 to 1000. Only 94 husbands had earned

monthly income ranging between 1001 to 2500. Among them, 16 husband's monthly income ranged between 1001 to 1500, another 16 husband's income ranged between Rs.1501 to 2000, 18 husband's income ranges between Rs.2001 to 2500 and lastly 44 husbands income was above Rs.2500.

243 (48.60 percent) of the respondents had received Old Age Pension (OAP). Income from occupation as wages was received by 183 respondents (36.60 percent). Only 12 respondents had earned income from property. 23 respondents who received compensation for the death of their husbands. More than 50 percent of them could receive income from occupation and compensation.

Only 397 respondents had family income. Of them, 60 belonged to young generation, 197 belonged to middle generation and 140 belonged to old generation.

255 respondents (51.0 percent) had spent less than Rs.1000 per month. In the second slab of expenditure, there were 163 respondents (32.6 percent). There were 44 respondents (8.8 percent) in the expenditure range between Rs.2001 to 3000. 18 respondents are in the fourth range of expenditure between Rs. 3001 to 4000 per month. 11 respondents fall in the expenditure slab of Rs.4001 to 5000 and nine respondents fall in the expenditure above Rs. 5000 per month.

Expenditure on food is an important item. Below Rs.500 expenditure per month was incurred by 194 respondents (38.8 percent). 274 respondents (54.8 percent) had spent between Rs. 501 to 1000 per month on food. Those who spent between Rs. 1001 to 1500 was 28 (5.6 percent). Only eight respondents had spent between Rs.1501 to 2000 on food.

There were 82 respondents who lived in rented buildings. Of them, 60 had paid monthly rent below Rs.500. 17 respondents (20.73 percent) had paid a monthly rent of Rs.501 to 1000. Five respondents who paid monthly rent ranging between Rs.1001 to 1500.

Cloth is an essential item next to food for human survival. 323 respondents had spent below Rs.500 annually for clothes. 169 respondents (33.8 percent) who spent annually between Rs.501 to 1000 on clothes. Seven respondents (1.4 percent) had spent between 1001 to 1500 per annum on clothes. Only one respondent had spent between Rs.1501 to 2000 on clothes.

240 respondents (48.0 percent) had spent less than Rs. 500 on medicine. 105 respondents (21.0 percent) had spent between Rs.501 to 1000 on medicine. 92 respondents (18.4 percent) had spent between Rs. 1001 to 1500 on medicine. Remaining 63 respondents had spent between Rs.1501 to 2500 per month.

114 respondents (22.8 percent) had spent below Rs.500 on education. 133 respondents (26.6 percent) had spent Rs.501 to1000 on education. 116 respondents (23.2 percent) had spent between Rs.1001 to 1500 per annum on education. 71 respondents (14.2 percent) had spent between Rs.1501 to 2000 on education annually. 60 respondents (12.0 percent) had spent between Rs.2001 to 2500 annually on education. Six respondents (1.2 percent) had spent above Rs.2500 annually on education. All the respondents, belonging to all the generation, had incurred expenditure on education. It shows their awareness about the importance of education.

398 respondents (79.6 percent) had spent less than Rs. 500 on fuel every month. In the next slab of Rs.501 to 1000, there were 84 respondents (16.8 percent). 17 respondents (3.4 percent) who had spent between Rs.1001 to 1500 monthly on fuel. Remaining one respondent, who belonged to middle generation, had spent between Rs. 1501 to 2000.

Among the total respondents, 44 respondents had used cosmetics. Of them, 20 belonged to young generation, 17 respondents belonged to middle generation and seven respondents belonged to old generation.

374 respondents (74.80 percent) had not under taken any travel during the year of interview. Only a small minority of 126 respondents had travelled. Their expenditure varies from Rs.100 to 500.

The quantum of investment varies from Rs.25,000 to more than Rs. One lakh (table 7.16). Out of the 22 respondents, 12 (54.54 percent) had invested below Rs.25000. There were three respondents who had invested between Rs.25,001 to 50,000. Two of the respondents had invested between Rs.50,001 to 75,000 and another two respondents had invested between

Rs.75,001 to 1,00,000. There were two respondents who had invested more than Rs.1,00,000.

Land was the preferred investment of the 10 respondents. Next priority for investment was livestock for nine respondents. Two respondents had invested in buildings and one had invested in jewels. The choice of investment made on land, building and livestock was productive while the investment made on jewels was not productive, which was made by a respondent.

Two of the respondents had reported to have saved, who formed only 0.4 percent of the total respondents. Other respondents had no strength to save. It was found that banks was their sources of savings.

200 respondents (40.0 percent) had borrowed, while 300 respondents (60.0 percent) had not borrowed. Among three generations, smallest borrowers belonged to old generation, 22.5 percent, followed by young generation 45 percent and lastly, 49.2 percent of the middle generation.

113 respondents (56.5 percent) who had borrowed below Rs.25,000. There were 10 respondents who borrowed between Rs.50,001 to 75,000, of them, six belonged to middle generation and four belonged to old generation. There were 17 respondents who borrowed between Rs.75,001 to 1,00,000. There were 19 respondents who had borrowed above Rs.1,00,000.

60 (30 percent) had used the borrowed money for meeting marriage expenses. 36 respondents had borrowed to meet medical expenses. 29 respondents had borrowed to meet day to day expenses. 28 respondents had borrowed for construction of houses. Education was the priority for borrowing for 24 respondents. 14 respondents had borrowed for the purpose of business. Nine respondents had borrowed for miscellaneous purpose.

Majority of them, 142 (71.0 percent), had borrowed from money lenders. It was followed by 31 respondents (15.5 percent), who borrowed from relatives. 24 respondents (12 percent) had borrowed from banks. A small number of three respondents had borrowed from financial institutions like

Land Development Bank and Tamil Nadu Small Industries Corporation.

Capacity of Mudaliar Widows to take Decisions

Only 47 respondents (9.4 percent) could take independent decisions in the matters of purchase of assets. When they are divided between regions, 21 belonged to rural areas and 26 belonged to urban areas. 93 respondents (18.6 percent) had reported that the decisions were taken by others. Of them, 62 belonged to rural areas and 31 belonged to urban areas.

141 respondents (28.2 percent) could take independent decision on the marriage of sons and daughters. As regards others take decision, there were 209 (41.8percent) respondents. It was not applicable to 150 (30.0 respondents) as they were young, as well as others who lived independently.

152 (30.4 percent) respondents could take independent decision on festivals. For 228 respondents (45.6 percent), decision to celebrate festivals was taken by others. There were 120 respondents for whom this question is not applicable because they were not participating in these festivals.

119 respondents (23.8 percent) had taken independent decision on ceremonies as against 209 respondents (41.8 percent) the decision was taken by others. 172 respondents (34.4 percent) had reported that it is not applicable to them.

41 (8.2 percent) respondents had exercised their capacity on investment. There were 74 respondents (14.8 percent) who dependent on others for taking decision on investments. 385 respondents (77.0 percent) had reported that it was not applicable to them.

473 respondents (94.6 percent) had not availed medical care, for, they did not take care of their health after the attainment of widowhood. Only 27 respondents had availed medical facilities either on their own or on the advice of others. There were 16 respondents who depended on others to take decision in order to avail health services.

482 (96.4 percent) had not engaged in management of business. So they refrained themselves from taking any decision. Two respondents, who had taken their own decision,

were belonged to one each to middle and old age generation. 16 respondents had to depend on others for taking decision.

Impact of Women Welfare Programmes on the Status of Mudaliar Widows

Only 243 respondents had received old age pension. Of them, 126 respondents belonged to urban areas as against 117 respondents belonged to rural areas. 44 out of 90 young respondents could receive benefit under old age pension scheme. In the case of middle aged respondents, 128 out of 250 could receive benefits the number of beneficiaries belonging to old age respondents were 71 out of 160. Thus the young and old respondents, who received benefits, were below 50 percent but the beneficiaries belonged to middle age were just above 50 percent.

Problems and Suggestions

81 respondent widows (16.2 percent of the total) had agreed for remarriage. 395 respondents (79.0 percent) had disagreed for re-marriage. There were 24 respondents who maintained neutrality with rergard to re-marriage.

373 (74.6 percent) respondents had agreed to take up employment after widowhood. Among those who disagreed to take up employment after widowhood was 111. There were 16 (3.2 percent) respondents, who were neutral with regard to employment after widowhood.

There were 16 respondents (3.2 percent) who were neutral with regard to participation in politics. The participants belonging to rural areas were more in number, 31, who agreed to participate in politics after widowhood compared to 22 respondents belonging to urban areas.

Out of 500 respondents, 94.4 percent were disagreed with participation in women's organisation, out of this, 86 were young, 232 were middle and 154 were old. 3.4 percent had agreed to participate in women's organisation. Only 2.2 percent were neutral.

92.8 percent respondents had disagreed to participate in local administration. Out of this 81 were belonged to young generation, 234 were middle and 149 were old generation.

88 percent had disagreed with education after widowhood. 9.2 percent had agreed with education after widowhood. Only 2.8 percent were neutral towards education after widowhood.

457 (91.4 percent) of the respondents had disagreed to receive help from male members. 6.2 percent of the respondents were agreed to receive help from male members. Only 2.4 percent were neutral to receive the help from male members.

Out of 500 widows, 94.8 percent of widows had disagreed to adopt children. 4 percent of the widows had agreed to adopt children and only 1.2 percent of the widows were neutral to adopt children.

Attitude of Others Towards Widows

315 parents (63.0 percent) of the respondents were affectionate towards them, 67 (13.4 percent) were considerate, 85 parents (17.0 percent) were helping and no response was recorded by 31 parents (6.2 percent).

17 respondents (3.4 percent) had expressed that the attitude of brothers towards them was affectionate. 181 respondents (36.0 percent) had reported that they had received help from brothers. 300 respondents (60 percent) had reported 'no response' regarding brothers attitude towards widows.

257 (51.4 percent) of the respondents had found their sisters affectionate, 105 (21.00 percent) sisters were considerate, 80 (16.0 percent) sisters were found to be helping. Only 58 respondents (11.6 percent) had no response.

16 (3.2 percent) respondents had reported that their brothers-in-law were affectionate. 10 (2.0 percent) respondents had reported that the attitude of brothers-in-law was considerate. To five respondents, the attitude of their brothers-in-law was helpful. But 300 respondents (60.0 percent) had reported that the attitude of their brothers-in-law was resentful. 169 respondents (33.8 percent) had not responded to the question.

12 respondents (2.4 percent) reported that their sisters-in-law were affectionate. Five respondents reported that their sisters-in-law were considerate. Only three respondents reported their sister-in-law were helpful.

350 (70 percent) of the sample respondents reported that their sons were affectionate. 50 (10 percent) respondents reported their sons were considerate. Helpful nature of sons were reported by 25 respondents (5 percent). Another 15 respondents reported the resentful nature of their sons. 60 respondents (30.0 percent) had not responded.

457 respondent's (91.4 percent) daughters were affectionate. 10 respondents (2.0 percent) had agreed that their daughters were considerate. 15 respondents (3.0 percent) reported their daughters were helpful. 18 respondents had not responded.

244 (48.8 percent) respondents reported that the co-workers were affectionate. 100 respondents considered co-workers as considerate. To 75 respondents, the co-workers were helpful. 25 respondents (five percent) reported that the co-workers were resentful. 56 respondents had expressed no response.

400 (80.0 percent) respondents are reported to be affectionate towards widows as against only 10 respondents (2.0 percent) who reported the shopkeepers as resentful. For 50 respondents, the shopkeepers were considerate and for another 15 (3 percent) respondents the shopkeepers were helpful. 25 respondents had expressed no response.

375 respondents (75 percent) had reported that women are generally affectionate towards them, as against 50 respondents (10 percent) reported that women were considerate and 25 respondents (5 percent) had reported that the women were helpful to them. Only 15 respondents (3 percent) had reported that the women were resentful towards them. No response was made by 35 respondents (7 percent).

380 respondents (76 percent) had reported that 'men were affectionate'. 'Men were considerate' was reported by 40 respondents (8 percent). 'Men were helpful' was reported by 50 respondents (10 percent).

Re-marriage Attempt

Only 12 respondents (2.4 percent) had reported attempt of re-marriage, of them, four belonged to young generation, six belonged to middle generation and two belonged to old generation. Even for those, who made remarriage attempts, the marriage did not take place mainly because of in-laws, parents and relatives.

Problems of Widows

448 respondents (89.6 percent) had economic problems like employment, income, debts, borrowings, source of investment and looking after the assets. The emotional problems were faced by 289 respondents (57.8 percent). Physical problems were faced by 29 respondents (5.8 percent). 43 (8.6 percent) respondents had faced mental problems. 13 respondents in the sample who had psychological problems.

Suggestions

209 respondents (41.8 percent) had given first priority to education. Second priority of the respondents had gone to self-employment, as it was suggested by 122 respondents (24.4 percent). It was followed by the suggestion of acquiring courage by 102 respondents (20.4 percent). Development of self-confidence was suggested by 36 respondents (7.2 percent). The other suggestions like talent by 12 (2.4 percent) respondents and hardwork by 8 (1.6 percent) respondents and 11 respondents (2.2 percent) had not made any suggestions.

Sample Widows Vision

250 respondent's (50.0 percent) expectation had gone to married sons. Aid from the government is the expectations of 121 respondents (24.3 percent). For 32 respondents (6.4 percent) parents are the main source of help. Married daughters are the source of help for 28 respondents (5.6 percent). 25 respondents (5.0 percent) had lot of expectation from the relatives followed by 12 respondents (2.4 percent) who had expectation from the society. Expectations from husband's families are expressed only by 7 respondents (1.4 percent) thus showing very little priority to them. 25 respondents (5.0 percent) had not expressed any expectations.

Conclusion

From the above findings the following conclusions are deduced.

1. The Mean age of marriage of the respondents was very much less than the age fixed by the government. It inter alia proves that those who marry early become widows at an early age.
2. Illiteracy was very high both among the respondents as well as their deceased husbands. The Hindu Mudaliar widows were not well-equipped educationally in the study area as it was declared by the Government.
3. As against the exposed belief, the respondent's age at marriage and their husbands age at marriage were negatively co-related.
4. The occupations, the respondents and their husbands preferred, were unskilled work such as coolies, domestic work, and other works. A good percent of the respondents in the three generations were non-workers, it results in low earning and low expenditure.
5. The analysis of the social status of the respondents reveals the following factors.
   (a) Majority of the respondents living in huts and tiled houses, shows that they are living below the poverty line.
   (b) In the matters of dress, food, use of cosmetics, use of jewels, entertainments etc.. young respondents are modern compared to the middle-aged and old generation.
   (c) In doing customary things, the young generation had greater preference than the middle-aged and old generation.
   (d) The role of the respondents in the family was characterized by the sole earning, self-cooking, child care, washing and cleaning and making purchases.
   (e) The middle-aged and old generation face exclusion and social stigma than the young generation.
6. The respondents were leading a very low economic status because of low income and unemployment. It reflects in the low expenditure on food, cloths, education, medical

care, electricity, transport, entertainment and cosmetics. The repayment of old debts is a big burden to them.

7. The decision-making capacity was found among less than 50 percent of the respondents and others were incapable of taking decisions.
8. They depend on parents, Governments, parents-in-law, sons and daughters for meeting daily expenses, for repayment of old debts and to receive compensation.
9. Those who had education had exhibited positive attitude towards remarriage, employment, participation in politics, participation in panchayats / municipalities, participation in women's organisation, education after widowhood, receiving help from male members and child adoption, others have negative attitudes towards these factors.
10. Regarding other's attitude towards widows, the attitude of parents, sisters, brothers, sons, daughters, men, women, and shopkeepers was positive, while the parents-in-law, sisters-in-law and brothers-in-law was negative.
11. Only a miniscule of respondents, whose husbands were employed, were aware of the government schemes and they could receive benefits after the death of their husbands. Those coolie widows, earning daily wages could avail old age pension. Others were not aware of the government schemes.
12. The re-marriage of widows has been restricted by their loyalty to their deceased husbands, lack of religious sanctions, and love and affection towards their children.

Suggestions

The following suggestions are given for the improvement of the social and economic status of widows in the study area.

1. Education is sin quo non for the progress and empowerment of women, to create awareness and to change their attitude and enable them to take decision. So education should be made compulsory for all category of women.

2. Employment will improve the economic status of widows and reduce their dependence. Therefore, training should be imparted to develop their skills.
3. In order to make the widows independent, ration cards, land pattas, group houses and pension should be issued by treating them as single women.
4. It is not enough to announce various beneficiary schemes by the government but the government should ensure that the benefits really reach the deserving.
5. Organising the widows by forming self-help groups is a pre-requisite for their empowerment. Non-government organisation could play a vital role in organising the widows.
6. The study reveals that most of the respondents were socially and economically backward. They were living below the poverty line. Therefore the government reservation should be based on social and economic criteria rather than on caste lines.

Scope for Future Research

The following areas require further indepth analysis by the researchers in the colleges and Universities.

1. The Psychological impact of the death of the husbands on the widows.
2. The emotional integration of widows to the family and the society.
3. The problem of single women including widows could be analysed separately because the number of single women in the community is on the rise.
4. The sexual relationship of widows is a subject for future inquiry as they are subjected to various kinds of harassment like eve-teasing, sexual-assault and forceful prostitution.

Action Plan for Empowerment of Widows

1. Educate the children and the public about widows by declaring 'myths about widows' as unreal and imaginary.

The widows are equal to any other women. Though they have lost their husbands, they have retained all the sterling qualities of women.

2. As income turned out to be a significant variable, influencing the respondent widows, measures may be adopted to augment their income. Most of them are assetless, jobless and homeless. Hence, they have been depending on the Old Age Pension. A separate fund may be created, from which, these widows may be paid monthly. It may be christened as Widows Pension Fund. All widows irrespective of their age should be paid pension from this fund with an exception of re-married women. This will protect the widows and it will reduce their dependence on others.
3. Education is another factor, which will empower widows. As the study reveals, educated widows are better placed compared to unedcuated widows. Universal literacy will remove this disability of widows. Of course, adult education, vocational education, human rights education may be extended to these widows during night time by employing women tutors.
4. Lack of skill appears to be a great drain in the personality of these women. Training may be extended to these widows taking into account their aptitude and the local needs.
5. Widows remarriage may be promoted by educating the male and through advertisement in marriage columns. Those men who come forward to marry widows and adopt their children may be provided all the assistance particularly finance and support in all their ventures.

BIBLIOGRAPHY

1. Maya Majumdar (2001), "Protecting Our Women", Vol.III., Domiant Publishers and Distributers, New Delhi, pp. 361 to 368.
2. Mukesh Ahuja (1996), "Widows - Role Adjustment and Violence", Wishwa Prakashan Publishers, New Delhi, p. 11.
3. M. Rajkumar (2000), "Encyclopedia of Women and Development", Vol.16, Anmol Publications, New Delhi, pp.1 -10.
3. D. Godavari (2000), "A Study on Deprivation of Hindu Widows", Gyan Publishing House, New Delhi. pp. 27 -29.
4. Sandhiya (1994), Widowhood: A Socic - Psychiattic Study, Mohit Publications, New Delhi, pp. 82-98.
5. N.S. Krishna Kumari (1987), Status of Single Women in India, Uppal Publishing House, New Delhi, p. 85.
6. Mukesh Ahuja (1996), Widows: Role Adjustment and Violence, Wishva Prakasham Publishing House, New Delhi, p. 35.
7. Serinity Young (1998), Encyclopedia of Women and World Religion, Vol.II, Macmillian Reference USA, New York, p. 1029.
8 N. Dutt (1968), Origin and Growth of Caste in India, Vol.I, Firma Publications, Calcutta, p. 247.
9. G.R. Lesile (1979), The Family in Social Context, Oxford University Press, New York, p. 614.
10. M.A. Fritz (1929), A Study of Widows in Sociology and Social Research, Vol.XIV, No.1, p. 553.
11. H.H. Hyman (1983), Of Time of Widowhood, Duke Press Policy Studies, Durham, p. 3.
12. Monica Das Gupta et.al (1995), Women's Health in India, Oxford University Press, Mumbay, pp. 267-268.

13. Godvari.D. Patil (2000), A Study in Deprivation – Hindu Widows, Gyan Publishing House, New Delhi, pp. 27 - 29.
14. Raj Kumar (2000), Encyclopedia of Women and Development, Vol.16, Anmol Publications, New Delhi, p.7.
15. M.C. Median (1999), Dictionary of Economics, Himalaya Publishing House, Mumbai, p. 132.
16. Lalitha Srinath (2000), An Indian Book Review, Vol.3, No.4, Sage Publications, New Delhi, p. 27.
17. Ranjana Kumari (1981), Widow Headed Households on Rural India, Radiant Publishers, New Delhi, p. 40.
18. D. Baskara Rao (1998), International Encyclopaedia of Women, Vol.I, Discovery Publishing House, New Delhi, p. 6.
19. M. Indra Devi (1987), Women, Education and Employment Family Living, Gian Publishing House, New Delhi, pp.130-132.
20. M. Rokeach (1979), Understanding Human Values - Individual and Societal, The Free Press, New York, p. 2.
21. Taruna Sareen (2001), Encyclopaedic Dictionary of Economics, Vol.2, Sarup and Sons, New Delhi, p. 378.
22. Ghodake (1985), Encyclopaedic Dictionary of Economics, Vol.3, Mittal Publications, New Delhi, pp. 640-641.
23. The Oxford English Dictionary (1978), Vol.VIII, POY-RY, Oxford, London Glasgow, p. .325.
24. P.A. Thomas and K.Padmanabhan, (1991), District Planning, Northern Book Centre, New Delhi, pp. 18 - 72.

Journals

25. Meera Chakravarthy (2004), Over Coming Barriers: Gandhi on Women, Southern Economist, Vol.43 (2), pp. 21,22.
26. Tusharkant Mishra (1988), "Make Women Equal Partners in Development", Yojana, Vol.32., May, p. 18.
27. M.A. Fritz (1979), "A Study of Widowhood in Sociology and Social Research", Yojana, Vol.XIV, No.1.,January, p. 53.
28. B.M.M. Aradhya (1987), What is Means to be a Widow, Social Welfare, Vol.XXXIV, No.9, p. 3.
29. L.A. Morgan (1981), Economic Changes at Midlife Widowhood – A Longitudinal Analysis, Journal of Marriage and the Family, Vol.43, No.4, p. 899.

30. Ram Singh (1994), Decision-Making in Home and Farm Related Activities, Kurukshetra, Vol.XLII, No.10, p. 37.

Reports

31. K. Malathi (2001), An Published Ph.D Thesis; Socio-Economic Status of Hindu Widows in Walajapet Taluk - A Three Generation Study, University of Madras, Chennai, p. 44.
32. Census of India 2001 - Tamil Nadu, (2001), Provisional Population Totals, Paper - 2 of 2001, Rural Urban Distribution, Series - 34, Controller of Publications, Civil Lines, New Delhi, pp.151-161.
33. Census of India 2001 - Tamil Nadu, (2001), Distribution of Workers and Non-workers, Paper - 3 of 2001, Series - 34, Controller of Publications, Civil Lines, New Delhi, pp. 154-157.
34. Tamil Nadu - An Economic Appraisal 1997-98, Dept of Evaluation and Applied Research, Govt of Tamil Nadu, Chennai, pp. S - 1-157.